The Civil Service

Radical reform of the civil service during the 1980s and 1990s has broken up the unified hierarchical structures, leaving a central core concerned with making policies, and peripheral agencies for implementing them. The Civil Service provides an up-to-date critical introduction to the working of these bodies, combining descriptive history and theoretical explanation, with an emphasis on public-choice theory.

The first part of the book concentrates on managerial issues. The second part focuses on policy-making and the role of the civil service in terms of theories about the modern state. Assessing the reforms in terms of the public-choice and managerial theories which underpin them, Keith Dowding uses budget-maximising and bureau-shaping models to predict the directions we can expect reforms to take in the future, and what their success might be.

Central to the argument in *The Civil Service* is an examination of the term 'efficiency' in the context of the reforms. Comparing public choice 'rent-seeking' arguments with more traditional 'pluralist' accounts, the book examines the constitutional role of the civil service and its part in policy-making. This combination of the theories of bureaucracy with an account of the modern-day civil service will be essential reading for students of British politics and for civil servants themselves.

Keith Dowding is Lecturer in Public Choice and Public Policy at the London School of Economics.

Theory and Practice in British Politics
Series editors: Desmond King, Jeremy Waldron, Alan Ware

This series bridges the gap between political institutions and political theory as taught in introductory British politics courses. While teachers and students agree that there are important connections between theory and practice in British politics, few textbooks systematically explore these connections. Each book in this series takes a major area or institution and looks at the theoretical issues which it raises. Topics covered include the police, Northern Ireland, Parliament, electoral systems, the law, cities, central government and many more. No other textbook series offers both a lively and clear introduction to key institutions and an understanding of how theoretical issues arise in the concrete and practical context of politics in Britain. These innovative texts will be essential reading for teachers and beginning students alike.

Other titles in the series

The Law
Jeremy Waldron

Electoral Systems
Andrew Reeve and Alan Ware

The Civil Service

Keith Dowding

London and New York

First published 1995
by Routledge
11 New Fetter Lane, London EC4P 4EE

Simultaneously published in the USA and Canada
by Routledge
29 West 35th Street, New York, NY 10001

© 1995 Keith Dowding

Typeset in Times by
Ponting–Green Publishing Services, Chesham, Bucks

Printed and bound in Great Britain by
TJ Press Ltd, Padstow, Cornwall

British Library Cataloguing in Publication Data
A catalogue record for this book is available from the
British Library.

Library of Congress Cataloging in Publication Data
A catalogue record for this book has been requested

ISBN 0–415–07567–X (hbk)
ISBN 0–415–07568–8 (pbk)

Contents

Figures

Tables

Preface

I would like to thank Phil Cowley, Oliver James, George Jones, Desmond King, Sonia Mazey, Christopher Pollitt and Alan Ware for their written comments; each has contributed to at least one sentence. I would especially like to thank Anne Gelling who has read the entire manuscript at least twice and forced me to rewrite large chunks of it. I would like to thank the civil servants both in Whitehall and Brussels who agreed to be interviewed. I am indebted to the Nuffield Foundation who funded my trip to Brussels (Grant no SOC/181(2243)) which contributed enormously to Chapter 7; they also funded the data collection exercise (Grant no SOC/100(302)) which contributes to the argument in Chapter 8. I would like to thank Norman Cooke and Helen Cannon who collected most of that data. This short book has taken much longer to write than it should have done, which during a period of rapid change caused me more headaches than I care to tell. I hope the factual information was correct at the time of going to press but believe that in this regard some errors remain. I believe that my opinions were correct at the time of going to press, but rather hope some are not.

K.M.D.
Barton, Oxford

1 Introduction

The civil service and the state

> It is impossible not to wonder at the inability of administrators and politicians in Britain not to recognize that to speak critically of their experience inevitably involves a species of theorizing: their ritual rejection of theory merely tends to ensure that such theorizing as they do indulge in is badly done.
>
> (Johnson 1978: 271)

There are many books on the civil service and on bureaucratic theory. There are not many which combine explanations of both bureaucratic theory and the civil service. There are a few books which empirically test theories of the bureaucracy by setting them against the evidence of the British civil service. Books of the latter kind, like those concerned with bureaucratic theory itself are often rather dry and hard to understand, which is fair enough. The world is hard to understand; and if it is made to appear simpler than it really is, we will be hiding as much of the world as we reveal. However, most of the books which provide easy introductions for the undergraduate or general reader merely describe the civil service and do not consider, other than in passing, the theories of bureaucracy which help us to explain the way the civil service works. They are too full of descriptions, opinions, anecdotes and personalities with not enough theoretical analysis explaining how these elements all fit together. Often the reason for this is that writers of the descriptive mode believe that the general theories of bureaucratic behaviour are badly drawn or inapplicable. They may be right in this belief. But if the existing theories are poor, then some better ones should be divised, rather than denying that theories can be used at all. As Nevil Johnson implies in the quotation above, to deny theory is merely to obscure the theory with which one is operating.

THE CIVIL SERVICE

This book is about the civil service in Britain, which is at the centre of British political life. Whilst the newspapers and television concentrate upon politicians and what goes on in the Cabinet and Westminster, many of the day-to-day decisions with which government is concerned are taken by civil servants. It is at the centre of a policy network comprising organized pressure groups, politicians, parties and government ministers. What do civil servants bring to this network? Do they dominate it, as Sir Humphrey Appleby used to dominate Jim Hacker in the TV series *Yes, Minister*? Or have politicians fought back and taken over policy, as Jim Hacker began to do in the later series of *Yes, Prime Minister*? For many commentators this did seem to be the case as Margaret Thatcher, the most dominant Prime Minister in living memory, carried out the most radical set of policies and reforms during her second and third terms of office. Indeed it was under her stewardship that the most recent and probably the most far-reaching civil service reforms began.

Twenty years ago writing a book on the civil service was a comparatively easy task. The service had remained largely unchanged for almost a century, acquiring new tasks and departments, a rearrangement here and there; but in the main historians of the civil service could stand on the shoulders of their predecessors. Originality in analysing the civil service a generation ago came through applying a different theory to explain the largely immobile object. All that has changed. During the late 1980s and early 1990s the civil service was rapidly and radically transformed. Its edifice has been altered from a straightforward hierarchical line structure to a complex form with a core of policy-making civil servants in Whitehall surrounded by a periphery of policy-executing agencies. Even at the time of writing the status of these agencies is under review, and some are likely to move from the public to the private sector. Even the role of the core Whitehall policy-maker is in question with some suggesting that private and politicized policy advice may be advantageous to the current career structure. Today, writing a book about the civil service is to describe a moving target; explaining how it works and why it is changing is even harder. This is the task of this book.

The evolutionary process which saw only minor changes has given way to a revolutionary process of change. At a seminar at the London School of Economics in 1993, a senior civil servant described these changes as 'permanent revolution'. The question that begs to be asked is: why is the bedrock of the British state now undergoing Maoist convolutions under a Conservative government? The answer is to be found in the character of the Conservative administration which gained power in 1979. Margaret Thatcher's government was no ordinary traditional Conservative regime committed to conserving the fundamentals of the state and unlikely to initiate changes to the constitution. Rather it was led by a Prime Minister who believed in the 'free market' libertarian doctrines of the 'New Right' (Bosanquet 1983). These New Right principles in the guise of public-choice arguments (King 1987) entailed a critique of the ever expanding state and a set of prescriptions for ending the malaise of Britain's decline. The public-choice critique of the state forms the theoretical centrepiece of this book. It is used to examine the civil service as it was, and to explain why such radical reform was thought to be necessary. It is then used to explore those changes and to question whether they will have the effects expected of them by their proponents.

MODELS OF THE STATE

There are numerous competing models of the state (Dunleavy and O'Leary 1987) and the public-choice account is not the only one that will be examined here. Three others will also be considered: the constitutional-representative government view; the pluralist account; the autonomy of the democratic state. Each implies certain ways in which the central pillar of the state – the civil service – should operate. For those upholding the constitutional-representative government vision of the British state, the civil service is a neutral machine wound up and kept ticking by an elected government itself supported by parliament representing the people. We see this idea in the justification of old-style hierarchical forms of bureaucratic organization usually defended by a Weberian model of the bureaucracy. We encounter this in Chapter 2 where we examine Weberian justifications of hierarchy (and find Weber has a more realistic account of the state than some of his advocates), and again in Chapter 8 where we probe the relationship between civil servants, ministers and parliament in terms of the constitutional model. This model of the state is recognized as 'fictional' even by its adherents. They realize that the relationships are more complex than the model describes, but believe that it is a useful guide to how things ought to be, and that it can help explain why some of the actors behave as they do. But we shall see that its 'fictional form' makes it virtually useless both as a prescriptive guide and as an aid to explanation.

The pluralist view of the state, despite decades of criticism, is still the dominant paradigm of political science. The target of much of that criticism is an idealized version which has much in common with the constitutional-representative government model. Like the latter, the idealized pluralist account of the state sees the civil service and other policy-making agencies of the state as a neutral arena where the interplay of political forces determines policy. The main difference between this and the constitutional view is that the role of interest group organizations is recognized as a far more important system of representation than parliament. This idealized pluralism sees government as just another force alongside competing group interests. This version exists only in the eyes of critics of pluralism (Dowding 1991); all modern pluralists have a more sophisticated account of the state. The role of interest group organizations is still seen as vital, but the central organizations of the state are also defined as interests in their own right. It is recognized that policy-making is segmented into different policy networks, sometimes crossing departmental boundaries, sometimes contained in small policy communities at the departmental or sub-departmental level (Jordan and Richardson 1987; Marsh and Rhodes 1992). These different policy networks are defined by the characteristics of their members and the nature of the relations between groups (Dowding 1994c, 1995).

Pluralism shades into the third model of the state: the autonomy of the democratic state. Like pluralists, state autonomists see policy-making as segmented into different policy networks, but they downplay the power and importance of different organized interests. According to state autonomists (Nordlinger 1981), group organizations only influence policy where government does not already have strong policy preferences. Group organizations may affect policy in open-issue areas, but where departments already have set out the parameters of their preferred policies only those groups which conform to these parameters are allowed into policy-influencing positions. In Chapter 6, which concentrates upon the policy-making role rather than the organizational structure of the civil service, we examine both the pluralist and the state-autonomist models of policy making.

The New Right model of the state differs from the others in that it is more openly normative, not only explaining how the state operates but also prescribing how it can be made more efficient. The book is necessarily dominated by this model, which provides the intellectual justification for the process of organizational reform the civil service is currently undergoing. The New Right model suggests that there is an internal dynamic which leads to state inefficiency and inexorable growth in the state machine. Where pluralist and constitutional-representative models see the interplay of political forces and interests as an essential, though not always desirable, feature of democracy, the

New Right sees this process as an unmitigated evil. What traditional constitutionalists call 'politics' and pluralists call 'group representation', the New Right calls 'rent-seeking'. Rent-seeking for the New Right is a process whereby some groups extract an economic rent, in the form of state subsidies, simply for being there. So farm subsidies under the Common Agricultural Policy are a form of economic rent for farmers, subsidized road-building programmes a form of economic rent for car drivers, and social security payments a form of economic rent for the poor. These demands for rent from all sections of society allow civil servants to promote certain programmes for their own departments. The overall tax burden goes up, ensuring a less efficient economy all round. Civil servants are also enabled to maximize the budgets of their own departments in their own self-interest, seen in terms of material welfare and influence over the direction of the state. This model of bureaucratic behaviour, together with more anecdotal critiques of civil service inefficiency within the traditional hierarchic structure, led to the current reforms of the civil service.

Chapters 2–5 are about the organization of the civil service; chapters 3–5 critically examine the New Right public-choice theory and civil-service reform. These chapters suggest the sort of success and failures we may expect to see following those reforms. Chapter 2 examines the justification of the hierarchical form of public-sector organization within the traditional representative government view. Using Weber's ideas as the traditional justification for such hierarchy, we see why it is supposed to be rational and efficient. Weber provides a good counterpoint to the New Right critique. We see in Chapter 3, the chapter with the most complex material, that the term 'efficiency' is used ambiguously as in much economic and public-administration writing. Weber's use of the term can be compared to that of modern economists. Furthermore, the notions of 'rationality' that Weber and the public-choice school utilize are not completely convergent. That too is worth examination. Despite its difficulty Chapter 3 is important in order to understand fully the New Right critique and thus the fundamentals of the reform process.

Chapters 6–8 are about policy-making. Chapter 6 examines the evidence of the relative powers of ministers, pressure group organizations and senior civil servants in the generation and implementation of policy. Here the pluralist and state-autonomy accounts are most fruitfully compared. Whilst the public perception is that the radical Conservative administrations since 1979 have been less influenced by outside pressures and that the civil service is more controlled by ministers, we see that the picture is more complicated. Chapter 7 is a closer look at the difference the European Union makes to both organization and policy-making in the civil service. Most books on the civil service pay only passing attention to the effects of Europe on the central element of the British state. Here I have tried to fill these lacunae, though Europe is developing so quickly that the descriptions in Chapter 7 may soon be out of date. Chapter 8 returns to the constitutional-representative government model with which we started. Essentially concerned with the accountability of the civil service, it examines the relationship between civil servants, ministers and parliament to see how strong and useful the thread of accountability really is. This chapter suggests that accountability has never operated as it is often claimed by constitutional writers, but in this chapter it is also argued that the agency reform process will have less impact than is often asserted.

2 Hierarchy
Weber and the old model

This chapter is concerned with the first model of the state mentioned in Chapter 1: the constitutional-representative government model. There it was described as a 'fiction', because it was not developed in order to explain the reality of the British system of government or its civil service but rather as a guide to such explanations and as a normative model of how well-functioning bureaucracies should behave. The Weberian model, with which this chapter begins, underlies the standard defence of the hierarchical and politically neutral form of the civil service as it has typically operated. This chapter describes the traditional organization of the civil service before the reforms of the 1980s and demonstrate how that fits in with conventional thinking on the operation of key issues in constitutional theory. This chapter provides a benchmark for later discussions of these issues, particularly in the light of academic concern that the recent radical reformations of the civil service create substantial problems for British constitutional practice. The chapter concludes with a critique of hierarchy which underpins the recent reforms.

WEBER AND BUREAUCRACY

Max Weber was a German sociologist writing in the early decades of this century. He has been very influential in the English-speaking world as well as in continental Europe. He is well known for his 'ideal-typical' account of bureaucracy, less well known for his criticisms of the way in which bureaucracies take on a political life of their own, reflecting the social-class interests of their members.

To understand Weber's project in creating an 'ideal-typical' model of bureaucracy, we need to appreciate the logic of the 'ideal-typical' approach, current thinking on bureaucracy when he was writing (and how bureaucracies were run at that time), as well as his overall aims.

We also need to describe Weber's rationalization method of social research, for it is a key to understanding his ideal-typical approach to bureaucracy and the underlying justification for the hierarchical form of the civil service.

The ideal type

Ideal types are abstract constructions that enable us to try to understand the social world. Weber suggests that it is impossible to understand any given phenomenon in its totality, rather we can only ever gain a partial insight. We need to identify certain key features from the totality of any given social object, such as a bureaucracy. The features that are important are those which contribute to explaining why bureaucracy works in the way it does and which distinguish it from other social organizations such as the firm. Thus in ideal-typical explanations we abstract the important and crucial aspects whilst suppressing others. In this manner we create an ideal type.

Weber does not think this process denotes the objective 'essence' of bureaucracy nor that we have produced a 'correct' description of its essential features. Rather the ideal type is a construct by which the particular questions being addressed may be answered. Which features are accentuated and which minimized varies depending upon the problem the investigator is considering and the questions asked. For example, if we ask why a one-inch square peg will not go into a one-inch round hole we could give either a geometric or an atomic answer. Which we choose to give depends upon the context in which the question is asked (Putnam 1978: 42) Similarly, if we ask a question about the power relationship between senior civil servants and politicians, whether we give a legalistic or a behavioural answer may depend upon the context in which the question is asked.

According to Weber, the ideal type thus constructed can then be used as a point of comparison with examples of bureaucracies around the world. Differences between actual examples and the ideal type can therefore become the focus of investigation. If a given bureaucracy does not work in ideal-typical fashion, we can examine why and explain the differences in the operation of actual bureaux as opposed to what is expected by the ideal type.

The ideal type is a general description which maps out the form of some social scientific concept. It gives the criteria which any object must satisfy to some extent if it is to count as an example of the concept. The ideal-typical bureaucracy thus maps out the general form of a bureau; any existing bureau conforms to that ideal to a greater or lesser extent. For Weber, a bureaucracy or administration has a definite form which allows it to perform its function in the most rational manner. 'Rational' is a key concept in Weber's account and we shall return to its definition.

Ideal-typical bureaucracy

For Weber a bureaucracy or administration in its most rational form has the following defining characteristics:

1 Individual officials are personally free, but constrained by their employment when performing the impersonal duties of their offices.
2 There is a clear hierarchy of officials.
3 The functions of each official in the hierarchy are clearly specified.
4 Each official has a contract of employment.
5 Officials are selected by professional qualification, ideally through competitive examinations.
6 Officials have a money salary, usually with pension rights, and reflecting their position in the hierarchy. Officials may leave their jobs when they desire and their contracts may be terminated under certain circumstances.
7 The official's post is his sole or major occupation.
8 There is a clear career structure with promotion by seniority or merit according to the judgement of superiors.
9 The official may not appropriate for his personal use the post or its resources.
10 The official is under a unified control and disciplinary system.
(Weber 1978: 218–19; cf. Albrow 1970: 44–5)

These propositions do not look very surprising. Number 6 for example, 'officials have a money salary . . . ', seems hardly illuminating at all, although when Weber was writing, the days of the amateur or casual civil servant were not long past. Similarly notions of officials having no other jobs, being selected by appropriate qualifications and so on, though becoming standard in Britain at that time had begun to be implemented in the home civil service only during the decades following the Northcote-Trevelyan Report of 1854. Before then, individuals were often given jobs within the civil service through personal or family contacts with politicians or civil servants.

The Northcote-Trevelyan Report established the civil service as one of the bedrocks of the British state. The Fulton Report of 1968 describes the home civil service as 'fundamentally the product of the nineteenth-century philosophy of the Northcote-Trevelyan Report'

(Fulton 1968: 9). At only twenty pages long the report is still worth reading for terseness and precision. Its recommendations were not accepted immediately and many of its aims were not accomplished for more than fifty years. Northcote-Trevelyan was produced after great parliamentary debate about the merits and efficiency of the home civil service during the nineteenth century. It suggested six main reforms which created the civil service in its modern form and are still in place today (though some are being changed following recent reforms):

1 The civil service should be divided between superior and inferior posts corresponding to intellectual and mechanical tasks.
2 Entry into the civil service should be for young men who are then trained 'on the job'.
3 Recruitment should be on merit based upon competitive examinations overseen by an independent central board.
4 Examinations should include as broad a range of subjects as is practicable and should include exercises pertinent to official business.
5 All promotion should be on merit.
6 The civil service should become less fragmented and allow individuals to move from department to department and be given a more uniform pay structure.

Of these six recommendations, four seem almost trivial today, whilst one may seem unfashionable. The most controversial in its day is the one now taken most for granted. The idea of merit-based intake and promotion horrified the aristocracy who perceived in it the seeds of their own destruction (Chapman and Greenaway 1980: 40–50; Hennessy 1990: 43–6), though that hardly came to pass. The recommendation, now increasingly out of favour, is the idea of training 'young men' rather than taking 'men of mature age, who have already acquired experience in other walks of life'.[1] Perhaps the most often repeated criticism of the higher civil service is the lack of interchange between the public and private sector. Civil servants, it is claimed, do not understand business. The reasoning of Northcote-Trevelyan is worth noting, however, for their views are not so much at odds with present thinking as might be imagined:

> In many offices . . . it is found that the superior docility of young men renders it much easier to make valuable public servants of them, than of those more advanced in life. This may not be the case in the higher class of offices, but it is unquestionably so in those where the work chiefly consists of account business. The maintenance of discipline is also easier under such circumstances, and regular habits may be

enforced, which it would be difficult to impose for the first time on older men. To these advantages must be added the important one of being able, by proper regulations, to secure the services of fit persons on much more economical terms.

(Northcote and Trevelyan 1853: 111)

Whilst Hennessy (1990) is correct that this attitude sowed the seeds of the tradition of an administrative class proceeding from their public school to Oxbridge to running the country, Northcote-Trevelyan distinguished between the advantages of on-the-job training for the lower, executive grades ('account business') whilst acknowledging the benefits of bringing in 'mature men' for the top positions. The idea of the 'superior docility of young men' fits very much with the Weberian idea of the administration as a machine, with each worker a noncognizant cog with no need for flair or imagination. How far a unified system is 'economical' depends more upon other economic conditions: during full employment it most certainly is, with high levels of unemployment it may make little difference.

Rationality and efficiency

In what sense is this system 'rational'? In what sense is it 'efficient'? To understand why Weber thought it was so, both the culture in which he was writing and his justification of hierarchy needs to be considered. This approach may seem to take us far afield from the British civil service today, but if we are to contrast modern conceptions of efficiency and rationality with Weberian ones, we need to understand the subtleties of both.

According to David Beetham (1975), Weber's account of bureaucracy has three elements.[2] First, bureaucracy is seen as a technical instrument. Secondly, it is seen as an independent force in society since it has an inherent tendency to overstep its proper function as a technical instrument. Thirdly, this inherent tendency develops because bureaucrats are unable to divorce their behaviour from their interests as a particular social group. Thus bureaucracy exceeds its proper function because its membership tends to come from a particular social class. The second and third aspects of Weber's account of bureaucracy, contained in his political writings, have been ignored by writers on public administration who concentrate upon the first aspect contained in his sociological writings. This has distorted Weber's views to such an extent that almost the opposite of what he believed have been represented as his theories. This chapter concentrates upon the technical aspects of Weber's account. Chapter 6 considers his political arguments.

THE BUREAU AS A MACHINE

A bureau is a rational response to a set of goals in so far as it provides the best means of attaining them. Bureaucrats should not establish the goals to be attained, for that is a political function to be fulfilled by their political masters. The model Weber has in mind is a machine, set up and ready to go: when given a task the machine mindlessly pursues the goals following set procedures and processes. Thus each individual civil servant is a cog in the machine, with no personality or interests. No civil servant need have any creative input to the process and hence no individual has accountability except to the degree that they carry out their proper function according to the rules and processes of the organization. In this way the civil service can serve as a neutral force with no class or group interests. The state can perform via its civil service the cypher role traditionally assigned to it by classical pluralist theory (Dunleavy and O'Leary 1987). The neutral aspect of the function of bureaucracy in Weber's thought was well known to the conservative thinkers of his age. Where Weber differed somewhat was in his account of the bureaucracy as a machine rather than seeing it as an organism contributing to the organic unity of the state. However, the second and third aspects of his account of bureaucracy contradict the prevailing contemporary view. He sought to demystify bureaucracy as a part of the state.

The dominant view amongst German scholars in Weber's time was that the bureaucracy formed an independent political force standing outside and above the competing political actors of the day. The bureaucracy was seen as neutral, not in the sense that it merely carried out the orders of its political masters, but rather in the assumption that it was not swayed by the sectional interests of party or class and was endowed with special expert wisdom and disinterestedness, which allowed it to decide what policies were in the best interests of the nation as a whole. German academics did not consider the bureaucracy to be perfect but believed its problems were technical which, with the correct administrative reforms, could provide an antidote to the special inter-ests which caused strife in the modern state. These academics were fearful of democracy, believing that democratic governments would rule not in the general interest but in the interests of those sections of the population which put them in power. They felt that the best government was essentially one of the wisest administrators advising a monarch – the perfect bureaucratic state.

Weber's account of bureaucracy should be counterpoised to this conservative Prussian position in order to be fully comprehended. He agreed with the conservatives that bureaucracy provides the best technical means of administration; however, he had no faith that it could provide a neutral political force above the sectional interests of the day. He was fearful that any political neutrality that might be hoped for from a set of experienced and technically equipped administrators would be overridden by their class interests. Like any other political force, bureaucrats would rule in the interests of the class of which the vast majority of them were members. Weber insisted therefore that bureaucracy should only be a technical instrument and that its neutrality could be assured only if it carried out the instructions of its political masters, whatever those instructions were. This neutrality is of a different kind from that claimed by the conservatives. Rather than being neutral between competing interests by ignoring those interests and going its own way, the bureaucracy would be neutral by doing whatever the dominant interests ordered. This version of bureaucracy as a technical machine of the government allows bureaucracy to be a tool of democracy. The dominant interests would be elected to power, and have the state machine available to carry out their policies in the most efficient manner possible.

We need to examine why Weber thought that hierarchical organization provided the state with the most efficient and rational machine and what he meant by 'rationality' in this regard in order to contrast the Weberian account with the rationality inherent in the 'rational choice' models examined later.

Rule-governed authority

The modern state for Weber was constituted by the creation of a 'legal-rational' form of authority. He identified three types of authority or legitimate domination in society:

1 'Legal-rational' authority which rests upon belief in the legality of the law and the right of those in authority to issue commands to the rest of society.
2 Traditional authority which rests upon the established belief in rules which have been exercised for generations and in those who traditionally command.
3 Charismatic authority which is invested in particular individuals

because of some exemplary character or action such as heroism.
(Weber 1978: 215)

Weber believed that in the modern age the first type of authority grew
in importance as the second two waned. Bureaucracy gained its
authority through being rational and legal. Beetham (1985: 67–9) points
out that there are two elements of the idea of 'legal-rational' authority
as applied to bureaucracy. The first is the legality of bureaucratic
decisions, which is attained through procedural correctness. Individuals
in a society will accept the decisions of any agent of the state as long
as they are assured that these decisions have been made according to
the correct procedures. This contrasts with pre-modern societies where
allegiance is given to those in authority either through tradition or
because of their charismatic personalities. In the modern state allegiance is to impersonal rules. Furthermore, procedural correctness is
important when a new law is introduced or an old law changed. If the
law is based upon tradition, then the scope for changing the law is
severely limited unless some charismatic ruler can start afresh. However,
in modern society new laws can be introduced more easily as long as
the process by which they arise itself conforms to the correct procedures. Thus both law itself and its implementation are governed by
the correct procedures. The authority of the state and the stability of
society can be maintained only if citizens are satisfied that procedural
correctness is guaranteed.

The second concept is rationality. Weber used the term 'rationality'
in several different senses. He formally distinguished between 'instrumental' and 'intrinsic' rationality. The first is the rationality of choosing
the best means to any given end. The second concerns the rightness or
bestness of any particular end. Bureaucracy is rational for Weber
primarily in the first 'instrumental' sense. It brings about ends, chosen
by its political masters, in the most efficient and effective manner. But
civil servants do not only act on the instructions of their political
masters; they also advise them on the ends to be achieved. This advisory
function is rational to the extent it is governed by explicitly formulated
rules and carried out by experts with the relevant knowledge.

Thus Weber specifically called bureaucracy 'rational' because it
involved control on the basis of knowledge, in particular, specialized
knowledge; because of its clearly defined spheres of competence;
because it operated according to intellectually analysable rules; because
of the calculability of its operation; finally, because technically it was
capable of the highest level of achievement (Beetham 1985: 69).

Whilst Weber believed there was a growing tendency for society to become more bureaucratized and therefore more 'rational' in this sense, it is a mistake to infer that he welcomed this growing 'rationalization' and bureaucratization of society. He feared that economic and political initiatives could be destroyed by an overwhelming bureaucracy, because the risk-taking role of the entrepreneur, so important for economic dynamism and technical progress, is the very opposite of the risk-aversion expected of the bureaucrat. Indeed, considering the subsequent stagnation of communist Eastern Europe and the Soviet Union, he made very prescient comments upon the dangers of a centrally planned society.

Weber saw bureaucracy as dangerous in another sense too. Not only could it stifle society if it took over too many of the functions of the private market, it was also potentially the most powerful political actor in the state. Indeed Weber recognized that the very factors which made bureaucracy rational were those very features which allowed it to gain powers to control and influence society. He saw clearly that modern society was to some extent dominated by bureaucracy: 'power is exercised neither through parliamentary speeches nor monarchical enunciations but through the routines of administration' (Weber 1978: 1393). He believed that this dominance would grow.

Weber talked about the bureaucracy in two senses: first as a set of individuals taken as a whole, and second as an organization or a set of routines. He believed that it is the bureaucracy itself which is the source of power, though individual bureaucrats actually wield that power. He defined power as 'the probability that one actor within a social relationship will be in a position to carry out his own will despite resistance, regardless of the basis on which this probability rests' (Weber 1978: 64).

So actors wield power, and individual bureaucrats therefore can be powerful, but the job itself imposes constraints. The bureaucrat

is only a small cog in a ceaselessly moving mechanism which prescribes to him an essentially fixed route of march. The official is entrusted with specialized tasks, and normally the mechanism cannot be put into motion or arrested by him, but only from the very top.

(Weber 1978: 988)

This complexity and systematization are bulwarks of bureaucracy, as would-be reformers discover when they take on the civil service machine.

Top civil servants, the policy-makers in the higher reaches of the administrative class, are indeed powerful and their power is based upon the resources they have available.[3] One of the fundamental bases of civil-service power, as Weber recognized, is knowledge:

> Apart from being rooted in the administrative division of labour, the power of all bureaucrats rests upon knowledge of two kinds: First, technical know-how in the widest sense of the word acquired through specialized training. . . . However, expertise alone does not explain the power of the bureaucracy. In addition, the bureaucrat has official information, which is available through administrative channels and which provides him with the facts on which he can base his actions. Only he who can get access to these facts independently of the officials' good-will can effectively supervise the administration . . . the bureaucracy's supreme power instrument is the transformation of official information into classified material by means of the notorious concept of the 'official secret'.[4] In the last analysis, this is merely a means of protecting the administration against supervision.
>
> (Weber 1978: 1417–18)

Bureaucracy has therefore to be controlled or it will dominate society. This view led Weber, unlike his conservative opponents, into the defence of democracy.

Weber believed that whilst growing bureaucracy was inevitable in a modern state, so was democratization. The very idea of a modern state included concepts of the equality of people, leading to the idea of universal suffrage. Weber had no utopian illusions about the nature of democracy. It would not alter the essential basis of political rule – oligarchy – rather it would alter the basis of selection of the elites who would rule. Elite rulers in the modern state can operate only with mass support, which is mobilized by organized political parties. Weber believed democratic processes were vital for controlling the oligarchic tendencies of elites to govern in their own interests. The need to seek support and maintain their position through elections forms an important check upon political leaders. As a part of this check upon oligarchy, a strong parliament is necessary. Weber also argued that as well as the right institutions, the right sort of politicians are required. These are people who are willing and able to take personal responsibility for policies and their consequences. It is right therefore that politicians direct the work of government, and bureaucrats implement it. Weber saw the British system of government as conforming most closely to this picture, and indeed the constitutional structure of ministers, parliament and the civil service conforms to Weber's ideal.

The next two sections will consider the British constitution and the duties of ministers and their servants.

DEPARTMENTS, MINISTERS AND CIVIL SERVANTS

It is a curious fact that what constitutes a department, a minister or a civil servant is not easily defined. The constitutionally minded might define a department as a structure of officials under a minister with the responsibility to report upon and answer questions on their activities in parliament. The importance of this definition was demonstrated by the Crown Agents Affair in 1978. The Crown Agents acted on behalf of dependent colonies and had been closely supervised by the Minister in the Colonial Office, but once those colonies became independent this supervision ceased. One of the conclusions of the Tribunal of Inquiry into the workings of the Crown Agents was that it appeared to be working outside of any department, since no minister seemed to consider the Crown Agents to be within their areas of responsibility and its accounts were not required to be laid before parliament (Ganz 1980). It was made a public corporation by the Crown Agents Act of 1979 and may be considered a quasi-governmental organization (a 'quango'). However, political scientists more interested in examining the workings of the bureaucracy define departments in a multiplicity of ways (Clarke 1975; Hood *et al.* 1978; Hood and Dunsire 1981; Pitt and Smith 1981; Pollitt 1984; Rose 1987; Dunleavy 1989a; Hennessey 1990; Drewry and Butcher 1991; Madgwick 1991; Smith *et al.* 1993).

There is no need to assume that there must be one all-encompassing definition. It may be more useful for different purposes to disaggregate government business – such as overall ministerial responsibility, or management control or tracing monetary trails. Moreover, around a quarter of the UK civil service lies outside departments headed by cabinet ministers (Hogwood 1993). Furthermore, over a third of public money is spent by extragovernmental organizations (EGOs) (Weir and Hall (eds) 1994).

Nor is what constitutes a civil servant any more clear-cut, and the lines are likely to become more blurred as the Next Steps reforms continue into privatization. An appendix 'Definition of a Civil Servant' to a 1977 report by the Expenditure Committee of the House of Commons confirmed that the definition is fraught with difficulties. It is worth quoting in full:

1 Apparently, the only legal definitions of 'civil servant' are those contained in Superannuation Acts. The Superannuation Act of 1965, s.98(2), reads as follows:

In this Act 'civil servant' means a person serving in an established capacity in the permanent civil service, and references in this Act to persons ceasing to be civil servants, to persons retiring from being civil servants and to retired civil servants shall be construed accordingly.

'Civil Service' upon which the above definition depends is defined in s.98(1) of the same Act as:

In this Act 'civil service' means the civil service of the State.

This is by no means a clear definition since 'the State' (as distinct from the Crown or various other institutions) does not seem to be an entity known to the law in the United Kingdom in any other context and 'the State' is not the employer of any civil servant. The Act itself seems to recognize this because it goes on to say in s.98(3):

For the purposes of this Act no person shall be deemed to have served in the permanent civil service unless he holds his appointment directly from the Crown or has been admitted into the civil service with a certificate from the Civil Service Commissioners.

This definition, though it is no doubt satisfactory for pension purposes, is most unsatisfactory in many other respects. It implies, for example, that there is an impermanent civil service the members of which are not civil servants and there are in fact many people commonly regarded as civil servants who do not fall within it. However, for what it is worth, there seem to be about 746,000 people who are civil servants in law.

2 Because of the difficulties mentioned above previous enquiries into the civil service have adopted a different definition, described in 1931 by the Tomlin Commission in the following words:

Servants of the Crown, other than holders of political or judicial offices, who are employed in a civil capacity and whose remuneration is paid wholly and directly out of moneys voted by Parliament.

Though it was adopted in 1968 by the Fulton Committee this definition too is, however, an unsatisfactory one since it implies that whether a person is a civil servant or not should be determined by whether he or she is paid out of monies voted annually by Parliament. Thus members of the Royal Household, for example, seem to be civil servants under the Superannuation Act but were not so regarded by the Tomlin Commission or the Fulton Committee, though it is difficult to imagine anyone who is more of 'servant of the Crown' than such members of the Royal Household. This Tomlin definition embraces 725,000 people.

3 The full difficulties of defining 'civil servant' are perhaps best realised by considering who in the working population is primarily

paid for his employment directly or indirectly from the Exchequer. That includes all local government employees and indeed in many countries, eg France, such employees – even including teachers – are regarded as civil servants, though they are not so regarded in Britain. Such a definition, if adopted in the UK, would add another 3 million people.

4 Even restricting the definition to exclude local government employees does not solve all the problems. There are also, under the central government, organisations with employees not paid from the Exchequer, eg nationalised industry corporations (1.9 million employees) and companies in the beneficial ownership of the Crown (400,000 employees). If an individual is employed by a subsidiary of, say, ICI, he usually regards himself as an employee of ICI as a whole and, although this may not be technically correct in law, it has an element of common sense about it since his salary will form part of ICI's consolidated accounts. Yet an employee of say, British Leyland,[5] probably does not regard himself as a civil servant and is not so regarded by others and in any case the UK has no consolidated accounts as such.

5 Apart from employees of organisations which are corporate persons in law, there are also employees of various other organisations the precise state of which is unique and even doubtful. The largest case of this is the National Health Service (1 million people) whose remunerated staff are not regarded as civil servants, although the head of the NHS is a Secretary of State. That staff also seems to be technically the employees of a variety of bodies, whilst general medical practioners, for example, contract with the Family Practitioner Committees. It is by no means clear to us why some at least of the administrative staff of the NHS should not be regarded as civil servants.

6 The importance of all this is that vagueness of definition has given scope for a fruitless juggling of statistics in which numbers of 'civil servants' are bandied about which are really almost meaningless for the purposes of sensible discussion. For example, until 1974 there were about 33,000 'civil servants' in the Department of Employment of whom 18,000 were transferred to the Manpower Services Commission and its agencies that year and thus disappeared from the statistics of civil servants. In 1976, the employees of the Manpower Services Commission and its two agencies, by then 21,000 strong, were all transferred back to the civil service thus reappearing in the civil service statistics (Civil Service Statistics 1976 and 1976).

7 We recommend that an agreed definition of civil servant which

would continue to be applicable irrespective of such changes in organisational structure should be worked out jointly by the CSD and our General Sub-Committee.[6]

The final recommendation has never been carried out and the exact status of civil servants remains unclear. Current reforms of the civil service make this a vexed and potentially important question, not only constitutionally in terms of ministerial responsibilities but also in terms of the contracts of employment and pension rights of employees (Fredman and Morris 1988).

THE FULTON REPORT

The Fulton Report, like Northcote-Trevelyan, was commissioned following doubts as to the efficiency of the civil service, particularly its ability to deal with modern technological society. It notoriously castigated the civil service as 'amateur', a controversy which diverted attention from some of its proposals. Essentially Fulton wanted to encourage the entry of more specialists such as economists or scientists. He recommended that preference be given to applicants with 'relevant' degrees and suggested that specialists should be given more encouragement to make it to the top of the hierarchy. He proposed more and better training, a Civil Service College to train administrators in management. He recommended widening graduate entry to correct the Oxbridge imbalance. Fulton wanted to see greater mobility between the private sector and the civil service. He also noted the complex grading systems in different departments which made it more difficult to transfer across departments.

Most of these recommendations were never fully implemented. Favouring relevant degrees was rejected. The Civil Service College was set up, but has not been a great success and training is still dominated by individual departments. Whilst some rationalization of grading systems occurred and there has been greater mobility between the private sector and the civil service, nothing like a unified grading structure ever came into being. Whilst the percentage of Oxbridge entrants did decline during the 1970s, the 1980s have seen reduced graduate entries and stagnant progress on this aim. Other recommendations such as hiving off certain departmental functions and making management more accountable had little impact until the fresh initiatives of the mid-to late-1980s, the Financial Management Initiative and the Next Steps (see Chapters 4 and 5).

All in all, the Fulton Report was a failure. It was overlong, poorly written and, since its execution was left in the hands of those whom it criticized, implemented patchily and without conviction (Kellner and Crowther-Hunt 1980: chs 4 and 5).[7] Nevertheless, it provided the starting-point of most discussions of the ills of the civil service until the advent of a Prime Minister, Margaret Thatcher, who believed in action rather than talk and began to introduce change without much discussion. Arguably, without the failings of Fulton, the Thatcher reforms may have made those self-same mistakes. By the 1980s and 1990s the junior civil servants of the 1960s and 1970s who tended to support Fulton were now senior mandarins much more willing to oversee change. Notably Thatcher's advisers warned her against the attempt to transform the civil service from within. The Thatcher reforms, still underway, are discussed in detail in Chapter 4.

THE CIVIL SERVICE AFTER FULTON

The Weberian account of bureaucracy offers a reasonably accurate portrayal of the British civil service as it operated from the implementation of the Northcote-Trevelyan reforms, or during much of the twentieth century. The British civil service has had a hierarchical form, in which officials have carefully demarcated duties and a clear career structure.

As the 'Definition of a Civil Servant' made apparent, many public-sector employees are not civil servants. No more than 10 per cent of public employees are usually thought of as civil servants. Other public-sector employees are found in the National Health Service, nationalized industries, armed forces, and traditionally the largest group of all, in local authorities. There are around 550,000 civil servants.[8] Ignoring the war-time peaks the civil service has grown enormously from its beginnings, as Table 2.1 demonstrates, though its numbers are now in decline (as indeed are local authority employees).

Shrinking numbers do not necessarily mean there are fewer people doing the same amount of work. Table 2.1 shows that civil servant numbers dropped by 163,000 between 1979 and 1989, but this includes over 100,000 industrial workers who left the civil service, many from the Defence Department. Many are still working on behalf of the civil service but are now not civil servants because their jobs have been privatized. Similar processes have affected non-industrial workers as certain functions, for example, cleaning and similar services, have been contracted out. In the early 1990s further reductions in numbers have occurred as sections have become extragovernmental organizations, – for example, English Heritage from the Department of the Environment.

Table 2.1   Civil servant numbers 1797–1993

Year	Number	Year	Number
1797	16,267	1911	172,352
1815	24,598	1914	280,900
1821	27,000	1922	317,000
1832	21,305	1944	1 164,000
1841	16,750	1950	746,000
1851	39,147	1960	643,000
1861	31,947	1970	701,000
1871	53,874	1979	732,000
1881	50,859	1986	594,000
1891	79,241	1989	569,000
1901	116,413	1993	554,000

Sources: Drewry and Butcher (1991: 48); Civil Service Statistics 1988–89 and 1993, London: HM Treasury.

Numbers may shrink further as new agencies are privatized or their functions contracted out. How soon and how far these agencies will be privatized is not yet clear.

The popular mythology of the civil servant takes no account of the thousands of those who work outside London or of the thousands of industrial or 'blue collar' workers who are civil servants. There are still about 50,000 industrial workers in the civil service or approximately 9 per cent, whilst only about 21 per cent of non-industrial civil servants work in London.[9] Furthermore, 55 per cent of civil servants work in the new executive agencies. Whilst the organization of non-industrial civil servants depends to some extent upon which departments they work in, we can map out general features of all departments. Before doing that we need to consider some important moments in the development of the modern civil service.

THE STRUCTURE OF GOVERNMENT

The general structure of the civil service as it relates to the government and parliament is shown in Figure 2.1. (Compare this with Figure 2.2, page 29, for the internal organization of the core department.)

This rather schematic figure presents the structure as more hierarchical than it is in reality. Networking occurs across these horizontal levels, and at the higher policy-making levels numbers are small enough for personal linkages. Many insiders talk about the 'civil service village' or 'club' (Heclo and Wildavsky 1974; Ponting 1986: ch. 1). This figure also ignores outside influences upon the civil service. The policy communities of civil servants, pressure groups and political parties

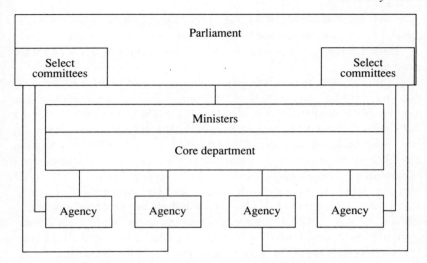

Figure 2.1 Accountability relations in the new civil service

Table 2.2 Non-industrial home civil servants in non-specialist grades, 1 April 1993

All non-industrial grades*	Men 259,300	Women 243,498	Total 502,798**	% women 48.4
Open structure				
Grade 1	36	2	38	5.3
Grade 2	112	10	122	8.2
Grade 3	421	45	466	9.7
Grade 4	269	33	302	10.9
Grade 5	2,210	343	2,553	13.4
Grade 6	3,954	568	4,522	12.5
Grade 7	11,438	1,898	13,336	14.2
Total	18,440	2,899	21,339	13.6
Administration group				
Senior executive officer	7,814	1,973	9,787	20.2
Higher executive officer (D)	168	110	278	39.6
Higher executive officer	18,723	10,213	28,936	35.3
Administration trainee	61	37	98	37.8
Executive officer	26,462	30,734	57,196	53.7
Administrative officer	28,197	62,465	90,662	68.9
Administrative assistant	11,808	29,225	41,033	71.2
Total	93,233	134,757	227,990	59.1

Note: * Includes part-time staff
** This figure is the addition of the two totals in column 3 and the total from Table 2.3
Source: Calculated from *Civil Service Statistics 1993*, London: HM Treasury.

which form around policy areas are very important to understanding the policy process at the higher levels and will be considered in Chapter 6.

Table 2.2 shows the breakdown of the civil service in terms of grades and gender.

Table 2.2 also demonstrates the unequal role of women in the civil service. Whilst almost half of the non-industrial civil service are female, their numbers as a percentage of the whole diminish as they go up the ladder to a derisory 13.4 per cent in the open structure and again their numbers drop dramatically in the higher grades. Only two women in 1993 were Grade 1 permanent secretaries. In 1971 the Kemp-Jones Committee recommended changes to help women do better in the civil service. Later reports also made suggestions for improving the position of women, which included job-sharing and greater part-time opportunities at all levels. Little progress has been made on any of these fronts.

Partly as a result of Fulton, qualified specialists as well as non-specialists may apply for posts in the open structure (hence the name). There is no formal classification of posts or individuals by occupational group in the open structure. This in part reflects the management responsibilities at this level and in part the desire for generalists rather than specialists in policy-making roles. Within the new agencies there is a more diverse set of grading structures, and there are plans to introduce a flexible set of gradings within the core departments as well (Cm 2627, 1994). In many ways the reforms contained in Next Steps (see Chapters 4 and 5) retreat from Fulton's aim of unified grades – certainly at the lower levels. What we may see in the future is unified grades in the core civil service and market-determined salaries in the periphery. However, since the open structure only applies to 5.3 per cent of all grades in the non-industrial civil service, this may not be as great a change as is often assumed. Policy-making grades may be defined as those at Grade 5 and above which constitute 0.8 per cent of the non-industrial civil service.

The lower levels do not have an open structure. Various specialist groups (such as scientists) have a different system of grading from the non-specialist posts. Different classes may exist in different departments, which impedes easy movement within the service. This is compounded by different methods of recruitment at different levels. Thus to move from an executive officer post to an administrative trainee one in order to enter the open structure may be impossible. Administrative officers, administrative assistants and other office staff such as typists are recruited directly by local offices. The Civil Service Commission takes responsibility for recruitment only at executive officer level and above. Under the age of 32, executive officers may apply to join the administration trainee scheme. Graduates comprised only 5 per cent of recruits at the executive officer level in 1965 but around half the appointments at this level by the mid-1980s. Fulton assumed that executive officers with degrees would have good prospects of going further in the civil service, right up to the top administrative levels. However, the proportion of internal candidates entering the administration trainee scheme is not as high as might be expected. During the 1980s less than 20 per cent of administration trainees were internal candidates and the percentages have shown a continuing downward trend during this decade. This has led to a large number of frustrated graduate executive officers who are over-qualified for the work they are doing, without opportunities for promotion.

Charges of elitism have always been made. Whilst only 15 per cent of those applying for high-ranked posts are from Oxbridge, they make up over half of the total who enter. Far greater numbers of arts graduates apply to the civil service, though over all those with a science background have a better chance of entering the service. This science bias on entry is lost as civil servants proceed through the open structure,

Table 2.3 Specialist component of the non-industrial civil service, 1993

Specialist group	Number
Driving and traffic examiners	1,730
Economists	195
Immigration officers	2,264
Information officers	887
Inland Revenue	49,546
Legal department	184
Librarians	428
Mapping/charting officers	2,979
Pharmaceutical officers	79
Photographers	293
Police category	4,451
Prison service	27,760
Professional and technological	18,828
Psychologists	279
Research officers	233
Scientists	9,869
Secretarial Staff	17,379
Social Security Group	43,714
Statisticians	201
Telecommunications	1,716
Others	70,454
Total	253,469

Source: Calculated from *Civil Service Statistics 1993*, London: HM Treasury.

there being a strong arts bias amongst permanent secretaries. Meanwhile grave doubts about new procedures for entry have been voiced by academics. Chapman (1993) has identified serious flaws in the Qualifying Tests (QTs) for entry. In future years the success of the new QTs may be assessed more adequately than is possible at present.

Table 2.3 is a selective look at the specialist component of the non-industrial civil service.

Specialists have always had fewer career opportunities than the generalist grades, a disparity which Fulton wanted to rectify. Specialists have been organized in two ways. Parallel hierarchies divide responsibility into generalist and technical functions. Generalist functions include such matters as finance and general policy decisions. Technical functions are provided by the specialists organized in a separate but parallel hierarchy (with a similar number of grades) to the generalist administrators. In a joint hierarchy an administrator and a specialist constitute joint heads with joint responsibilities, but at lower levels the parallel separation of functions occurs.

These parallel hierarchies have been justified on the grounds that specialists are too deeply involved in technical matters to take a detached view. It is true that there is a well-known logical problem associated with specialist advice, the 'technocrats' paradox'. If one is a specialist then one will favour one technical solution over another because of one's particular expert beliefs. Thus neutrality between competing expert opinions is not possible if the arbiter is an expert and thus part of that debate. Yet, in order to be able to make a rational choice between two sets of conflicting advice, one needs to be able to understand the technical data: hence one cannot be a neutral observer of the technical debate. The only way out is to allow non-specialists to make informed, though not necessarily expert, decisions. Thus the argument for parallel hierarchies. This solution relies upon the neutrality of generalist officials with regard to policy-making, which we may rightly view with scepticism. Policy formulation in many areas requires understanding of technical matters and thus requires the integration of specialists. If they demonstrate themselves adept at policy issues, then there should be no reason why they should be at a disadvantage with regard to generalists. It is apparent besides that creating a parallel hierarchy for specialisms does not overcome the supposed bias problem, as expert advice may become distorted upwards through the specialist hierarchy before the parallel generalists receive it. If ministers, isolated from technical matters, are advised by their permanent secretaries who are not themselves experts, then distortion may not be detected or at least competing views will not be brought to the attention of the minister. Fulton recommended the ending of parallel hierarchies, but only in a few sub-departments has this happened. Whilst specialists are making headway in the higher reaches of the open structure (around 40 per cent of the posts), they tend to fill specialist positions such as Chief Planner at the Department of the Environment. Few have attained Permanent Secretary level and those only in the role of Second Permanent Secretary.

ORGANIZING DEPARTMENTS

There is no standard way of organizing a department but all are organized along similar lines. Government departments are under the control of a minister who is directly responsible to parliament. Each minister is assisted by a number of junior ministers who are assigned particular responsibilities. The Department of the Environment has the largest number of junior officials: as well as the Secretary of State for the Environment, there is a Minister of State for the Environment, Countryside and Water, a Minister of State for Planning, a Minister for Local Government, and four parliamentary under-secretaries including the so-called Minister of Sport. Other departments come under the overall control of another department. Thus the Foreign Secretary is formally responsible for the Overseas Development Administration, though it is headed by a sometimes-Cabinet-level Minister for Overseas Development. Ministers will also have their private political office separate from the rest of the ministry, though located within its buildings.

Below these political appointments come the civil servants in strict hierarchy. The most senior civil servant is the permanent secretary, who has four main areas of responsibility. First, he is the minister's immediate adviser on policy.[10] Secondly, he has the role of a managing director ensuring that the business of the department is carried out each day. Thirdly, he is responsible for the organization of the department and its staff. Finally, he is the department's accounting officer. In this role the permanent secretary is directly responsible to parliament for the legality and efficiency of departmental expenditure and he appears before the House of Commons Public Accounts Committee to answer points raised by the Comptroller and Auditor-General's reports. In this regard the permanent secretary can state in writing disagreement with ministerial proposals which he feels cannot be defended before the Parliamentary Accounts Committee. This situation happened in 1975 when Peter Carey, the second permanent secretary at the Department of Industry, wrote such a disagreement with his Minister Tony Benn's proposal to provide funds for the Kirkby Workers' Cooperative.[11] More recently Sir Tim Lankester, then permanent secretary at the Overseas Development Adminstration, refused to sign the cheque for the Pergau Damn project, saying in a memorandum to Lady Chalker, the Overseas Aid Minister: 'Implementing Pergau now would impose a cost penalty to the Malaysian economy of over £100 million, compared with alternative gas Turbine projects. Thus, far from aid contributing to the development of Malaysia, it would at best be offsetting the extra cost of Pergau.'

Under the permanent secretary are deputy secretaries whose work covers broad areas of responsibility co-ordinating the activities of the department. Each department is broken down into branches often called divisions or, confusingly, departments, which deal with a major part of the department's functions. Each branch is headed by an under-secretary who is an extremely influential figure, often the ultimate target of most pressure group activity within policy areas. Most departments have statistics, legal, finance, establishments and organization branches. Each department's finance branch is headed by a principal finance officer of deputy or under-secretary level who is responsible for the department's financial and accounting policies and procedures. The principal finance officer deals with costing and estimates of the department's functions for the Public Expenditure Survey and prepares parliamentary estimates. The principal finance officer will also have most dealings with the Treasury and will thus be under pressure to limit departmental spending. Each branch is sub-divided into a number of units called (again rather confusingly) divisions, each headed by an assistant secretary, and these may be further sub-divided into sections controlled by a principal. Assistant secretaries handle the minutiae of policies and they are perhaps the civil servants who are most directly concerned with producing detailed policy advice. Whilst many of the branches or divisions do policy-oriented work, including policy-formation and the preparation of legislation, case-work or answers for the minister on parliamentary questions and so on, other branches are concerned with management functions which have less to do with the department's responsibilities as a whole. Figure 2.2 shows a stylized map of a hierarchy of a department. A complete geography of all departments is contained in Hennessy (1990).

This traditional civil service organization by and large conforms to Weber's hierarchical model of a large bureaucracy organized into departments, themselves organized into sections and sub-sections. Each civil servant has specified tasks carried out to a set of rules. At the apex are those civil servants within the open structure with each department headed by a permanent secretary answerable to its minister,

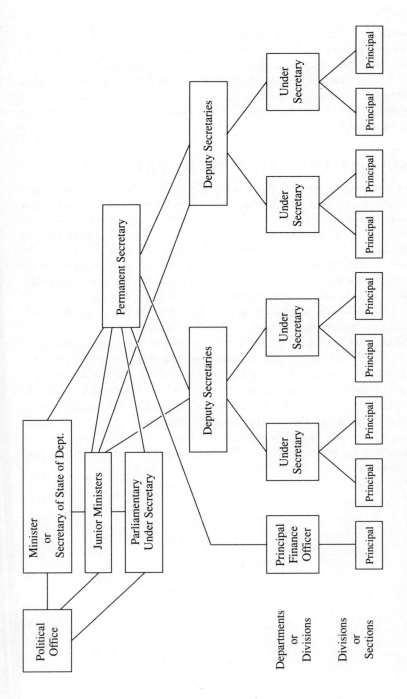

Figure 2.2 The hierarchy of a core department

who in turn is answerable to parliament. In the Weberian model this final accountability is the most important. Parliament provides the ultimate check upon civil service power. How this works in practice will be discussed in Chapter 8. The new agency structure, discussed in Chapter 4, has altered the lower reaches somewhat (see Figure 2.1), but organization within the core Whitehall departments has remained largely unaltered.

RATIONALITY AND EFFICIENCY IN THE CIVIL SERVICE

The number of investigations into the civil service over the years suggests that it does not have the reputation for efficiency or rationality that it would like. Many different explanations for its failure to meet the standards desired have been propounded. First, it is argued that the general standard of the administrator is low. The type of person who rises to the top in the civil service is not the sort of dynamic or managerial individual who can run a tight ship. The generalist philosophy breeds the amateur spirit described by Fulton. Too much recognition has been given to policy advisers and not to good general managers. Secondly, it is argued that the civil service has become too unwieldy. It has taken on too many, too diverse functions for any set of hierarchically organized managers to maintain control. Thirdly, it has become subject to too many pressures from outside government and too many political constraints imposed by elected governments. Efficiency and democracy do not sit well together, it is argued. Fourthly, it is asserted that public-sector organizations are inherently inefficient because they are unable to provide the sorts of incentives which drive efficiency in the private sector. These are the arguments we shall now consider.

3 Efficiency

Its meaning and its abuse

INTRODUCTION

The rational-choice or public-choice school has produced very influential explanations and criticisms of the nature and growth of bureaucracy under democratic rule. The most famous and influential of these models of bureaucracy is that of William Niskanen (1971, 1973), though the earlier work of Anthony Downs (1967) is also important. Patrick Dunleavy (1991) has described Niskanen as a 'New Right' thinker and Downs as a 'pluralist'. This tells us something about their conclusions. At first glance Downs and Niskanen seem diametrically opposed, Downs (1960) concluding in an early article that 'the government budget is too small', whilst Niskanen argues that bureaucracies are inefficient and budgets much larger than they should be.

Niskanen's conclusions are part of a wider set of New Right arguments about the outputs of governments under democracy. His and similar rational-choice accounts (Tullock 1965; Borcherding 1977; Brennan and Buchanan 1980; Buchanan *et al.* 1980; Pirie 1988) have been a significant influence within both academic and political circles. They provide much of the impetus and justification for recent reforms of the civil service in Britain (see Chapter 4). This chapter explains these theoretical models and analyses the distinction between bureaucratic and market provision which underlies some of their arguments. It will also adapt these models, as far as possible, from the context within which they were created – the US system of government – to the somewhat different British case.

ECONOMIC MODELS OF BUREAUCRACY

The assault upon public bureaucracy launched by the public-choice school in the United States has been instrumental in bringing about political change. James Buchanan, Gordon Tullock and William Niskanen have all argued that bureaucracy inexorably grows and stultifies capitalism by taking resources from the productive sector. Their arguments utilize rational-choice assumptions of egoistic individuals acting in their own self-interest and suggest that the structure of the modern democratic state is the major cause of the growth of the public sector. They argue that the Weberian model requires the absurd assumption that bureaucrats, unlike other people, act from selfless motives of concern for pure public interest. Rather than use such utopian assumptions, the rational-choice school views civil servants in the same way as economists see everyone else: rational maximizers. This critique of the 'utopian' nature of the Weberian hierarchical form of efficient bureaucracy must be borne in mind when we consider the ideal-typical economics model – the perfectly competitive market. It would be wrong to criticize the Weberian ideal-typical hierarchy on the grounds that it does not stand comparison with reality, if we replace it with another ideal-typical model which is also unrealistic. The true comparison should be with realistic models of hierarchy and realistic competitive models of bureaucracy.

Public-choice models consider four main groups of actors in the governmental sphere: first, the public or voters; secondly, factions within the public represented by organized pressure groups; thirdly, the government, itself split into the executive and the legislature; finally, the bureaucrats who are supposed to serve the others. The growth of the public sector in these models has two major determinants. First, there is the very nature of modern democracy and the structural relationships between voters, pressure groups and the government. In this argument the bureaucracy itself does not cause the government budget to grow but rather the relationship between the four sets of actors. The cause of the growth in public spending is external to the bureaucracy itself. Secondly, the very nature of bureaucracy also causes public spending to rise. This second argument is the 'budget-maximizing argument', where internal forces lead bureaucrats to maximize their budgets. The second set of arguments are examined in Chapter 4. This chapter examines external reasons for public sector growth.

The external reasons for growth can be split into two closely related arguments: log rolling (or vote-trading) and rent-seeking. Both shall be examined before proceeding to consider Niskanen's model.

EXTERNAL ARGUMENTS FOR PUBLIC-SECTOR GROWTH

Log-rolling or vote-trading

Log-rolling or vote-trading arguments imply that governments provide more goods than the public actually wants. At their simplest these arguments suggest that political parties try to win elections by making a multitude of different promises to different sections of the electorate to secure their votes (Downs 1957). All these promises together produce a set of goods which cost more than the sum total that the electorate as a whole would be prepared to pay if they purchased those services privately for themselves. This process is particularly prevalent in the USA, where budgets are set by committees of politicians in Congress who are more subject to the fragmented pressures of many diverse interest groups than are MPs in the centralized and unitary British system of government. Thus whilst politicians generally support cuts in the overall budget, they tend to support budget increases in particular policy areas.

Log-rolling was recognized as an unwelcome element in American politics long before public-choice analysis was explicitly used to explain political processes (Schattschneider 1935), but the economic method helps to explain how it occurs. Generally speaking, log-rolling is thought to be a pernicious feature of democracy, but it is not true to say that it always produces a welfare loss to society. Some argue that vote-trading can act like a private goods market (Buchanan and Tullock 1962; Tullock 1970), though it has also been shown that vote-trading can lead everyone to lose through trading votes (Riker and Brams 1973) and that it can make everyone better off (Schwartz 1975). The concern here is less dramatic, merely illustrative of the problems of comparison. Two simple examples of vote-trading are demonstrated in Tables 3.1 and 3.2 in which individual gains and losses can be compared.

Table 3.1 Vote-trading policies: total welfare gain

Voters	X	Y	X + Y
A	-1	-1	-2
B	+5	-1	+4
C	-1	+5	+4
Total welfare	+3	+3	+6

In Table 3.1 we have two policies: X and Y; and three voters: A, B and C.[1] If policy X is enacted, then it brings a welfare gain of +5 to B and a welfare loss of −1 to each of A and C. Similarly policy Y would bring a welfare gain of +5 to C but a welfare loss to A and B. If each policy were to be considered and voted upon separately, there would be a majority against both X and Y. However, if B and C agree to trade votes and vote for the policy which brings their new coalition partner welfare gains, then both policies will be enacted to bring a relative welfare gain to both B and C of +4, a welfare loss to A of −2 and a welfare gain to society of +6. Now consider Table 3.2. Here again both policies will be enacted because the relative welfare gain to B and C of vote-trading is +2, but there is an overall welfare loss to society of −2.

Table 3.2 Vote-trading policies: total welfare loss

Voters	X	Y	X + Y
A	-3	-3	-6
B	+5	-3	+2
C	-3	+5	+2
Total welfare	-1	-1	-2

Table 3.1 thus demonstrates an overall welfare gain to society through log-rolling, whilst Table 3.2 demonstrates an overall welfare loss. In each case notice that vote-trading occurs because the trade gives a relative gain to each vote-trader and is unrelated to whether or not there is an absolute gain or loss to society.

Does Table 3.2 show in this case that vote-trading was bad? Many people would argue it does, even though a majority of the voters gain by trading their votes. If you think the outcome in Table 3.2 is wrong because there is an overall welfare loss, then you are taking some form of utilitarian stance in the belief that what matters for good government is the overall utility or welfare of each potential policy.[2] Some people who oppose vote-trading do so on the grounds that the results of Table 3.2 occur more frequently than those of Table 3.1. They argue that the structure of links between voters, pressure groups and politicians means that the government tends to provide benefits to small groups of people or firms, bringing about an overall welfare loss to society. However, some opponents go even further and hold that vote-trading is also wrong in the case of Table 3.1. They argue that it is not right that voter A should lose out through a combination of the self-interests of B and C. Underlying this view is a normative commitment to the idea of Pareto-efficiency.

It is worth pausing here to consider the term 'efficiency', which is the key concept in the debate over civil-service reform. Yet, in the history of the social sciences there are few words upon which so much confusion has been bestowed by so many.

EFFICIENCY AND EFFECTIVENESS

Pareto-efficiency

The Italian social scientist Vilfredo Pareto (1848–1923) was a positivist who believed that it is possible to create a social science which does not include normative judgements about how the world should be but just describes and explains the world as it is. He believed that the cardinal addition of utilities in the manner of Tables 3.1 and 3.2 is unscientific, for there is no objective way of measuring interpersonal comparisons of utility. That is, we can never be sure whether the pleasure one person derives from the government's policy X is twice as much as another person's, half as much again, or just the same. We can never be sure since individual utility is not open to external inspection.[3] According to Pareto (1971) all we can ever measure is the order in which individuals rank alternatives – an ordinal ranking. If we are to assume that every individual's preferences should each count for the same in a social welfare ranking, then we can count only ordinally. In Pareto's view all that can reasonably be stated by an objective social science is that if there are two possible worlds X and Y containing the same people and resources, and if no one prefers world X to world Y but there is one person who prefers world Y to world X, then Y is preferable to X. We can uncontroversially believe that Y is preferred to X because we do not have to inspect personal utilities in this test.

Figure 3.1 shows how Pareto-comparisons can be made. Here the utility of person A is measured along the vertical axis and the utility of B along the horizontal axis. Any logically possible world in which it is not technically feasible to increase one person's utility without decreasing the other person's utility is said to be Pareto-optimal. The line A_u–B_u represents such possible worlds of which there may be an indefinite number; it is the 'optimality surface' or 'Pareto-frontier'. All possible worlds can be classified into the Pareto-optimal set along that A_u–B_u line, with the Pareto-sub-optimal set inside it.

The Pareto-criterion can also be used to classify changes in possible worlds. A movement from point v to point w is Pareto-efficient since it moves the individuals from a point inside the Pareto-frontier to a point on it. A move from point v to w increases A's utility without decreasing B's, whilst a move from v to x increases B's utility without decreasing

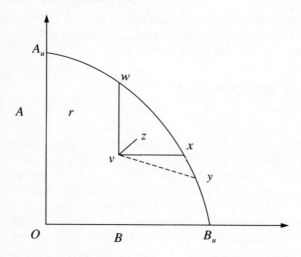

Figure 3.1 Pareto-moves

A's. However, a move from *v* to *y* is not Pareto-efficient even though it moves the individuals from a point inside the Pareto-frontier to a point on it, because although this increases *B*'s utility, it decreases *A*'s. Any move within the triangle *vwx*, such as *v* to *z*, is Pareto-efficient, since one individual is made better off without making the other worse off. In this case both individuals are better off. Once we are on the Pareto-frontier we are in one of the Pareto-optimal worlds, and all moves from this point, including moves along the Pareto-frontier, will be Pareto-inefficient since they will make one of the individuals worse off.

The constraints under which Pareto-comparisons can be made should be noted. The Pareto-frontier A_u–B_u can only be drawn *given technical constraints*. Beyond that line there is an indefinite number of points which are Pareto-superior to all lines upon it. In so far as these points are 'logically possible' they are Pareto-superior; but in drawing the Pareto-frontier, we are assuming that these points are not possible in the sense that technically they are unfeasible. Given new technologies, a whole host of new possibilities may arise and a new Pareto-frontier may be drawn. Figure 3.2 shows a number of Pareto-frontiers: *B–B* is preferred to *A–A*, whilst *C–C* is Pareto-incomparable to both *A–A* and *B–B* since it crosses both.

Pareto-moves as so far described are historically contingent. Figure 3.1 shows moves to *w*, *x*, *y* and *z* from *v*. If there was another point from which to start, say point *r*, very different calculations as to the Pareto-efficiency of moves to *w*, *x*, *y* and *z* would be made. Here only

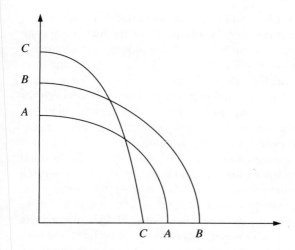

Figure 3.2 Different Pareto-frontiers

w of the marked points would be a Pareto-efficient move. Thus not every point on the Pareto-frontier is Pareto-preferred to each point within the frontier.

A world is said to be Pareto-optimal if there exists no other feasible world in which no one is worse off and at least one other person is better off. There could also be two worlds which are Pareto-incomparable if some people prefer world *A–A* and some world *C–C*. In such a case Paretian welfare economics simply cannot say which is preferable. Some writers claim these Pareto-incomparabilities never occur, for in these cases compensation can be paid. The winners in *C–C* could pay compensation to the losers, making them winners as well.[4] But such arguments misunderstand the nature of comparison across possible worlds because the world in which compensation is paid is a *different* world from one in which it is not paid. Why not simply move to that Pareto-preferred world, rather than moving to *C–C* and then paying compensation?[5]

Some economists assert that the Pareto-principle is a 'very weak ethical postulate'. Buchanan and Tullock (1962: 172) state: 'Clearly this postulate must be accepted by those who accept any form of individualistic values, that is those who consider the individual rather than the group to be the essential philosophical entity.'

Only a little thought reveals that the Pareto-principle is a very strong normative principle, and the idea that anyone holding individualistic ethics must agree with it is nonsense. In Figure 3.1 where the

Pareto-frontier crosses the horizontal axis, *A* could be receiving his zero utility where *B* gets her maximum. Similarly where the line crosses the vertical axis, *B* receives zero utility and *A* maximum, but any move from that point is Pareto-inefficient. So if moving from a situation where one person is starving whilst all others are well fed requires taking from the well fed some small morsels of food, it is concern for the starving person *as an individual* that would justify such redistribution even if some or many of the well fed objected. Pareto-optimality as an ethical postulate is a very strong one.[6]

This diversion into Pareto-comparisons is necessary to understand the arguments of Niskanen and others about the externally generated inefficiencies of bureaucracies. The inefficiency of bureaucratic as compared to other decision processes is Pareto-inefficiency. Yet there is a strong moral component in these arguments. Hidden behind the pretence of a morally neutral science of economics, or at least one with only a 'weak moral postulate' obvious to all who care about individuals, is a commitment to the idea that any form of redistribution which is not agreed by the person losing is morally wrong. This strong moral stance is concealed behind the argument that any such process is 'inefficient'.[7] Moreover it boosts arguments for market processes since, as we shall see, markets are held to produce Pareto-efficiency since they involve uncoerced trades. The willingness to trade is thought to prove that individuals believe they are better off in the post-trade world than they were in the pre-trade world.

Other uses of 'efficiency'

The technical sense of Pareto-efficiency is not how most of us ordinarily understand the term 'efficiency'. When many academics – and probably all politicians – suggest the civil service should be made more efficient, it is not Pareto-efficiency in this sense that they have in mind, but rather some subset of it.

Christopher Pollitt (1992) discusses six criteria by which policies or services can be evaluated. They are economy, productive efficiency, allocative efficiency, effectiveness, cost-effectiveness and equity. Economy simply means minimizing inputs or spending as little as possible. Making a process more economic in this sense does not necessarily bring Pareto-efficiency, because spending less may mean lower outputs which could be disadvantageous to some people. Productive efficiency is the *ratio* between inputs and outputs. We can improve productive efficiency by holding inputs steady whilst increasing outputs or by holding outputs steady whilst reducing inputs. When politicians demand greater efficiency of the civil service, they mean productive efficiency.

Pollitt suggests that effectiveness is a different kind of criterion altogether, and one much discussed by civil servants themselves. It is 'the degree to which the final outcomes (not outputs) of a service or policy match the original objectives for that service/policy. The closer the match, the more effective the policy' (Pollitt 1992: 24). If the policy is to help British firms win export orders, and government reduces regulation within Britain, thus lowering costs and helping win export orders, the policy may be effective. Cost-effectiveness occurs when one chooses the cheaper of two equally effective policies. Subsidizing industry to cope with regulations may be equally effective in helping win export orders, yet be less cost-effective than simply doing away with regulations.

Allocative efficiency is usually concerned with the way in which outputs are allocated to the public at large. If some people get more of a good than they really want, whilst others get less, then the allocation is said to be inefficient. Universal provision of family allowance is often deemed allocatively inefficient because some families do not need the money whereas other families need more. Paying out the same total amount targeted on needy families is said to be allocatively more efficient. This use is closely tied to the use of Pareto-efficiency. The market is usually considered to be allocatively efficient since people pay what they are prepared to spend on goods in a market, though this assumes a link between wealth and utility. Non-market methods mean we cannot be sure how much of a good people want, except by the cruder methods of democracy. Equity is simply the prescription of equal treatment which is often held for the allocation of resources paid for through coerced taxation. Thus the police are supposed to treat all equally according to their needs, and the military in maintaining the defence of the realm defend all equally. Figure 3.3 links Pollitt's criteria together.

A policy can be viewed as a means by which a particular set of inputs (staff, money, equipment) are combined to produce a certain set of outputs. These outputs are designed to produce a desired set of outcomes but, as Pollitt points out, outcomes may be analytically distinct from outputs. Most of Pollitt's types of efficiency are subsets of Pareto-efficiency, as shown in Figure 3.4, which depicts the relationship between the types of efficiency.

Along the top row is equity and effectiveness, which can be competing or complementary aims of government policy. Equity may be the

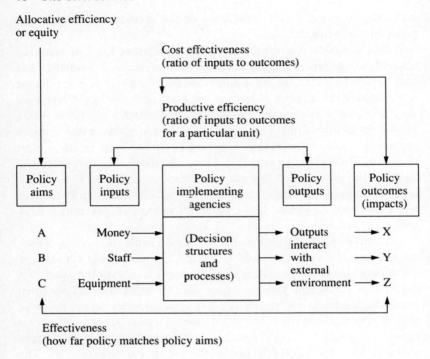

Figure 3.3 Different aspects of efficiency on policy outcomes
Note: Modified from Pollitt (1992: 24)

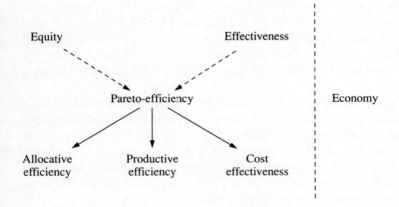

Figure 3.4 The relationship between types of efficiency

priority with all efficiencies subsumed under it. Pareto-efficiency thus becomes a part of the aim of equity, and a policy is Pareto-efficient subject to the constraint of equity. The figure links the two with a dotted line, however, since an equitable policy is often claimed to be allocatively inefficient, as earlier shown with universal provision of family allowance. Thus Pareto-inefficiency (in its subset allocative efficiency) is often used to criticize equity.[8] Pareto-efficiency may be attained subject to the constraint of the policy aims – its effectiveness – though again, government aims are often criticized on Pareto grounds, so once more the line is dotted. Allocative efficiency, productive efficiency and cost-effectiveness are all subsets of Pareto-efficiency. Cost-effectiveness is related to effectiveness directly as well as through Pareto considerations. Economy is not logically related to any of the other principles and so is left to one side in the figure.

RENT-SEEKING

Rent-seeking is the process by which money is spent trying to persuade the government to provide special benefits for a firm or industry or any other group (Buchanan, Tollison and Tullock 1980). It is held to be inefficient for three reasons. First, rent-seeking industries or firms try to persuade governments to provide them with special privileges which allow them to compete on more favourable terms. Such terms shield them from the rigours of the competitive market and allow them to be less productively efficient than they would be under perfectly competitive conditions. Second, resources (money, time, effort) spent by the company or industry on the rent-seeking activity could be better spent on other activities such as increasing productivity through capital investment (Tullock 1990: 198). Finally, the response of government officials to rent-seeking activity is a cost to society; their energies could have been allocated to other uses.

The rent-seeking argument is important but, like the log-rolling argument, it needs to be distinguished from claims that bureaucracy is internally or inherently wasteful and inefficient. The processes of democracy, and particularly the US version of it where these arguments originate, may be wasteful and include Pareto-inefficiencies, but these processes may be helped along by a very efficient bureaucracy.

Rent-seeking arguments are about inefficiencies generated when resources are not used to the best effect. The underlying assumption is that competition always ensures that sources are used to best effect. As Chapter 4 shows, that assumption forms the bedrock of recent reforms of the civil service. However, if the assumption is false and competition does not always ensure that resources are spent in the best possible way, then rent-seeking might occur under competitive conditions where it would not have done so under hierarchical conditions. Chapter 5 returns to this point.

The US and the British case

Log-rolling and rent-seeking arguments were developed by American political scientists and are well known in US politics. They are relevant to Britain, though it has a different political structure. Log-rolling and rent-seeking take a different form in Britain. Log-rolling is much more common in the US than in Britain. Legislation, whether initiated by Congress or the President, needs to pass through both the House of Representatives and the Senate. Rules in both houses allow it to be amended by members to the extent that all sorts of conditions can be added to the original proposal. For example, amendments to the defence budget might include conditions that so much money must be spent in a certain state or on a particular project. The lack of control over members by the party hierarchy, including the President, and the members' strong constituency interests makes log-rolling easy and Congressmen and Senators good targets for lobbyists. In Britain such scope for log-rolling is severely limited. The fact that legislation is almost entirely initiated by the government, strong party discipline and the whipping system in the House of Commons allows the government to force through legislation in much the form it desires.[9] This is not to say that a form of log-rolling is not possible, but in so far as it occurs it is much more informal and behind the scenes. MPs are therefore less of a target for lobbyists than in the US. Though with the rise of professional parliamentary lobbyists (Jordan 1991), and of select committees and as a result of a smaller government majority, British MPs do face increased lobbying.[10]

Similarly in the US rent-seekers see Congressmen and Senators as important targets. Whilst MPs (and particularly certain MPs) are also targeted in Britain, rent-seekers generally understand that the bureaucracy and members of the government are the better targets for their aims. So while log-rolling is not as important in Britain as in the US, rent-seeking is, though in Britain rent-seekers behave in slightly different ways to achieve their aims. Whilst rent-seekers lobby both elected politicians and civil servants, less attention is directed at the legislature in Britain.

NISKANEN'S EQUILIBRIUM ARGUMENT

We turn now to the rational-choice models of bureaucracy proper, beginning with that of Niskanen.[11] There are two aspects to Niskanen's model: the *equilibrium argument* and the *behavioural foundations*. The equilibrium argument is supposed to follow from the behavioural foundations, though both stand independently of one another. Most of the criticisms directed at Niskanen's model by political scientists focus on the behavioural foundations. Both theoretical arguments and empirical evidence have been marshalled against his conclusion that bureaucrats attempt to maximize their budgets.[12] Nevertheless, Niskanen's equilibrium argument will be considered first since it has not been thoroughly understood by many commentators in politics.

Niskanen's model is designed to show how bureaucrats influence the efficiency of resource allocation and how bureaucracy compares in (both productive and Pareto-) efficiency with firms in competitive markets and private-sector monopolies. Niskanen makes certain assumptions about the behaviour of bureaucrats. Equally important to his model are the constraints upon bureaucratic behaviour created by the environment in which civil servants find themselves. These include the relationship between bureaucrats and politicians, particularly the government, and the relationship between these two sets of actors and the public. Essentially the relationship between bureaucrats and the government is a bilateral monopoly. A government department supplies a set of goods in exchange for a budget:

> The primary difference between the exchange relation of a bureau and that of a market organisation is that a bureau offers a total output in exchange for a budget, whereas a market organisation offers units of output at a price.
>
> (Niskanen 1971: 25)

There are no general solutions to bilateral monopoly bargaining, because the outcomes depend upon the relative bargaining strengths of each side. In the government-bureau bargain the bureaucrats have the advantages of a near monopoly of information about production and costs, a longer average length of tenure, and the possibility of utilizing public opinion and/or pressure groups against the government. Governments have the legitimacy of their elected position, often enhanced when they are elected on specific election pledges. The length of tenure of Mrs Thatcher was an important factor in her reforms of the civil service.

There are several important points to note. The first is that the equilibrium account (see below) has several aims, one of which is to compare the outputs at equilibrium of different sorts of organizations. Niskanen's general demonstration is that public bureaucracies produce at equilibrium up to twice the amount that firms operating under competitive conditions would produce. He demonstrates this in his formal model by assuming that the bureau offers the government output as zero or at almost twice what the government wants. Since the politicians dislike underspending and overspending equally, they will settle for output at almost twice that which they prefer. This ability to offer a take-it-or-leave-it situation derives from a power in the formal model not actually enjoyed by bureaux. Rather they have greater information which allows them to manipulate budgets. It is this information control that Niskanen uses to defend his model verbally. Unlike a profit-making monopoly which produces less at a higher price than would firms in competition the bureaucracy produces more at the same price.[13] The comparison is between the bilateral monopoly bargaining solution and the competitive solution.[14] A naïve criticism argues that in the absence of a price mechanism it is impossible actually to collect the data necessary to test the model empirically. But, *for some purposes*, this misses the point. If it can be theoretically demonstrated that the very nature of the beast causes inefficiencies, then this gives us a reason for preferring market solutions over bureaucratic ones even in the absence of empirical demonstrations to that effect. Theoretical demonstration in the absence of empirical evidence is a scientifically valid approach. After all theory rather than empirical experience often leads us to ignore certain possible solutions and attempt others.[15]

In perfectly competitive markets the price and quantity of goods are determined by supply and demand curves. The demand curve represents the quantity of goods the public is prepared to buy at any given price. The supply curve represents the quantity of goods industry is prepared to produce at any given price. The quantity and price of the goods provided is the point where the demand and supply curves cross. This is the equilibrium point. This equilibrium may change as other factors change. If people become richer, they may be prepared to buy more at higher prices, shifting the demand curve upwards; or if firms reduce their costs, they may be prepared to supply more at lower prices, shifting the supply curve down. At equilibrium the market clears. Above it there is unsatisfied demand, so suppliers can increase their charges; below it goods are left unsold, and prices must be reduced and thus fewer will be produced. Equilibrium price (P) and equilibrium quantity (Q) are marked.

The market process is Pareto-efficient, by definition, at equilibrium

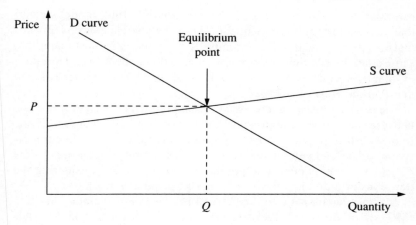

Figure 3.5 Equilibrium in a market

because under these conditions when the market clears there is no actor wanting to buy more or produce more at that price. No one wants to move away from the equilibrium point. But saying that this is Pareto-efficient is not to say that everyone is perfectly satisfied and that no one would prefer a completely different state of affairs. In Figure 3.1 (page 36) *B* would prefer to move from *w* (a Pareto-optimal point) to *z*. In Figure 3.2 (page 37) there could be more gainers than losers from a move from *A–A* world to *B–B* world, whilst some would prefer *C–C* world to *B–B* world and some *B–B* world to *C–C* world. Most people would want more of the good supplied to them than they get – it is just that they do not want more of the good *under those conditions* and *at that price* given their current wealth. Similarly it is not that firms do not want to produce more or less; it is just that they have no desire to produce more or less *under those conditions* and *at that price*.

One way of understanding this is to say that the Pareto-efficiency of the market process is 'path-dependent'. What constitutes Pareto-efficient trades depends upon initial starting points. It depends upon the resources of the firms and consumers at the start of the process. With a different set of initial resources, the market might have produced a different number of goods, or the same number of goods at a different price or not produced any goods at all. We are not able to produce Pareto-comparisons between the Pareto-efficient outcomes across different possible markets, for Pareto-efficiency is path-dependent. (Again consider the Pareto-efficient moves from *v* in Figure 3.1 page 36.)

Understanding this aspect of Pareto-efficiency in these models is

essential if we are to assess the Niskanen equilibrium model's claim
that bureaucracy is inefficient. To claim that bureaucracy is Pareto-
inefficient, one has to make a comparative claim. One must claim that
some other distribution of those resources is efficient. What is the nature
of that claim? It is that the market can produce a more efficient
distribution. How is this so?

The market process is supposed to yield productive efficiency in firms
because they all wish to produce goods more cheaply than their rivals
in order either to make more profit on goods sold or to undercut their
rivals' prices and enlarge their market share, thereby increasing profits
overall. We can explain this productive efficiency by considering the
decisions of individual firms to supply goods at any given price.

A firm in a competitive market will produce until the marginal cost
(MC) of production – the cost of producing the last good – equals
marginal revenue (MR) – the price they receive for that good – (see
Figure 3.6). At that point they maximize their profits. When firms are
in perfect competition, the demand curve is horizontal because by
definition the firm cannot affect price by increasing output. With perfect
competition marginal revenue (MR) and average revenue (AR) are
identical: that is, the additional revenue of selling another unit is the
price of that unit. (With less than perfect competition the demand curve
slopes downward and is closer to the horizontal; and demand is more
elastic, the greater the competition.)

However, with a monopoly the demand curve is the demand curve
for the industry and thus, typically, slopes downward more sharply. In
this situation marginal revenue (MR) and average revenue (AR) are not

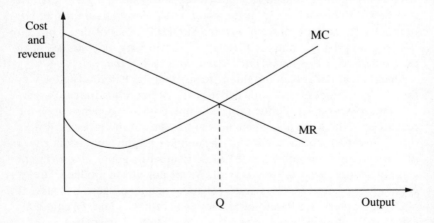

Figure 3.6 Marginal cost and marginal revenue

identical, but profit is still maximized when MC=MR. If MC < MR, profit can be increased because marginal units are adding less to costs than to revenue. If MC > MR, profits can be increased by producing less because marginal units are adding more to costs than to revenue. Thus in Figure 3.7 the output which maximizes profits is OA where MC and MR are at Ad. The price is Aa and the average cost per unit is Ab. The average profit per unit is ab. Total revenue of the firm is the rectangle AOap and total profit is ebap (which is the profit per unit multiplied by the number of units sold).

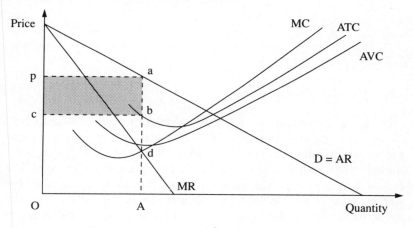

Figure 3.7 A firm's production in a competitive market

The important difference between competition and monopoly is the absence of a proper supply curve for the monopolist. With perfect competition there is a unique relationship between price and quantity which gives rise to supply curves for each firm and thus by aggregation for the industry as a whole. Under perfect competition we know the industry short-run supply curve as soon as we know the marginal cost curves of each firm, because profit-maximization involves firms equating marginal costs and marginal revenue. So if marginal costs are known, predictions can be made as to how much will be produced at each price. But under a monopoly there is no unique relationship between price and quantity supplied. Whilst the monopolist equates marginal costs and marginal revenue, the latter is not determined by the price at which the market clears. Totally different demand conditions (given in Figure 3.8 by D_1 and D_2) give rise to the same output but at different prices. Monopolies can gain super-normal profits by restricting output and gaining a higher price per unit.

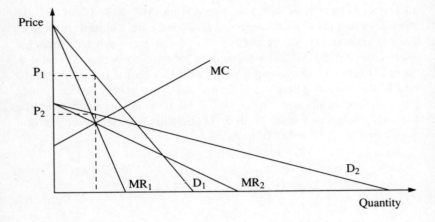

Figure 3.8 Monopoly production

In Figure 3.9 the marginal cost curve (MC) crosses the demand curve for society at point E. Here marginal costs will equal marginal revenue and so a perfectly competitive market should produce goods here. Nobody wants to trade further and so Pareto-optimality is reached. The bureau, however, does not act as firms do in a perfectly competitive market: it is a monopoly in a bilateral trading situation with the government. Nor is the bureau quite like a monopolist, for it is not driven by profit-maximization, although like the monopolist it has no incentive to produce at equilibrium E. Whilst demand is not completely

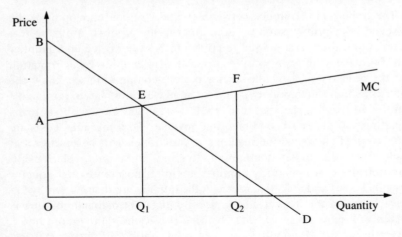

Figure 3.9 Bureau production

irrelevant in the bureau's decisions to expand output, it is not relevant in the straightforward and dynamic way as in the situation of a competitive market. The bureau will only cease producing more when the government tells it to do so. It is difficult for both the government and the bureau to know where the D curve lies, since the only signals they get are through the ballot box and the lobby system. Such signals are not as clear as those received through the market. According to Niskanen, bureaucrats take advantage of uncertainty over the true position of the D curve to push output to the higher level of point F, producing quantity Q_2 rather than the optimal Q_1. The benefits of these outputs are worth less than the marginal costs of producing them. The area EFQ_2 is waste, because more is produced than would be produced in the perfectly competitive market. A monopoly produces less at a higher unit price; conversely the monopolist bureau produces more at the same cost.

In Figure 3.9 the D curve is *essentially theoretical* and impossible to measure empirically. It represents the *amount society would purchase if the product were being sold to private individuals at the price each would be prepared to pay*. But this notion is problematic. First, not all goods supplied by government can be conceived of as being supplied to private individuals a 'bit at a time'. Secondly, not all the goods supplied by government are paid for by those who benefit from them. Thirdly, we pay for a whole bundle of goods when we pay our taxes. In the private goods market, if the equilibrium price of an item is £10 and the customer is prepared to pay only £8, then she does not purchase it at that price. Price signals the meaning of Pareto-efficient allocation, which in this case means that the customer demonstrates that she/he does not want any more of the goods at that price, all other things being equal. This does not mean that the customer does not want any more of the goods at another price or that she does not want more if other conditions change (such as income).

What does the D curve mean when price does not signal individual decisions to buy or not buy? Does it stand for individual decisions to buy or not buy if, contrary to the reality, such decisions could be made? It does not, for the demand curve represents what individuals are forced to pay through their taxes for goods they (or subsets of them) have demanded through log-rolling or rent-seeking behaviour. But would that demand curve be different if the goods could be provided by systems which did not involve log-rolling or rent-seeking? Buchanan, Tullock and others argue that it would. But the question has to be considered precisely as to what it means and whether their reasons for answering in the affirmative make sense.

Consider once more Table 3.1 (page 33). What are the three individuals demanding? Two of them, acting as a coalition, are demanding the policies X and Y. One, A, is demanding neither X nor Y. Given the voting rules, they get X and Y to the benefit of B and C and to the detriment of A. Would the market have provided X and Y? Only if B was prepared to pay for X on his own, and C prepared to pay for Y on her own. Let us imagine that B and C are not prepared to pay for X and Y on their own, assuming the same price for those policies. The market demand curve is different. Which situation – the market or the government intervention – is Pareto-superior? The answer is neither: they are Pareto-incomparable since A prefers the market solution and B and C prefer government intervention. Neither is Pareto-efficient. We have counteractually compared two situations and found that the Pareto-principle cannot recommend which is best. In an equilibrium model the difference between comparing the market versus government intervention solution and looking at market-clearing is that the first is counteractual but the second is not. What we are considering when we apply Pareto-efficiency to Figure 3.5 (page 45) is that, all things being equal, the market clears at the equilibrium point. But we are not comparing that equilibrium point with any other point where different conditions hold. However, when Figure 3.9 is compared with Figure 3.5, *necessarily* all things are not equal, for it is things other than the price mechanism which are being compared. Therefore the Pareto comparisons made within a model of perfect competition are not available. We are left comparing situations such as those illustrated in Tables 3.1 and 3.2, about which Pareto claims any objective scientist must remain silent. These can only be choosen for moral rather than social scientific grounds. The comparison between market and bureaucratic ways of producing certain goods must remain Pareto-incomparable.

If governments intervene in a market, then the market may be expected to clear at some point. When it does, Pareto-efficiency is at the equilibrium point. This new equilibrium may produce many inefficiencies, welfare losses or welfare gains; whatever else it is, this equilibrium is Pareto-incomparable with the market clearance under a perfect market situation with no government interference. In other words, government intervention and pure markets cannot be Pareto-compared any more than such comparisons can be made about the examples of vote-trading as on pages 33–4.

CONCLUSIONS

The claim of the external argument that bureaucracies are less efficient than market processes has been shown to be false. It rests on a confusion between two different types of comparison: that between equilibrium and non-equilibrium levels of production within a market model, and that between the equilibrium of the market and the equilibrium of bureaucratic production. Bureaucratic and market production are Pareto-incomparable. Concomitantly it cannot be maintained by such an argument that bureaucracies are more efficient than markets. It is fatuous to attempt to compare the incomparable in this way. We may wish to maintain that the levels of production attained under market processes are superior or that those under bureaucracy are superior; but to do so we will need explicitly normative accounts.

Critics of inefficiencies within the British civil service may consider as irrelevant comparisons between the market and bureaucratic modes of production. But the comparisons underlie the whole argument of the Next Steps and Market Testing programmes of the Conservative administrations of the 1980s and 1990s. These programmes may or may not help cost-effectiveness and productive efficiency (which will be examined in subsequent chapters). However, the idea that market methods can demonstrate demand for goods in an allocatively and hence Pareto-efficient manner has been shown to be false. The idea that the market is the preferable producer of the sorts of goods that governments traditionally provide is simply dogma.

4 Budget-maximizing
Evidence of and ending it

INTRODUCTION

The hierarchical model of bureaucracy with its assumptions of a set of disinterested, politically neutral and public-spirited civil servants came under increasing attack in Britain during the 1960s and 1970s. The left argued that the social-class background of civil servants led them to give partial advice and that they were opposed to the more radical policies of left-wing Labour ministers during Wilson's two administrations (Kellner and Crowther-Hunt 1980; Benn 1981; Freeman 1982). The memoirs of former Labour ministers and political advisers added fuel to this criticism (Crossman 1976, 1977; Haines 1977; Castle 1980, 1984; Falkender 1983; Benn 1987, 1988). Whilst this left-wing analysis did lead to a certain amount of tinkering with the civil service machine, the general complaint was about the quality of civil servants and the role they adopted, rather than a critique of the nature of the civil service itself. It was a question of people rather than organization.[1]

The New Right (Bosanquet 1983; King 1987), developed a much more thorough going and radical critique of state bureaucracy. It influenced the incoming Thatcher government much more than the sniping from the left had influenced successive Labour governments and was also influential abroad. It was a developed critique, with a theoretical pedigree based upon sustained economic analysis developed by the 'public–choice school'. The public-choice school utilizes the assumptions of economists to develop simple models of political institutions to predict how they behave and explain how they work.[2] Writers of this school argue that the modern democratic state has a built-in tendency to grow stultifying individual freedom and enterprise. They consider that the traditional public-administration assumption of civil-service disinterested 'public-spiritedness' is naïve. But rather than seeing civil servants as creatures of their social class, as the left and indeed Weber did, the public-choice school regards them as self-interested.[3] The public-choice theorists assume that everyone, civil servants included, is self-interested; and this assumption needs taking into account when explaining the workings of institutions.

As we saw in Chapter 3, public-choice models consider four main groups of actors in the governmental sphere: first, the public or voters; secondly, factions within the public represented by organized pressure groups; thirdly, the government, itself split into the executive and the legislature; finally, the bureaucrats who are supposed to serve the others (Buchanan and Tullock 1962; Tullock 1965; Niskanen 1971, 1973; Brennan and Buchanan 1980; Buchanan *et al.* 1980). The growth of the public sector has two major determinants. First, there is the nature of modern democracy and the structural relationships between voters, pressure groups and the government. In this argument it is not the bureaucracy itself, which causes the government budget to grow but the relationship between the four sets of actors. In other words, the cause of the growth in public spending is *external* to the bureaucracy itself, as was examined in Chapter 3. Secondly, the nature of bureaucracy also causes public spending to rise. This second argument is the 'budget-maximizing argument', where *internal* forces lead bureaucrats to maximize their budgets.

This chapter will consider the budget-maximizing side of the New Right critique, concentrating upon the work of Niskanen. Even if the critique of the external argument given in Chapter 3 is correct, the internal or budget-maximizing argument is still potentially valid. Niskanen's first book (1971) has been described as the 'most significant work yet produced by an economist on the role of bureaucracy' (Mitchell 1974: 1775) and is one of the most cited studies of bureaucracy (Bendor 1988). His second book (Niskanen 1973) was published in the UK by the Institute of Economic Affairs, a right-wing think tank which proved enormously influential in the Thatcher government. As well as inspiring the views of many of her private advisers (such as Alfred Sherman and Madsen Pirie) and politicians (such as Sir Keith Joseph and Nicholas Ridley), it was set as required reading for civil servants in the early 1980s (Goodin 1982). Yet much of the academic response to the book in Britain has been critical. Evidence for the model shall be examined. Did it stimulate reform despite being false? Or does the evidence justify the use of the model to prompt change?

NISKANEN'S BEHAVIOURAL MODEL

Most of the British literature on Niskanen concentrates on the budget-maximizing argument (the exception being Jackson 1982). It can be considered quite separately from the equilibrium model examined in Chapter 3, though this is supposed to rest upon his behavioural budget-maximizing foundations. Niskanen's behavioural model provides a dynamic explanation of why bureaucracies over-produce. The fact that these conclusions about inefficiency and the ever-expanding nature of bureaucracy fit perfectly with popular perceptions of civil service waste helps explain their great influence.

Niskanen's behavioural model of bureaucracy is founded upon the basic assumptions of neo-classical economic theory. Under capitalism firms are assumed to maximize profits as far as possible. Profit-maximization is the motive force of their managers. People in business maximize profit for two reasons: (a) rationality – it is rational for them to maximize profit if the labour they contribute is independent of their income; (b) survival – it is rational for them to maximize profit, for it helps the firm to survive.

It is this model of the firm which Niskanen uses as the basis of his model of bureaucracy. Bureaucracies are defined as non-profit-making organizations that exist to provide those services which, ordinarily, are not provided by the private sector. In the absence of profit what determines the behaviour of bureaucrats? Niskanen reasons that bureaucrats will attempt to maximize their budgets. In explaining why he draws an analogy with the motivation of managers in firms who maximize profit in order to survive and to increase their personal welfare. Similarly bureaucrats want to survive and promote their own welfare. A larger budget will: (a) provide more jobs for bureaucrats, thereby improving promotion prospects; (b) tend to strengthen the demand for services, making the bureau easier to run; (c) increase the prestige and patronage opportunities of bureaucrats; (d) generally provide more chances to deliver funds to individual's pet schemes and private goals.

Of course, bureaucrats do not have a free hand in maximizing their budgets: there are constraints. These constraints are determined by government which sets the output the bureau is expected to produce and supervises its expenditure. Rational-choice writers on bureaucracy have generally treated the demand and supply of government goods and services much as classical micro-economics treats the demand and supply of traded goods and services. The demand for the bureau's services comes from government; and in a democracy this is in some way related to the expectations of the electorate as revealed through the electoral process. Bureaucrats are able to maximize via the process of external demand, Niskanen assumes, because they have a near monopoly of information. They are therefore able to demand the budgets they desire in order to pretend to provide the service politicians think the public are demanding.[4]

This is not to say that there are no incentives for bureaux to seek out and implement the most efficient combination of resources; but these incentives are not as strong for public bureaucracies as for firms in competitive markets. There are a number of reasons for this:

1 The relationship between costs and profit is less direct for bureaux. For example, a firm that makes a 5 per cent profit can cut its costs by 5 per cent if it can increase its profits by 100 per cent. However, a 5 per cent reduction in costs for a bureau does not increase profits and probably entails less than a 5 per cent increase in spending power, as the government will try to claw back most of the savings. Wildavsky (1964: 93–4) argues that efficient bureaux are often 'rewarded' with reduced budgets.
2 The factor costs, such as wages, fringe benefits, fees, rents and so on, are generally lower than their full value in the public sector because the civil service has certain exemptions from taxes, rates and so on. Therefore their over-used factors of production are under-priced.
3 Some bureaux, especially those in which demand grows very rapidly, have no marginal incentive to improve productive efficiency.

Bureaucracy therefore is inefficient and expensive. It has an inexorable tendency to grow, the state sector gets too large, and too many non-productive workers stultify the dynamism of the productive private sector. Niskanen argues that a new way of organizing the governing machinery is required in order to stop the growth of the state.

The arguments of the New Right, developed during the 1960s and 1970s found a ready audience in Thatcher's Conservative Party. They fitted with the ideological presuppositions of the right and with popular wisdom about civil-service inefficiency. But how much evidence is there that civil servants attempted to maximize their budgets during the 1970s and early 1980s?[5]

EVIDENCE FOR BUDGET-MAXIMIZING

It is difficult to test whether or not bureaucracies attempt to budget-maximize.[6] Whilst increasing expenditure and staffing suggest that civil servants are maximizing, they do not tell the full causal story. In order fully to demonstrate that a public bureaucracy is maximizing, we need to be able to gauge the constraints. In fact it is easier to see whether civil servants are pursuing their self-interest in times of retrenchment, when there are great pressures upon the public purse, rather than in economically more buoyant times. Andrew Dunsire and Christopher Hood (Hood, Huby and Dunsire 1984; Dunsire, Hood and Huby 1989,

1989; Dunsire 1991) have collected evidence of the nature of bureau growth and decline from the mid-1970s to the mid-1980s, a period of retrenchment in the public sector in Britain. The time-scale is a good one for testing Niskanen's argument against the hierarchical form of organization. Later in the 1980s, with the Next Steps transformation of the civil service, the applicability of Niskanen may be open to question. But how well does it stand up to scrutiny in the earlier period?

Dunsire and Hood argue that the concept of the self-interested budget-maximizing bureaucrat in Britain (what they call the Adam Smith bureaucrat) does not stand up very well to scrutiny, and their data indicates the limitations of the Niskanen model. The problem, though, is not so much the self-interested assumptions of the model, but rather Niskanen's unrealistic description of bureaucratic organization especially as applied to Britain.

Drawing on public-choice theory, Dunsire and Hood derive a set of implications about bureaucratic behaviour during retrenchment and compare these with implications which may be drawn from Weberian models. The public-choice approach includes the following implications:[7]

1 During the early stages of retrenchment cuts will be selective.
2 Spending will be cut before staffing.
3 Capital rather than current spending will be cut.
4 Spending on grants and transfers rather than on goods, services and salaries will be cut.
5 The top rank will face fewer cuts than middle and lower ranks.
6 Specialists will be cut more than generalists.
7 Part-time rather than full-time staff will be cut most severely.

In Dunsire–Hood bureaumetric analysis it appears that departments protect their self-interest. They confirmed that departments will defend those programmes most strongly that are associated with primary-role and principal resources and cut where they interact with other departments and are outside their primary role. Dunsire and Hood also discovered that keeping a low profile on their programmes and having political clout were also resources to be used by departments against cutbacks.

Hood and Dunsire demonstrate that whilst the Thatcher governments were successful in reducing civil-service employment, they did not reduce public expenditure. Of course, as they point out, what matters is the counteractual, how much would public expenditure have risen without the government's cutback management?

Hood and Dunsire discuss the Jørgensen (1987) model of cutback management.[8] This descriptive model suggests that however an organization attempts to cut costs, the cost-cutting exercise itself entails expense. Obviously as long as savings from cost-cutting are greater than the expense, the exercise may be deemed worthwhile. However, any programme of cost-cutting finds it harder to make further cuts as time goes by: the fat is cut, then the meat, then the bone. Jørgensen suggests that each phase of cost-cutting winds up costing and not saving money. This is seen in Figure 4.1.

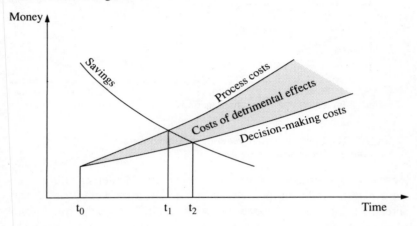

Figure 4.1 The Beck Jørgensen model – reform processes

As one programme expires – it can make no further progress – political masters determined to cut further need to bring in a new programme. The first phase is the incremental stage where cosmetic and small cuts are made, then we have the managerialist phase of the Financial Management Initiative, and finally a strategic phase where more radical changes are made under the Next Steps programme.[9] This is expressed in Figure 4.2.

Though Hood and Dunsire find the Jørgensen model difficult to verify empirically, it is suggestive of the type of rationale that engenders the programme of reform which has taken place in the civil service in the past fifteen years.

Hood and Dunsire's evidence on where major staff cutbacks occurred in the 1980–5 period strongly supports the rational-choice model. They report that whilst cosmetic changes provided most of the cutback figures in the early stages, after continued political pressures the civil service began genuine pruning. About one-quarter of these cuts were made by dropping functions (Thatcher's preferred policy) and only one-eighth covered productive efficiency gains through streamlining current programmes. But most interesting is the spread of these cuts. In de-

Money

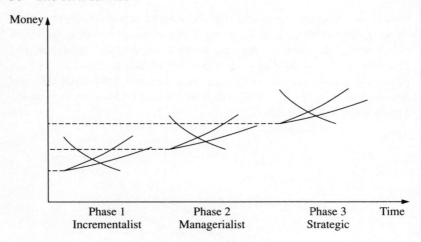

Phase 1   Phase 2   Phase 3   Time
Incrementalist   Managerialist   Strategic

Figure 4.2 The Beck Jørgensen model – phases of reform
Source: Dunshire, Hood and Huby 1989.

partments concerned with policy matters (the Whitehall clique) cuts were made mostly through streamlining. The cuts were more evenly spread in departments concerned with 'public service', 'trading and repayment services' or 'general support services'. In other words, policy staff, who make decisions on cutbacks, were unable or unwilling to cut their own functional roles; they saved by streamlining. Policy staff in departments which had service functions found ways of cutting the service side of the department whilst streamlining themselves. This suggests that those making the decisions did so in their own self-interest. Niskanen's simple model has to be re-interpreted, for he makes no distinctions between different sorts of staff. Patrick Dunleavy (1985, 1986, 1989a, 1989b, 1991) in a series of papers and a book makes a set of damaging criticisms of Niskanen in this regard and produces a more complex model of bureaucratic self-interest.

The major reason why Niskanen's model seems inapplicable is that he sees all bureaucracies as simple line agencies where the authority proceeds upwards and there is no internal conflict. He says:

> Among the several variables that may enter the bureaucrat's utility function are the following: salary, perquisites of the office, public reputation, power, patronage, output of the bureau, ease of making changes, and ease of managing the bureau. All of these variables, except the last two, I contend, are a positive monotonic function of the total *budget* of the bureau during the bureaucrat's tenure in office.
>
> (Niskanen 1971: 38)

But ease of making changes and managing the bureau for a top bureaucrat is not the same as ease of life for a lower one. Power is, often, zero-sum, and one civil servant's gain may be another's loss. Dunleavy assumes that there is a distinction between different levels of civil servants and that each level will respond differently to assorted pressures. The higher the rank, the more likely a preference for personal contracts; the lower the rank, the more probable a preference for general salary increases. Given that decisions over cutbacks are made at the higher levels, it does appear that Hood and Dunsire's evidence of where cutbacks occurred is consistent with the self-interested assumptions.

Dunsire and Hood argue, however, that when we look at which staff have been cut, the Adam Smith assumptions do not necessarily hold. Given that decisions are made at the higher ranks, we should expect the higher levels to be cut less than the middle and junior ranks (hypothesis 5). Table 4.1 shows that in percentage terms the top ranks were cut more heavily than lower and middle ranks.

Table 4.1 Percentage reductions in staff, 1980–85

Rank	Percentage
Top	19.0
Middle	7.2
Lower	10.4
Blue collar	34.0

Source: From Dunsire 1991: 187.

Blue-collar workers saw the greatest decline. This was part of a long-term reduction of staff (see Table 2.1 on page 22), and much of this was due to a reduction in numbers rather than to workers leaving the workforce. Many blue-collar workers at naval shipyards lost their civil service status through privatization. Dunsire (1991: 188) suggests that 'Top brass certainly did not preserve themselves at the expense of all others, as would have been expected had they been self-regarding; indeed, they were the first cut (in 1976) and the most heavily cut of all in percentage terms'. However, these gross figures do not demonstrate that higher civil servants were cutting themselves, rather they were not replacing themselves following natural wastage and early retirements (often to lucrative private sector appointments).

Indeed, not promoting from middle to higher ranks, can be a self-interested action for those already at the higher levels. As C. Northcote Parkinson (1958) argues, a top bureaucrat wants to increase his immediate inferiors, but not to introduce rivals at his own level. This interpretation is buttressed by decline in the middle ranks (which was reversed during 1975–80). Contrary to Dunsire and Hood, therefore, these figures do not support the 'Weberian' model.

Similarly there is no reason to suppose that generalist administrators have any greater desire than do specialists to see more of their numbers or to support the introduction of part-time workers if this means that more can be done by them for lower costs.

The main problem with the Dunsire–Hood 'bureaumetrics' approach to testing the Niskanen model is that the gross statistics they collect are open to various interpretations and that a finer-grained analysis of the interests of top bureaucrats and their strategies may reveal different conclusions. For example, Hood and Dunsire consider the proportions of budgetary increase expended upon civil servants' salaries. The major theoretical problem with their statistical analysis of salaries, both when they consider salaries as a percentage of overall budget and when they compare them to the private sector, is that they take no account of the constraint side of the equation. Civil servants do not make decisions simply in terms of what they desire but in the terms that are set for them by their political masters (see Hood and Peters 1994). In fact far fewer constraints exist in the private than in the public sector, and so we should expect to see lower salary increases in the latter (demonstrated in Hood 1992). The civil service pay system designed by the Priestley Royal Commission of 1953–55 operated until October 1980 (becoming the Review Body on Top Salaries in 1971) which was designed to be 'outside politics', providing a rationale for pay rises throughout the service. In fact, ministers repeatedly intervened at the final stages of pay negotiations. The review body was suspended 1976–78 during the Labour government's pay freeze (Fry 1983). Nevertheless, civil service pay did keep largely in line with overall public spending and increased more than prices in the same period (Dunsire, Hood and Huby 1989: 100–1).

The indirect statistical evidence does not demonstrate a lack of self-interested behaviour, for it cannot take account of the constraints on pay rises. In fact there is direct evidence that at a time of severe pressure on civil service costs, top civil servants did protect their own salaries. Christopher Monckton, formerly a member of the Prime Minister's Policy Unit, writes:

> When the Review Body on Top Salaries recommended a large increase in the salaries of top civil servants in 1985, all the papers relating to the Report were given a national security classification as though the matter were a military secret which could, in the wrong hands, endanger the safety of the State. Members of the Prime Minister's Policy Unit are cleared to see papers classified up so far

as Secret. We were, therefore, unaware of the existence of the Report or of any of the papers relating to it until we saw the Cabinet Minute recording that the Report had been agreed. At this point we at once protested at this scandalous abuse of the classification system and made enquiries which eventually revealed that the Prime Minister had taken our silence as acquiescence. It is no secret that the Prime Minster has realized that the wrong decision was taken.

(Cited in Fry 1988: 12)

Almost exactly the same story is told by Joe Haines (1977: 18–22) of his time in Harold Wilson's Policy Unit. Then, though, the papers were not given such a high classification so he managed to get a peep at them before the Cabinet met and thereby slowed down by two weeks the decision to award the high salary increases. Tactics do not change much at the top.

There is little evidence that Niskanen's behavioural argument is false. The egoistic motivational assumptions have not been disproved, though the evidence from the 1980s certainly suggests that budgets have not been continually increased, as Niskanen's argument seems to suggest. Why is this? One reason is that the Niskanen model of bureaucracy is too rudimentary. Bureaucracies are simply not organized in the way that Niskanen imagines. His model assumes that each department is run by a senior official whose job includes deciding the budget for that department. The budget thus becomes the private good of that senior civil servant and the utility of the department is equated with the utility of that senior official. This is manifestly not realistic. There are many senior civil servants in each department who all, despite hierarchical structures, have a hand in preparing budgetary claims but do not all share exactly the same interests. At any given level in the hierarchy there will be civil servants in competition with each other for promotion and recognition. As they are in control of different aspects of the department's work they will have objectives which may be at variance with those of their colleagues. Many departments have up to eighty staff at Assistant Secretary level or above. Officials may pursue their own objectives, ranging from the individually private to the collectively public: for example, vertical promotion in the bureau, promotion across departments, upward regrading of their particular job, workload reduction, diversion of money to their own pet schemes, general improvement in working conditions, general pay increases across all levels of staff, budget maximization and so on. In other words, pursuing self-interest may not always lead to budget-maximization. Indeed civil servants may gain approbation through cutting budgets.

Clive Ponting received plaudits from Margaret Thatcher for his work under Derek Rayner (see below) in cutting bureaucratic waste long before he received public recognition for other activities less welcomed by the Prime Minister.

Budgetary excess may be achieved other than through special initiatives. Each year there is conflict between the Treasury and the spending departments over the size of their budgets. Here the Niskanen model is at its weakest when applied to Britain and seems to fail through simple equivocation. Niskanen argues that bureaucrats will always favour budgetary increase, for it is in their interests to do so, and that one cannot hope to contain this pressure from within because bureaucrats are required to check up upon other bureaucrats' budgetary estimates. This argument looks like a simple syllogism:

> bureaucrats gain through budgetary increase
> bureaucrats monitor budget claims
> *ergo*   bureaucrats will always favour budgetary increase.

But the syllogism is false. The term 'bureaucrats' does not mean the same thing in the first and second lines. Consider the following:

> DfE officials gain through DfE budgetary increase
> Treasury officials monitor DfE budget claims
> *ergo*   . . . .

Finish how you will, but Niskanen's conclusion plainly does not follow. What may follow is Downs 'law of ever-expanding control'. Downs (1967: 150) suggests that 'The quantity and detail of reporting required by monitoring bureaus tends to rise steadily over time, regardless of the amount or nature of the activity being monitored'. In order to be able to make a fully balanced decision on the budgetary claims of a department, the monitoring official must have at hand all the information available to the monitored department, plus relevant contrary arguments from other sources. This problem of ever-expanding control is often handled in a much more elementary, indeed primitive, manner than civil servants would ordinarily like to admit. One Treasury official described to Leo Keliher a test for requests for money for a specific programme from the Department of Trade and Industry:

> We often subject what the DTI submits to us by way of these key technology proposals to a 'Red Jelly Test'. If we can substitute 'Red Jelly' for, say, optoelectronics without any damage to their case, then we don't think the DTI has presented a very good case because it doesn't discriminate between one technology and another. . . . It's a good exercise to go through because you come up with statements

like 'We should support Red Jelly because the Red Jelly producers are risk averse' or 'There are fantastic externalities from Red Jelly'. Bullshit.

('Treasury Official' quoted in Keliher 1987: 109–10)

It may appear that such tests are absurd, and of course they may backfire. The ever-expanding cost of Concorde in the 1960s was a result of back-of-the-envelope monitoring by Treasury officials, and more recently the costs of Trident have far exceeded the claims of those who supported its development. It is easy to be dismissive of this type of monitoring exercise but hard to provide ways out of the law of ever-expanding control. The Rayner scrutinies described below was one response, and one which again was too easily dismissed by critics despite undoubted savings. Introducing market tests may be another response to the problem of monitoring, though market methods have their own problems.

Chapter 5 will examine a more realistic and complex model which shares Niskanen's behavioural assumptions but produces different predictions, ones that may fit the events of the 1980s and early 1990s more closely. First however, we shall consider the background to the reforms of the 1980s and 1990s, and their causes.

THE THATCHER REFORMS

Thatcher appeared to have no idea of what to do about the civil service when she entered office other than to distrust it. She thought it inefficient as an institution and suffused with a misguided ideology of its own. Brought up on a second-hand diet of New Right arguments about the inevitable growth of bureaucracy and first-hand experience of the civil service which she had found unpalatable, she was determined that the civil service was not going to stand in her way. Hennessy (1990: 592) writes:

> Mrs Thatcher is a great believer in the 'guilty men' theory. In her demonology it is the protagonists of the failed Keynesian-Beveridgite consensus who have brought Britain low. She appears to treat them, almost as a Marxist might, as a class with their own values. And those with the biggest horns in this demonology are the permanent politicians, the senior civil servants who assisted at the birth of that consensus and who had succeeded in capturing every Cabinet, Labour or Conservative for its own cause from the mid-forties to May 1979.

And she had good cause to treat the senior civil servants thus. Most of the published memoirs of Labour politicians and policy advisers of the

1964–70 government suggested an undirected but nonetheless conspiratorial civil service thwarting their plans (Crossman 1975, 1976; Haines 1977; Castle 1980, 1984; Falkender 1983), whilst Leslie Chapman (1978, 1982) was writing his popular books on civil service waste and advising Thatcher during the 1979 election campaign. It was also at this time that Peter Kellner and Lord Crowther-Hunt (1980) wrote and published their 'elite conspiracy' account of the failure of Fulton. Thatcher's views were bolstered by her own junior ministerial experience of civil servants' approach to ministers:

> I saw it vary from Minister to Minister. I used to sit there sometimes and say 'That's not what you said to my last Minister. You are giving him totally different advice. Why?' And gradually they said 'Well, the last one wouldn't have accepted that advice.' I said, 'Well you're now trying it on with my present one.'
>
> (Margaret Thatcher quoted in Hennessy 1990: 630)

Indeed, as so often, Thatcher's views of the civil service encapsulated the popular wisdom of the time – the civil service is wasteful, inefficient and the true masters of the nation.

For all her distrust she had no grand strategy though her ideology does suggest a general game plan. The ideology is that the private sector is dynamic and efficient, the public sector passive and wasteful. All forms of organization which exist to defend interests are conspiracies and therefore to be opposed. The other element in the game plan which derives from the ideology but which is not unique to it is the desire to stop government expansion and reverse the growth of the public sector.

Thatcher's first move was to set up under Sir (now Lord) Derek Rayner a small unit of around six civil servants based in her Private Office. The Rayner scrutinies started a process which led to the creation of the Financial Management Unit (FMU) later the Joint Management Unit (JMU), the Financial Management Initiative (FMI) and finally the programme of budgetary devolution and agency creation, usually referred to as the Next Steps initiative after the title of the report written under the tutelage of Rayner's successor, Sir (now Lord) Robin Ibbs (Jenkins *et al.* 1988). I will describe these stages in some detail, for the reforms are an outgrowth and yet a radical departure from them. Given that rational-choice models suggest that reform is difficult, if not impossible, the measures leading up to 'Next Steps' are instructive. The full story is worth telling, for the stages of radical reform were piecemeal and took a decade to institute.

Holding down public sector pay was a key policy issue in the early 1980s – as indeed it had been in the 1970s and 1960s – but with Thatcher at the helm there was to be no backing down. The civil service unions suffered from the attacks upon trade union organization, as had all trade unions; the ending of trade union recognition at GCHQ, Cheltenham, in 1984 was a side show but a significant ideological stance. The aim to major reductions through privatization and contracting out, particularly amongst blue-collar workers. As we saw, this is in keeping with rational-choice expectations.

The civil service remained a great bulwark of the large state, operating much as before. What Thatcher wanted was a complete change of culture amongst the civil service, and the only way to bring about cultural change is through institutional change. Next Steps is both a radical departure from previous Thatcherite reforms, and at the same time the logical extension of them, given her game plan. Try to make your civil servants more manageable by making them more managerial. Do this by bringing in new managerial techniques, but when this fails – or at least fails to bring about radical cultural change – try to introduce what the game plan really dictates: the market.

Saving money

Essentially the objective of Rayner's unit was to stop the type of waste described by Chapman (1978, 1982). Rayner's job was to save money. The objectives he laid out in The Scrutiny Programme (Rayner 1982) were just a fancy way of stating that aim and how it was to be implemented: (a) to examine a specific policy or activity, questioning all aspects of work normally taken for granted; (b) to propose solutions to problems and to make recommendations to achieve savings and increase efficiency and effectiveness; and (c) to implement agreed solutions, or to begin their implementation within 12 months of the start of the scrutiny (Rayner 1982: para. 2.2).

Rayner believed that it was vital that a strict and short programme of implementation should always be agreed by departments to ensure that his proposals did not merely gather dust on Whitehall shelves. He set up various ways of scrutinizing departmental activities, each of which followed a series of stages. First a strategy was created. All departments were expected to suggest areas in which a scrutiny could be conducted. Secondly, the investigation of that area was to be carried out, usually by the department's own staff, and a report submited to the minister within ninety working days. Thirdly, an action plan was to be created which summarized ideas for implementing savings. This had to be approved within three months of receipt of the initial report. Fourthly, the savings had to be implemented. This was the responsibility of the permanent secretary within each department. Finally, two years after the initial scrutiny, an implementation report was to be drawn up to see whether or not the expected savings had in fact been achieved.

Whilst Rayner was not given any rights of access to departments and could not himself force departments to take part, appropriate pressures were put upon senior civil servants to allow the necessary access. In the first six years a total of 26 reviews was completed, identifying annual savings of around £600 million with a further £67 million of one-off savings. Many of the economies were trivial in themselves, but together they mounted up. By the end of the Rayner scrutinies in 1986, over £950 million of savings were identified against only £5 million of costs. However, many critics have argued that the identified savings were often not carried out, and others have suggested that the savings were minuscule in relation to the overall budget. Rose argues that savings in 1982–3 were only 0.4 per cent of total government expenditure and that a better measure is savings against running costs which looks more worthwhile at around 6 per cent (Rose 1987: 258). If the figure of £950 million is correct, then this is a large saving which should not be dismissed lightly and represents genuine productive efficiency gains. To argue that in percentage terms the figure is trivial is to assume that genuine efficiency savings have to be higher. That assumes that the civil service is productively inefficient; but if Rayner-type scrutinies could not identify bigger savings, this may indicate that inefficiency is not as rife as some assert. The type of inefficiencies identified by Chapman (1978, 1982) are genuine, and it is these which Rayner hit; but in overall percentage terms they may not be that large.

Norman Warner (1984) gives a good insider's account of a Rayner scrutiny in the Department of Health and Social Security (DHSS). His brief was to see if savings could be made in the payment of social security. All staff dealing with social security payments were informed and invited to make suggestions. Over fifty sent letters, and the scrutiny team spoke to staff at all levels in various local offices, the two central offices in Newcastle and North Fylde and at the Reading computer centre. The team also consulted various consumer organizations, clearing banks, National Girobank and the Post Office as well as commissioning market research in order to hear from mothers and elderly people. The draft report was completed by October 1979. The total cost of administering benefits in 1979 was about £750 million compared to the £15 billion cost of payments themselves. The scrutiny established that approximately one-third of the costs were entailed by the method and frequency of paying benefits. For example, around £167 million was paid to the Post Office to meet encashment charges and postal costs, enabling recipients to cash social security order books and girocheques at post offices. The scrutiny team suggested that benefits should be paid less often – child benefit monthly and all other benefits fortnightly. People should be encouraged to receive their payments direct into bank accounts. The team also identified some scope for simplification of internal procedures. It estimated that these proposals would save around £50 million annually in administrative costs (assuming a constant number of recipients). Nearly £23 million would come from the reduced frequency of paying pensions and by offering the option of payment direct into banks. Around £12.5 million would be saved by improved administrative procedures, and the rest from reduced frequency of paying child and other benefits. In fact, the scrutiny team's report was leaked to the press (incorrectly according to Warner) and many special interests moved to block some of the proposals. For example, the National Federation of Sub-Postmasters was worried that the changes would put small, particularly rural, post offices out of business. There is no doubt that the proposals involve policy formation and do not simply involve policy-implementation. Is it important that the proposals move business from Post Offices to banks? Are the recipients likely to suffer or gain through being paid monthly rather than weekly? Leaving such questions aside, the Rayner scrutinies show that sometimes it is helpful for outsiders to come in and ask original questions or try to provide novel solutions. This was the strength of the scrutinies.

It should be noted that for all of the problems of such scrutinies – the smallness of the savings in regard to the overall budget of the civil service and so on – they are the best, if not the only, method of overcoming the problems of monitoring without overbureaucratizing and ever-expanding control pointed out by Downs (1967). Perhaps such small 'hit teams' going into departments and agencies looking for savings should be a permanent feature of the civil service. Later attempts to institutionalize them within departments was probably a theoretical and practical mistake.

The success of the Rayner scrutinies in different departments depended largely upon the enthusiasm of the permanent secretary or the minister. One of the most enthusiastic ministers was Michael Heseltine at the Department of the Environment. Following a Rayner scrutiny, the DoE introduced a managerial system known as the Management Information System for Ministers (MINIS). MINIS was supposed to let ministers know what was happening and who was responsible for it. Using MINIS involves three stages. First, each section head identifies the activities, staff, achievements and so on within the section. They

also prepare a set of 'performance indicators' for each staff member –
time spent per task, average cost of each task and so on. Secondly, these
reports are looked at by senior civil servants and their ministers who
question section heads about their objectives and the performances in
this regard. Finally, the minister and his servants will make suggestions
to section heads for improving performance. MINIS involves an annual
cycle of such performance measurements of the previous year and
expectation for the forthcoming year. This system, simple though it
seems, provided ministers with a much more comprehensive account of
the activities of their departments than had previously been the case
with briefings for ministers in response to specific questions. For the
first time, perhaps, it enabled ministers to manage departments. Following the introduction of MINIS, the DoE was reorganized and manpower
was reduced by around 15,000 or 29 per cent (Heseltine 1987: 18).

The Financial Management Initiative

The Financial Management Initiative (FMI) was the natural continuation of the Rayner scrutinies. Its aim was to produce a system
which gave managers at all levels greater responsibility and control.
Each manager should have a clear idea of his or her objectives which
would be developed under specific priorities. All did so, but the
objectives were often exceedingly vague. Departments found it much
easier to establish objectives for administrative costs – which make up
on average 13 per cent of total costs – than for the bulk of their
programme costs.

The Financial Management Unit (FMU) – which later became the
Joint Management Unit (JMU) – was set up by the Management and
Personnel Office (MPO) and the Treasury in 1982 to help all twenty-
one departments to examine all aspects of their work and develop
programmes to improve financial management. Departments followed
the lead of the DoE and set up management systems. It is worth noting
that the 21 departments which set up management systems produced 16
different management systems. The justification for this was that each
had unique problems and procedures, but part of the point of a
management system is to produce generally applicable procedures
for measuring effectiveness and efficiency. Of course, the different
management systems had the advantage for some departments of
making it harder to compare and contrast the performance of departments one with another. Thus already the civil service had perverted
one of the purposes of the introduction of such management systems.

As a part of FMI the departments were divided, where possible, into 'cost centres' with control of their own budgets. For example, the Department of Health and Social Security (DHSS) (which was split into two departments in 1988) had over eight hundred cost centres (many of them local social security offices) each with a manager responsible for the budget. In this way the government hoped to create a set of incentives to create savings. The problem with incentives, as the Civil and Public Service Association pointed out, is that they make managers care more about saving money than about providing good service. The Citizen's Charter, ten years later, is an attempt to fill that lacuna.

To implement FMI, departments developed ways of measuring their performance and that of their employees. Any measuring technique requires a scale by which to compare relative performances. The difficulty lies in creating a valid scale. Some tasks are easily quantifiable. Running costs such as postage, staff travel costs, photocopying and so on can be used to measure throughput, such as the number of cases dealt with and their unit costs. These measures can then be used to identify areas of underperformance, to set targets, and to form the basis of staff appraisal. But such savings are relatively trivial and so the process turned to programme measurement, which is much more difficult. First, the costs may be spread across various divisions or even departments. Secondly, many programmes are simply difficult to quantify. If collective goods are being produced then the benefits yielded are not easily measured; indeed, they may not even be recognised until the programme has been dismantled and problems emerge, perhaps many years later. Problems that result from programmes are more easily seen, as it is easier to find the causes for events which have occurred than it is to identify the causes for those which have not yet occurred. To quantify such effects, proxy measures are often used, but these have two drawbacks. The first is simply that proxy measures estimate the proxy and not the effects that are actually wanted. Sometimes the proxy and what it is approximating are not very similar. Secondly, and more importantly, the proxy may be more than misleading; it may be downright wrong. One notorious example is the practice of reducing hospital waiting lists by cutting the length of time patients stay in hospital. This may impair patients' health and lead to inefficiencies as people have to be re-admitted when problems emerge. But re-admittals are categorized as 'new patients' under accounting procedures, so the inefficiency of reducing the length of stay in hospital does not emerge. And despite the fact that this is a readily acknowledged failure in the accounting procedure, it is in neither the hospital managers' nor the government's interests to change the procedure because both are able to defend their records with the (discredited) figures. This is an example of what may be called an 'accountability conspiracy'.

An accountability conspiracy may occur when those who are being accounted and those doing the accounting share the same interest in what is being examined. In the example cited above new accounting procedures were introduced in order to bring about a more efficient health care service by increasing the numbers of patients being treated and thereby reducing waiting lists. The Department of Health therefore puts pressure on health authorities who in turn pressurize hospital managers who pressurize doctors to increase throughput. Once throughput is increased, however, and problems emerge as a result, who wants to advertise the fact? The managers of hospitals, the health authorities and the government are all happy to announce that they have increased throughput. Accountability upwards suffers from the fact that all those involved have similar interests with regard to the figures, and it is up to the doctors, the media and parliament to point out failures.

Accountability conspiracies are a type of problem called 'moral hazard', which occurs whenever those paying for some action are not in a position to judge whether or not that action is being carried out efficiently. This occurs when the interests of the decision-maker are different from the person who wants the decision made, and over-sight of the decision-maker is difficult.[10]

In fact, proxy measures create incentives for employees to satisfy the proxy and not what it stands for; and the programme can then become completely distorted. At root, the problem occurs either because variables are not open to quantification or are quantified in a fashion that is simply too crude. Indeed what is not often recognized by the proponents of the new public management is just how expensive proper measuring techniques can be. One can spend so long trying to measure output, that output is itself affected. In other words, technically speaking, what is not recognized is that new public management is not Pareto-efficient.

Finally, the drive for efficiency via performance measurement is not a policy-neutral device. Performance evaluation is value-laden by the sort of criteria which are used to choose those things to be evaluated (Pollitt 1986). Departments may concentrate on short-term managerial innovations and agenda management rather than upon long-term policy goals.

The policies of the Conservative administration leading up to and beyond FMI require a new type of civil servant, one trained in personnel management. In 1985 a new course was developed for those at under-secretary level to help them learn how to work collectively to solve management problems. Also in 1985 the first performance-related pay was introduced for all staff in grades three to seven, whilst new productivity agreements were offered to officials at deputy-secretary and under-secretary level to compete for discretionary payments. The incentives of civil servants are being altered. Formerly expected to behave as cogs in the machine and work smoothly without causing difficulties for the machine, civil servants are being asked to innovate with pay and promotion as the carrot. Logically the next step is to introduce the stick in the form of removing job security. The Next Steps programme has started this process which will be completed by market testing. To these subjects we now turn.

THE NEXT STEPS

In 1988 under the supervision of Sir Robin Ibbs, the government published a document *Improving Management in Government: The Next Steps* (Jenkins *et al.* 1988). This report was produced within the usual ninety-day deadline for scrutiny after the Efficiency Unit had spoken to a number of civil servants at various levels. The report took the idea of new management in the civil service further than FMI and sketched out the idea of creating agencies to implement government policies.

There are two broad views about the radical changes brought about in Britain under the the title of 'Thatcherism'. One view, fuelled by the writings of insiders, is that the Thatcher programme was mapped out in advance as a steady progression of ever more radical programmes to mould society into the desired dynamic, entrepreneurial capitalist one. Another view is that the governments of the 1980s staggered from one policy initiative to another, introducing new legislation when the previous programme had proved ineffective or even before it had had a chance to work. Government reform of the central executive can similarly be interpreted under either the 'stagger' or the 'policy continuation' viewpoint. Thus Next Steps can be viewed as a continuation of FMI or as its replacement, created to achieve what FMI had patently failed to do. The latter view is the official line most effectively argued by Peter Kemp, the sacked Project Manager and Permanent Secretary. The first is the view argued by a number of sceptical academics (Hennessy in HC 481, 1989–90: 60; Jordan 1992a: 8).[11]

The major thrust of the Next Steps programme is the breakup of the unified civil service. The uniformity of pay structure, of grading, and of the nature of civil servants are being changed and a two-tier civil service created with a policy-making core and a policy-implementing periphery. The latter is hived off into agencies which may or may not eventually be privatized. The report said:

> The aim should be to establish a quite different way of conducting the business of government. The central Civil Service should consist of a relatively small core engaged in the function of servicing Ministers and managing departments, who will be the 'sponsors' of particular government policies and services. Responding to these departments will be large numbers of agencies employing their own staff, who may or may not have the status of Crown servants, and concentrating on the delivery of their particular service, with clearly defined responsibilities between the Secretary of State and permanent Secretary on the one hand and the Chairman or Chief Executives of the agencies on the other.
>
> (Jenkins et al. 1988: para. 44)

At first there was some dispute over whether the agency process would break up the civil service. Anne Mueller (1987) at the Treasury thought so, suggesting that a two-tier civil service would develop with a 'core' enjoying job security and career prospects and a 'periphery' staffed under a wide range of conditions of employment. Peter Kemp in his report to the Treasury and Civil Service Committee 1989–90 stated that the status of civil servants would not alter. Later Kemp changed his tune:

> There will always be a sort of core of people – and perhaps the most senior people will be there . . . who will be advisers to Ministers and who will be looking after the agencies. They will have relatively standard terms and conditions and will be relatively transferable. Then, I think, there will be agencies . . . [with] varied systems for recruitment, varied non-pay arrangements and varied financial regimes . . . a core-periphery system is how I see it coming out.
>
> (HC 496, 1989–90 para. 415: 102–3)

During the initial stages the precise relationship between agencies and parent departments had to be worked out and financial issues still govern their relationship (Hogwood 1993). Their ability to introduce 'more flexible' pay conditions is still dependent upon national agreements over pay rates, and recent evidence (Hogwood 1993) suggests that many agencies are not keen to take on full responsibility for pay and conditions of staff. Some agencies are in the process of privatization, which may be speeded up in the future. This clearly spells the breaking up of the civil service as formerly constituted.

Agencies are set up with a chief executive who signs a 'framework agreement' with the parent or core department. These framework agreements vary in character but each 'involves the selection of a range of performance indicators which will enable the Department to judge productivity, financial performance, quality of service and so on' (HC 348, 1988–89: para 66; Evidence, Q. 272). Sir Robin Butler claimed that all of these initiatives would create a civil service 'unified but not uniform'. This statement is a typical example of old-fashioned civil service aphoristic nonsense or 'mandarinese' (as described by John Garrett, MP (HC 481, 1989–90: para. 178). The civil service is now unified only by virtue of the fact that it is a civil service – with the term civil servant covering a multitude of sins (see pages 17–20). Furthermore, as some agencies are privatized, some of those sins will be removed from the public sector. The sins are multiplied by Next Steps, with the term 'civil servant' conveying a wide variety of contracts, pay scales, negotiating rights, pension schemes, job structures and prospects and the likelihood of the practice of '*pantouflage*' between the public and private sectors (see Chapter 6). The hierarchical system, for all its faults, was unified by at least a salary structure (though not one as unified as Fulton would have liked) and common negotiating and pension rights. It embodied the idea of the state as the ideal employer. The public service ethic also unified the system; and whilst that ethic was not in itself enough, of course, to provide the kind of service the public requires, many within the service fear that the new managerialism will also diminish that aspect of the unified service. Nor can a unified service ethic exist when the agencies have differing relationships with the public with regard to their commercial activities – some able to offer many commercial services, some perhaps none. Civil servants are unified only to the extent that, by whatever circuitous route, ultimate accountability to parliament rests with the minister of their, or their parent, department. This fact of a rather weak unification has been belatedly acknowledged by the former Project Manager Peter Kemp:

> [The Civil Service] is directly accountable, through Ministers, to Parliament; and I think that that will remain for as long as we have agencies within the Civil Service . . . I think that public expenditure will remain the essential piece of the 'glue'. There is one banker; and we remain with that. Then, I think, there is the question of probity, of standards and of a proper standard of care . . . for the public . . . the Civil Service always does what nobody else wants to do . . . it does things which the private sector does not want to do, or will not do. And it does things for people who usually have no choice and it does things for people who very often do not pay and it gives a special

quality to how you have to do it. I think these are things that will
have to hold the Civil Service together. After that, I am not sure how
much else there is, actually, at the end of the day.

(HC 496 1990–91: 102–3)

This statement admits that there is not much substance in the idea of a
unified civil service other than the fact that it is the agent of the
government, paid for by the government and doing what the government
wants it to do. But then there are other non-governmental agencies
which carry out tasks for the government. In the case of agriculture, for
example, much of the policing and care of standards is carried out by
the National Farmers' Union rather than civil servants, but that hardly
unites the NFU with the public sector. Charities carry out functions for
people who have no choice and do not pay; like governments they fill
in where market failure occurs. Some charities receive government
money for services they provide, having been drawn into that provision
as government has cut public expenditure. But that does not unite them
to the public sector. We are left then with the fact that agencies are
accountable 'through the minister' to parliament. Leaving aside the
contradiction with statements about chief executives appearing before
committees of the House over operational matters without consulting
the minister, we are left with the idea of accountability 'as long as we
have agencies within the Civil Service'. Does this statement mean that
if agencies are privatized, their activities are no longer accountable?
Must accountability, that most nebulous of all the concepts in the
British constitution, do all the work of unifying on its own? It's not
much of a unity.

There are many advantages in creating a periphery of workers paid
at current market rates rather than having unified national pay structures. National pay structures make little or no welfare sense where
there are vastly different costs of living in different areas of the country.
Furthermore, market rates should mean that posts which are hard to fill
must be offered at higher rates of pay in order to attract staff of a high
enough calibre. Lower salaries can be paid in areas where there is a
ready supply of workers. But this does not mean that overall salary
levels will fall, and we should expect inflation of salaries at the higher
levels of the civil service, especially amongst chief executives who will
use the market argument to justify this. Without competitive rates of
pay the civil service could end up with the 'dregs of all other
professions' as feared by Charles Trevelyan (1856: 89) almost a century
and a half ago. The theory of the unified civil service was that the
working conditions and excellent pension schemes together with the

idea that the government is the 'model employer' (Beaumont 1981) allowed the state to employ high-calibre people at levels much below market rates, though rates for middle-ranking employees were once generous in comparison to the private sector that has been eroded over the past 25 years. The perks of index-linked pensions, the award of honours and the simple pleasure of power as policy-makers were supposed to allow top civil servants to be paid at below-market rates; but as the inflation rate amongst top businessmen increased over recent years, the perks seemed less advantageous. Moreover, the danger of the agency process – with its separation of policy-making and policy-implementation – is that chief executives would have to be paid far more than under a unified structure. If the intention is truly to encourage both *pantouflage* between the public and private sector and cross-over between the agencies and the core civil service, then salary inflation within Whitehall is a likely consequence. The Treasury has recognized this and has attempted to block proposals to allow chief executives control of salary levels within agencies and to keep its control over pay throughout the civil service and associated agencies.

The Next Steps report defines an agency as 'any executive unit that delivers a service for government' (Jenkins *et al.* 1988: para. 19). In this broad sense there have been agencies before, but the main difference between these and the current creations is the framework agreements negotiated between the agency and the core departments. The idea is to create a network of accountability between the chief executive, the core department and the Treasury. The framework agreement can be seen as a corporate plan establishing current and future objectives and policy including the financial arrangements governing running costs; the personnel issues and basic conditions of employment; plus the review procedures by which the sponsor department will monitor the agency. Chief executives are responsible for all day-to-day executive functions which are the raison d'etre for the agencies. The agency should be 'left as free as possible to manage within this framework . . . to strengthen operational effectiveness, there must be freedom to recruit, pay, grade and structure in the most effective way' (Jenkins *et al.* 1988: para. 21).

Evidence given to the Treasury and Civil Service Committee makes clear that whilst the operational responsibilities of the agencies are established through the framework agreements, there is little room for manoeuvre by chief executives in the setting of targets within these agreements. Peter Kemp stated that whilst chief executives could talk, argue and remonstrate in private with the minister and the permanent secretary, at the end of the day:

these Chief Executives (whether they come from the outside or from the inside) are civil servants. They are operating under discipline and they actually have the choice of doing one of two things. They can buckle down and do what the Minister has asked them to do; or they can resign.

(HC 496, 1990–91: 106)

Given the fact that chief executives now reply to Parliamentary Questions, this statement cannot be strictly true, though they should not wilfully reply in a way of which the minister would not approve. But the Civil Service Committee reports (after quoting the above) that the allocation of responsibilities is clearer since the implementation of Next Steps.

The 'Stagger' and the 'Strategic Advance' views of the Conservative Governments' reforms of the civil service in the 1980s are not completely incompatible. Underlying Next Steps is a market model, though not a particularly good one. It would be wrong to say that Next Steps introduces market processes, but it does try to introduce the sorts of incentives to civil servants that managers have in the market.

Table 4.2 Next Steps agencies: by department and date created

Date created	Department
	Department of Trade and Industry
03–10–88	Companies House
18–04–89	National Weights and Measures Laboratory
30–10–89	Laboratory of the Government Chemist
01–03–90	Patent Office
21–03–90	Insolvency Service
02–04–90	Radiocommunications Agency
03–07–90	National Physical Laboratory
05–10–90	National Engineering Laboratory
01–10–91	Accounts Service Agency
	Ministry of Agriculture Food and Fisheries
02–04–90	Central Veterinary Laboratory
02–04–90	Veterinary Medicines Directorate
01–10–91	ADAS Agency (also Welsh Office)
01–04–92	Central Science Laboratory
01–04–93	Pesticides Safety Directorate
	Ministry of Defence
02–04–90	Meteorological Office
06–04–90	Hydropgraphic Office
01–04–91	Chemical Biological Defence Establishment
01–04–91	Defence Research Agency

Table 4.2 (contd)

Date Created	Department
01–04–91	Directorate General of Defence Accounts
01–04–91	Military Survey
01–04–91	RAF Maintenance
24–04–91	Service Children's Schools, North West Europe
01–04–92	Duke of York's Military School
01–04–92	Naval Aircraft Repair Organisation
01–04–92	Queen Victoria School
01–07–92	Defence Analytical Services
01–07–92	Defence Operational Analysis Centre
17–07–92	Defence Postal and Courier Services
01–04–93	Army Base Repair Organisation
	Department of Environment
06–07–89	QEII Conference Centre
02–04–90	Building Research Establishment
31–10–91	The Buying Agency
01–04–92	Planning Inspectorate (also Welsh Office)
	Welsh Office
01–04–91	Cadw – Welsh Historic Monuments
01–10–91	ADAS Agency
01–04–92	Planning Inspectorate
	Cabinet Office
06–06–89	Civil Service College
02–04–90	Occupational Health Service
01–04–91	Recruitment and Assessment Service Agency
01–04–93	Chessington Computer Centre
	Department of Transport
01–08–88	Vehicle Inspectorate
02–04–90	Driver and Vehicle Licensing Agency
02–04–90	Driving Standards Agency
02–04–90	Vehicle Certification Agency
01–04–92	Driver Vehicle and Operator Information Technology
01–04–92	Transport Research Laboratory
	Employment Department
02–04–90	Employment Service
	Home Office
01–04–91	Forensic Science Service
02–04–91	UK Passport Agency
01–04–92	Fire Service College
01–04–93	HM Prison Service
	Treasury Solicitor
01–04–93	Government Property Lawyers

Table 4.2 (contd)

Date created	Department
	Department of National Heritage
01–10–89	Historic Royal Palaces Agency
01–04–93	Royal Parks
	Scottish Office
01–04–91	Scottish Fisheries Protection Agency
01–04–92	Scottish Agricultural Agency
01–04–93	Historic Scotland
01–04–93	Scottish Office Pensions Agency
01–04–93	Scottish Prison Service
	Department of Health
01–04–91	NHS Estates
11–07–91	Medicines Control Agency
20–11–92	NHS Pensions Agency
	Overseas Development Agency
02–04–90	Natural Resources Institute
	Department of Social Security
24–05–89	Social Security Resettlement Agency
02–04–90	Social Security Information Technology Services
10–04–91	Social Security Benefits Agency
10–04–91	Social Security Contributions Agency
05–04–93	Child Support Agency
	Department for Education
01–04–92	Teachers' Pensions Agency
	Inland Revenue
30–09–90	Valuation Office
	Foreign and Commonwealth Office
01–04–91	Wilton Park Conference Centre
	Non-Departmental
14–12–88	HM Stationery Office
02–04–90	Intervention Board
02–04–90	Mint, Royal
05–04–90	Information, Central Office of
06–04–90	Registers of Scotland
01–05–90	Ordnance Survey
02–07–90	Land Registry
01–04–91	Customs and Excise
19–11–91	Central Statistical Office
01–04–92	Inland Revenue (excluding Valuation Centre)
01–04–92	Public Record Office
01–04–93	Scottish Record Office

5 Bureau-shaping

The new model and the new manager

INTRODUCTION

From the late 1950s to the early 1980s Niskanen, Buchanan and other New Right public-choice writers argued the state's inexorable tendency to grow. From the mid-1970s the state apparatus stopped growing and seemed to retract. In part it did so because there was a political will at the highest levels to see the boundaries of the state recede. This political will was in part engendered by the New Right ideology – the arguments about the inevitability of state growth stopped that ostensibly relentless process. These arguments virtually self-referentially disproved themselves. But if the seemingly inexorable tendency to state growth could be altered by simple political will at the highest levels, what does this teach us about the usefulness of general models of bureaucracy? Dunleavy (1986: 18) suggests that 'There cannot be any necessary quality about bureaucratic over-supply and budget-maximization if simple change of political will at the helm of representative institutions is enough to make the state apparatus operate in a basically different way.' This criticism goes straight to the heart of the logic of rational-choice modelling. But it reveals a very deterministic attitude towards rational-choice theory which does not have to be adopted. We could try to explain how bureaucrats who try to budget-maximize may be defeated. Whilst there is pressure upon politicians to make promises to different sections of the population, thus enabling bureaucrats to budget-maximize, once the costs of bureaucracy get too high, the gains from promising the electorate wholesale reform will outweigh the benefits of making specific election pledges to different sections of the population. Niskanen argues that bureaucrats prefer larger budgets to smaller ones and that it is difficult to control their exaggerated claims because of the nature of pressure groups' rent-seeking. But this difficulty is not an iron law of logic, just a difficulty demonstrated by his model.

Margaret Thatcher came to power in 1979 explicitly on (amongst other things) an anti-rent-seeking ticket. Furthermore, the Conservatives refused to make many pledges in 1979 on the grounds that they needed to 'look at the books' first. Since then the Conservative Party has made a virtue of not promising very much other than tax cuts and has continued to promise to reduce the cost and influence of the state. So successful has this tax-cutting appeal been to the electorate that the other parties now cost their policies carefully to argue that they will not increase the overall tax burden. But it was largely the length of her tenure that enabled Thatcher to reform Whitehall. There has been no other prime minister this century who approached her three consecutive terms amounting to eleven years, the next longest being Harold Wilson's six years 1964–70 and Churchill's five years 1940–45 (when, incidentally, the civil service was transformed, though for rather different reasons (Hennessy 1990: ch. 3). Thatcher had a passionate desire to transform society, including the civil service; but the truly *radical* reforms of the service did not start until after her third election victory in 1987. The time factor is important to the bilateral bargaining relationship. As we noted above, such bargaining does not have a determinate solution but rather depends upon the resources of each actor. One of the major resources of bureaucrats is their near-monopoly of information and their longer length of tenure. Thatcher broke that monopoly by setting up a task force to look at bureaucratic waste and she lasted long enough to get the cutback started. There is nothing in her success that a rational-choice theorist need worry about.

Dunleavy's complaint against Niskanen is also unfair. Rational-choice models of mass behaviour, using general behavioural assumptions, cannot be expected to explain the behaviour of actual people. This requires a much more complex, empirically grounded account of their beliefs and desires. In order to explain the success of Thatcher in reforming the civil service, we do not need to waive all of Niskanen's motivational assumptions; we need simply to provide a more comprehensive explanation of the behaviour of key individuals This is a perfectly acceptable method. The logic of rationally explaining the behaviour of people such as Margaret Thatcher or Robin Ibbs is very different from the logic of rationally explaining that of a large number of people within a given institution. In the first case rigid utility maximizing tends to produce paranoic explanation, but the assumptions required to explain actual individual behaviour are far too complex to handle and completely inappropriate to explain the behaviour of a large number of people in a specific institutional context. Shifting from one sort of explanation to the other when explaining bureaucratic behaviour or the behaviour of a particular individual such as Margaret Thatcher is perfectly acceptable and indeed necessary when explaining the course of actual historical events (Dowding 1991: ch. 2; Dowding 1994a; Dowding and King 1995).

Thatcher was able to chip away at the civil service till eventually she put into train what she wanted. The major idea underlying Next Steps is to introduce the sort of managerial techniques which exist in the private sector. The ideology underlying this is that competition makes for greater efficiency. As outlined in Chapter 3, there are great dangers in the too-simple move from hierarchy to market efficiency. Efficiency in markets means Pareto-efficiency, but much of the role of the civil service is to provide services which are redistributive provided for, reasons of equity, or because the government, for whatever reason, has deemed they should be provided. The competitive drive between firms may help create productive efficiency within firms, and it is this drive that government wishes to instil within the civil service. 'New managerialism' in the public sector is about trying to provide such productive efficiencies. Whether they can be provided within organizations without the need for them to be in competition with other organizations is one question that needs to be addressed. Whether or not competition is desirable apart from any encouragement it provides to productive efficiency is another matter.

Niskanen (1979) in a later article suggests that competition can help to end bureaucratic over-supply, by taking away the monopoly of information from bureaucrats, thereby strengthening the hand of the government. He writes:

> Competition among bureaus supplying a similar service increases the amount of information available to the politicians and the public, because the competition for budgets is forced to [sic] the public arena. A monopoly bureau, in contrast, is more effective in suppressing information about costs, failures and risks.
>
> (Niskanen 1979: 519)

Competition is therefore seen as the panacea *because it leads to more open government* and therefore the true productivity of state provision is made clear. This chapter examines the Next Steps reforms from this perspective. Do they introduce the sorts of incentives which encourage the type of managers who exist in the private sector? Is there really any analogy with the competitive market?

THE BUREAU-SHAPING MODEL

These questions will be answered by developing Dunleavy's 'bureau-shaping model'. It is far more descriptively accurate than earlier rational-choice accounts, making it closer to 'descriptive theory' than 'predictive theory' (Stinchcombe 1968) for the simple reason that the greater the number of variables, the harder it is to produce unambiguous predictions. The bureau-shaping model assumes that rational self-regarding bureaucrats will try to modify their bureau in ways which increase their overall utility: 'rational bureaucrats ... pursue a bureau-shaping strategy designed to bring their bureau into a progressively closer approximation to "staff" (rather than "line") functions, a collegial atmosphere and a central location' (Dunleavy 1991: 202–3). Bureau-shaping may well include, under the right conditions, budget-maximizing; but other strategies are just as important to civil servants' overall utility. The major problem for Dunleavy is that 'bureau-shaping' is an amorphous concept which requires specific empirical interpretations in order to be useful. His model is tautologous if it is used in such a way that any form a given bureau takes is explained by officials' bureau-shaping. For this reason Dunleavy claims to use 'hard-edged' assumptions (that is, ones which produce easily falsifiable predictions).

According to Dunleavy, there are two basic sources of utility to bureaucrats: higher income and better working conditions. The first may come about in a variety of ways: through personal promotion, job regrading, general salary rises, and perhaps, for those who think they may gain from this process, a move to individual contracts (Dunleavy 1991: 175). The second source involves the bureau taking on more 'staff' as opposed to 'line' functions, a 'collegial atmosphere' and a central London location, and, most importantly, the type of work involved. It is assumed that most career civil servants are more interested in policy-making and 'strategic management' than in the day-to-day administration of their departments. An ideal bureau will have a good mix of policy and managerial tasks, and the further a bureau is from the civil servants' ideal mix, the more they will try to shape it that way.

The first set of assumptions looks hard-edged, though it should be noted that the move to individual contracts and general salary rises may operate in contrary directions, making it more difficult to generate predictions. For this reason Dunleavy assumes a distinction between different levels of bureaucrats – high, middle and lower ranks – to stand in lieu of their probable response of these different strategies. The higher the rank, the more likely one is to prefer personal contracts; the lower the rank, the more likely one would prefer general salary increases, though of course 'more likely' entails that this response is not the same for all individuals at each rank. Certainly, advantage has been taken by senior mandarins to argue that the new agencies require 'market salaries' up to twice the level of permanent secretaries (Butler 1993). Given that 65 per cent of chief executives appointed by early 1994 have been internal appointments (half through 'open' competition) the true need for such high salaries is highly questionable.

Dunleavy's second set of utility-enhancing strategies does not, however, look very hard-edged. How a 'collegial atmosphere' may be created and how far individual bureaucrats will be prepared to trade it off against their core budget remain unspecified. It is also questionable whether a 'central location' is unambiguously a common goal. Some senior bureaucrats may find the prospect of being a big fish in a smaller pond at least as attractive as being just one of a large number of sharks cruising around Whitehall or Brussels. Indeed, it seems likely that attitudes amongst senior officials are changing, encouraged by the fact that standard civil service salaries will go much further in, say, Newcastle or Bristol than in Central London. The prospect of running the new agencies in regional outposts will also contribute to this shift of perception.

Behavioural assumptions alone cannot generate the bureau-shaping model. Three important sets of distinctions characterize bureau-shaping: first, a simple distinction between levels of officials who may view government initiative rather differently; secondly, a distinction between four different elements of a bureau budget; thirdly, a distinction between types of bureaux. The heart of the bureau-shaping model is contained in its distinctive account of bureau budgets and its distinctive typography of types of bureaux.

TYPES OF BUDGET

Dunleavy argues that whilst officials have a common interest in having as big a budget as possible, they each also have an interest in getting as much as possible of the budget finally allotted to them diverted to their own divisions or sections or spent on their own pet schemes. Civil servants will at best be indifferent to budget increases in other departments but are more likely to be opposed to them, because, first, another department gains in prestige *vis à vis* their own, and, secondly, their own department will probably get less money. There is also the added collective action problem. Individual civil servants will only press for a greater budget if they think that their own demands stand a certain probability of being met. The costs of making their demands must be lower than the expected benefits of the increase multiplied by their evaluation of the probability that their advocacy will be decisive in bringing about a change. The lower the official in the hierarchy the lower the probability of the success of their advocacy (Dunleavy 1991: 177–80). This will lead us to expect that the lower the rank, the more conservative the attitude towards change.

However, Dunleavy surely exaggerates the collective action problem of senior civil servants, who consist of about forty or so first permanent secretaries. Insider accounts of the civil service talk of it as a 'village community' (Heclo and Wildavsky 1974; Ponting 1986): just the sort of network in which collective action problems can most easily be overcome (Taylor 1987; Raub and Weesie 1990, 1994). Dunleavy assumes here that overall budgetary increase benefits junior officials more than senior, though he does not make clear why this should be so (Dunleavy 1991: 178). Whilst he suggests that tenured and senior staff already have well-established positions and that budgetary changes do not affect their individual salaries and job security to the same extent, senior staff have experienced much higher salary gains than junior officials in the past twenty years. Concentrating on salary levels also skews the argument away from Niskanen's original intentions. Individual benefits are an important part of a bureaucrat's utility function but not its only component. It might be argued that budgetary increase is more likely to be spent in ways which affect junior officials' work to a greater extent than senior officials'. That is, it affects their pet schemes or makes their jobs easier. For example, more money to be paid out to social security claimants means less hassle for officials staffing the desks at the social security offices. But we must remember that individual utility provided by extra money has to be shared out – not necessarily equally – between the greater number of juniors. And surely the Niskanen assumption that top officials would sooner be in charge of a larger rather than a smaller bureau, *ceteris paribus*, still gives top officials an incentive to go for more money. Nor does Dunleavy consider the costs to those higher up the hierarchy of resisting the demand for more money from their juniors.

The costs of advocating budget increases are also exaggerated for the following reasons. First, much of the budgetary argument between officials of spending departments and the Treasury is done in the back rooms between people who know each other well and know the rules of the game well. The costs are low. Secondly, where agreement cannot be reached, the battle is moved to the political realm, and it is the minister who advocates budgetary increase in the Cabinet and cabinet committees and it is he or she who will take most of the Treasury and Prime Ministerial flak. Dunleavy excuses himself from such a bargaining model on the grounds that it would be too complex to be applied empirically (Dunleavy 1991: 177). However, even if that is true, the recognition of bargaining effects does weaken the arguments against senior bureaucrats' budget-maximizing.

On the issue of individual maximization not enough account is taken of institutional inertia and individual conservatism. Individuals, including bureaucrats, often oppose change for apparently no other reason than the fact that it is change; and this can be explained by means of rational choice: the costs of working out what the changes will mean for one's personal welfare, the greater uncertainty surrounding the future and the greater instability of the present. Once the changes are in motion, however, bureaucrats may well bureau-shape to ensure that their personal welfare levels are maintained or increased. Downs's model brings out some of these points, introducing factors such as the personality of the individual and the age of the bureau. Downs suggests that there are five personality types for bureaucrats: climbers, who want to maximize their own power and prestige; conservers, who desire a quiet life and stability; zealots, who are strongly committed to certain personal plans and elements of the programme of their department; advocates who have a more general commitment to their departmental programmes; and statesmen who are more like the bureaucrats of the 'Weberian' model of Chapter 2. Downs believes that individual civil servants may go through the whole gamut of personality types during their lifetime and the character of departments may alter as the mix of bureaucrats within them changes. Specifically, the longer a given bureau or agency is in operation, the more conservative it will become as advocates and zealots give way to conservers and statesmen. This would suggest that any dynamism of new agencies which depends upon the strength of the personnel rather than its organizational form, will be short-lived.

Downs's model provides few predictable propositions beyond some generalizations such as the 'law of increasing conservatism' or the 'law of hierarchy' (that coordinating large-scale activities requires hierarchy if market solutions are not adopted). As Goodin (1982: 29) has noted, these are more like 'maxims of bureaucratic folk wisdom' than truly testable propositions. This does not make them any less true, and Downs's book is still worth consulting for ideas about the nature of bureaucracy.

As discussed above, Dunleavy objected to the simple budget-maximizing assumptions of Niskanen on the grounds that they cannot explain the cutback management of the 1980s. This overly deterministic interpretation of public choice misses its target, but Dunleavy has a better critique of unadorned budget-maximizing. Simply expressed, a bureau's budget is complex and the money is spent on a multitude of different things. Bureaucrats are not interested in spending more in all areas of possible expenditure, only in some of them. We therefore need to fragment the budget into separate categories in order to gain a better understanding of what it is that bureaucrats wish to maximize. Dunleavy's major advance on Niskanen is his breakdown of bureau budgets into four categories (in fact, most of the work is done by the first three budgets, the final being a late addition to the model to scoop up monies not covered by the three sub-budgets).[1] The categories are:

1 Core Budget (CB) – money spent by the bureau on its own operations – staff, accommodation, day-to-day activities, personal equipment and so on.
2 Bureau Budget (BB) – those parts of the programme for which the department is directly responsible to the government.
3 Programme Budget (PB) – all of the expenditure over which the bureau exercises supervision or control.
4 Super-programme Budget (SB) – consists of the department's programme budget plus any other spending by other departments from their own budgets over which this department has some control or exercises some responsibility.

These budgets can be represented diagrammatically (see Figure 5.1).

According to Dunleavy, the benefits to each bureaucrat of budgetary increase are mostly associated with the core budget or the bureau budget. The costs of increasing the budget (in terms of time spent, the level of external criticism by the government and public) are associated with the programme budget. For example, if education costs in local education authorities rise sharply, the burden of defending their record in Cabinet and parliament falls on the Department for Education (DfE), especially in the annual round of negotiations over the following year's budget. This money is generally under the control of local education authorities rather than the DfE. Thus civil servants at the DfE have little incentive to defend the programme budget, as it is outside their control and their welfare is not determined by it. At the same time, they have little incentive to be efficient about their own core and bureau budgets if most of the criticism is directed at the much larger programme budget. Civil servants at the DfE will react to pressure to cut expenditure by trying to cut the programme budget, while leaving the core and bureau budget intact. Alternatively, the bureaucracy may try to take over control of as much of the programme budget possible, so that the bureaucrats themselves can benefit from increases in that budget.

A key explanatory variable of bureaucractic response to the continuous pressure to restrict spending is the relationship between these four elements of the budget. Four criteria are important. First, the size of the overall budget, as in Niskanen's model, plus three ratios: bureau budget:programme budget ratio; core budget:programme budget ratio; and core budget:bureau budget ration. Together these determine the behaviour of civil servants following any government decision to cut public expenditure.

While all departments may face pressure to cut their overall budget, the three ratios should explain how given bureaucrats respond. Essentially, the greater the ratio between the programme budget and the bureau budget and/or the core budget, the easier egoistic bureaucrats find it to

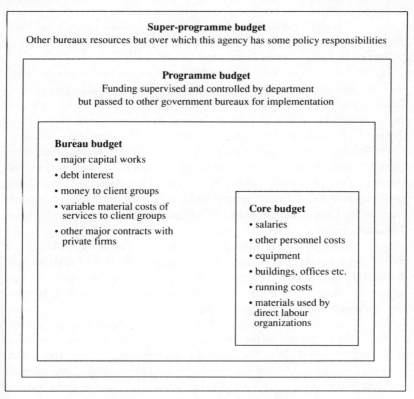

Figure 5.1 The relationship between different budgets

cut overall budgets. Where the core budget and programme budget are virtually identical bureaucrats should be expected to defend their budget. Budget-maximizing of the core budget here is much the same as overall budget-maximizing. However, bureaucrats could still attempt to maximize their core and bureau budgets and cut their overall budget if the first two were a relatively small proportion of the third. Indeed, Dunleavy suggests that in this case bureaucrats might well be happy to see responsibility for programme budgets hived off to others, as will be discussed later.

Dunleavy produced a descriptive typology which suggests that the three budget ratios are linked to the type of work bureaux do. He lists eight types of bureaux and examines their budgets to see if his predictions about budget ratios hold true. These 'bureaux' are not synonymous with departments (under any of the many definitions!); rather they may represent divisions, sections or departments as a whole. Dunleavy calls them 'agencies', though they will be referred to here as 'bureaux' to distinguish them from the new agencies created by 'Next Steps'. The type of 'bureau' may also apply to the new agencies.

The eight categories of bureau are as follows.[2]

(a) *Delivery bureaux* are like those described by Niskanen. They directly undertake the production of goods and services to citizens. Implementation is carried out by delivery bureau employees whose core budgets contain almost all of their bureau and programme budgets. An example of this type of bureau is the Department of Health.

(b) *Regulatory bureaux* control other bureaux and private firms. They do not directly produce material benefits themselves and are able to pass many of their costs on to those they regulate. They are largely inspecting and 'paper-moving' organizations and hence their core budget contains most of the bureau and programme budget. The Ministry of Agriculture, Food and Fisheries (MAFF) comes into this category.

(c) *Transfer bureaux* manage subsidies to private individuals or firms. Typically administration costs are only a fraction of their budget, hence the core budget is very small in relation to the bureau budget which contains most of the programme budget. The Department of Social Security is such a transfer bureau.

(d) *Contract bureaux* develop service specifications for capital projects for tendering to private companies. Their staff are concerned with the research and development of projects, whilst the actual implementation is carried out by the private contractor. Core budgets are small in relation to the bureau budget which would contain most of the programme budget. Defence procurement divisions within the Ministry of Defence are examples of such bureaux.

(e) *Control bureaux* allocate budgets and supervise activities of others. The core budget is only a small part of the programme budget, and so too is the bureau budget. The Department for Education is such a control bureau.

(f) *Taxing bureaux* are self-explanatory. Here core budgets absorb almost all bureau and programme budgets, for example, as in the case of the Inland Revenue.

(g) *Trading bureaux* are full governmental organizations controlled by political appointees. They deliver services to other sectors on a commercial basis. The Forestry Commission is such a bureau.

(h) *Servicing bureaux* provide collective facilities or services to other governmental bodies on a basis which cannot be easily or fully costed. What they produce is a collective benefit to a number of different departments within the civil service. The Cabinet Office (MPO) is an example of a servicing bureau.

Dunleavy's empirical work in this area has concentrated on demonstrating that the descriptive framework of budget ratios and types of bureaux is empirically accurate (Dunleavy 1989b). Dunleavy (1985: 320–4, 1991: 225–78) recognizes that there is a great potential for examining bureau-shaping strategies as an explanation of reorganization but does not actually take up this task. Oliver James (1994) has attempted to produce an empirically verifiable model and identify bureau-shaping strategies by distinguishing core-budget maximizing from maximizing policy work. In James's model bureaucrats wish to maximize the core budget *per* senior bureaucrat. However, the constraint is that the higher the core budget per senior civil servant, the more time they are expected to devote to managerial work. Therefore senior civil servants trade off extra amounts of core budget for policy work. This is represented by the preference curve P_1–P_2 touching the constraint curve X–Y (at point A) in Figure 5.2.

James argues that as managerial demands increased under efforts to increase productive efficiency in the 1980s, represented by a shift in the constraint curve to X–Z, bureaucrats grew keener to shift executive functions to outside agencies in order to attain a higher indifference curve at point C, rather than point B. James is currently testing this model against the evidence from selected departments and agencies.

More generally, there are different responses to the Next Steps process depending on the nature of the departments. The budget ratios specify the bureaucrats' reactions to budgetary cutback; the functions of their agencies specify the manner in which they are able to bureau-shape. Table 5.1 rather crudely specifies how different bureaux should be expected to respond.

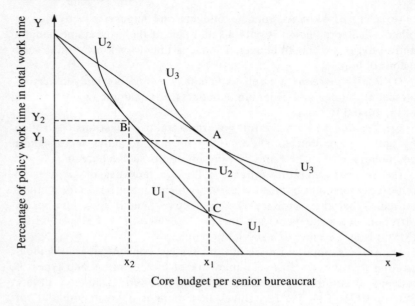

Figure 5.2 Effect of political changes on senior bureaucrat activities
Source: James (1994: 352)

Table 5.1 Bureau responses to budget constraint

Bureau type	Budget relationships	Bureau response
Delivery	CB most of BB and PB	Defend budget
Regularity	CB most of BB and PB	Defend budget
Transfer	CB small part of BB which is most of PB	Maximize CB, shape or hive off BB and PB
Contract	CB small part of BB which is most of PB	Maximize CB, shape or hive off BB and PB
Control	CB most of BB which is small part of PB	Maximize CB, shape BB, hive of PB
Taxing	CB most of BB and PB	Defend budget
Trading	CB small part of BB which is most of PB	Maximize CB shape or hive off BB and PB
Servicing	CB most of BB and PB	Defend budget

Delivery, Regulatory, Taxing and Servicing bureaux all have CBs which contain most of the BB and PB. One would expect bureaucrats within these bureaux to defend their budgets in order to defend themselves. However, the relationships of these four types of bureaux to other parts of the government machine are not the same. The pressure on them from civil servants in other parts of their departments may lead the bureaucrats within them to defend their budgets in different ways.

Transfer, Contract and Trading bureaux all have a CB which is only a small part of the BB. The BB and PB are almost identical. Again bureaucrats within these bureaux will want to maximize their CB and will respond to cutback management by shaping that part of the bureau covered by the BB and PB or hiving off the more troublesome parts under pressure from the Cabinet Office and the Treasury to do so. Control bureaux will do likewise, shaping the bureau and hiving off the troublesome parts of the PB. Again the particular response to be expected depends in part upon the structural relationship each bureau has to other parts of the overall bureaucracy.

Given that the Next Steps process is still underway, it is rather premature to attempt to produce a fully specified empirical test of the bureau-shaping model. However, it does seem that many elements of the bureau-shaping strategy predicted by Dunleavy's model are emerging. According to Table 5.2 the Department of Health is a delivery agency which should defend its budget. However, the overall health budget is too complex to be seen simply in terms of the core budget of the Department of Health and rather needs to be disaggregated into its component parts across these various departments and agencies which have some interest in it. Delivery bureau employees should defend these budgets, which they seem to do, whilst shaping their bureax, in this case hospitals, to maximize the core budget, cutting aspects of the bureau and programme budgets where necessary. As the health service creates self-governing trusts, there is a massive expansion of the bureaucracy within hospitals and a massive growth of managerial salaries. With expensive services such as casualty and intensive care wards being cut and rationalization across units within trusts, a cost-cutting exercise in health care has emerged.

The Ministry of Agriculture, Food and Fisheries has also managed to defend its budget largely through the offices of Brussels and the Common Agricultural Policy, though MAFF does argue in Europe that this budget needs to be cut. Again more detailed analysis of this budget is required to see how closely it conforms to Dunleavy's model. The Department of Social Security quickly moved its direct transfer services to agency status: the Resettlement Agency was created in May 1989, the Information Technology Services in April 1990, the Benefits Agency and the Contributions Agency in April 1991, and finally the Child Support Agency in April 1994, leaving a rump of fewer than 3,000 staff in the core Whitehall department (less than 4 per cent of total former DSS staff). The Ministry of Defence has also shed many service bureaux to agency status, though again the evidence of contract bureaux bureau-shaping is mixed and requires further analysis. The Department for Education, an example of a control bureau was discussed on page 86, whilst the taxing bureaux are expected to behave as Niskanen predicts. Their budgets are small and the room for saving is small. The evidence for trading bureaux is complex and incomplete, especially as plans for privatization complicate predictions. Servicing bureaux are also expected to behave much as Niskanen predicts. The Cabinet Office has shed four agencies, the Civil Service College, the Occupational Health Service Agency, the Recruitment and Assessment Service Agency and the Chessington Computer Centre. Its core budget has been protected, however. Dunleavy's model is complex and multi-faceted, and it will be some time before it can be fully analysed as predictively successful. It does suggest a set of plausible responses to cutback management from senior civil servants. One element it does not predict is a changing status for senior policy-making mandarins. Recent proposals from the government (Cm 2627, 1994) suggest that senior civil servants may also find themselves on flexible contracts with a greater number of outside and politicized advisers being brought in.

NEW MANAGERIALISM

New managerialism is hard to define. It is a basket of methods which differs from writer to writer, but its essential feature generally includes providing new sorts of motivations for managers, encouraging innovative practices, decentralizing decisions, creating new and wider responsibilities lower down the hierarchy, breaking up simple line hierarchies into more complex networks of responsibilities, as well as more cultural aspects such as creating new dynamism, team spirit and work ethic. Often new management books deteriorate into catalogues of anecdotes showing how this manager or that was able to increase the efficiency of her operation by some devilishly clever but simple trick which has little general application beyond suggesting that all managers need to be innovative; this is a type of policy advice little different from 'try harder' – possibly good advice but not terribly helpful. Christopher Pollit (1993: 1) says: 'Managerialism is a set of beliefs and practices, management will prove an effective solvent for a wide range of economic and social ills.' He defines it in terms of the following five beliefs.

1 Social welfare can be maximized by continued economic growth.
2 Economic growth can be sustained through productivity increases using technological innovation including organizational and information technologies. The large multi-functional corporation or state agency is the dominant form of organization.
3 New technologies require a workforce devoted to increasing productivity.
4 Management is an important and distinct function.
5 Good management is creative and dynamic.

These five aspects of managerialism add up to the belief that good management brings important productive efficiencies and entails a constant search for new and better means of organizing service delivery in the public sector. Managerialism searches for new incentives to encourage productive efficiency amongst the workforce and to measure that productivity through regular monitoring procedures. Monitoring is an important part of new managerialism. Whilst it should allow us to discover whether new techniques do in fact bring about productive efficiencies, the most important aspect of monitoring is to produce efficiency. The very act of monitoring never allows workers to forget that productive efficiency is what is required of them. Monitoring is a part of the efficiency drive rather than a way of finding out if the efficiency drive is succeeding.

The idea of the science of management in the public sector is not new. The Weberian rational bureaucrat is a version of this idea. But critiques of the apparent irrationality of the civil service grew in the post-war period. This was partly a result of the idea that the civil service was simply old-fashioned but more particularly that it was not organized in a manner which allows for the type of general strategic pattern of decision-making that was required in a modern economy. This led first to the creation of super-departments; latterly, perceived policy failures have led to the very opposite, breaking up departments into smaller units. However, these two approaches are not necessarily rival. The idea of super-departments was to ensure strategic thinking across policy domains. Breaking up departments into the agency structure is about producing efficiencies once the strategic objectives have been decided. Critics of agencies point out that in so far as the administrative efficiencies of smaller units actually impinge upon broad strategic considerations, the two are incompatible.

The new managerialism of the 1980s began with the ideological dominance of the private sector.[3] It was thought that better management was displayed in the private sector than in the public and that the latter could learn from the former. The private sector manager was typified by a few self-publicizing risk-taking entrepreneurs (Edwards 1984; Iacocca 1984, 1988). To what extent the public sector really resembles the private sector was not fully addressed. In part this is understandable in Britain where so much economic activity concerned with private goods was nationalized during the 1960s and 1970s (mostly as a consequence of deficiencies in British industry). Nevertheless, the key functions of the civil service are rather different from those of, say, car manufacturers (such as the once nationalized British Leyland) or North Sea oil production. Where civil servants deliver services, they face different organizational imperatives, many of them politically inspired. It is the private-sector model, notwithstanding, which has come to dominate public-sector management.

New managerialism springs from the same economic message that celebrates the individual, the free market and capitalism. Individuals could be liberated from the shackles of the state; corporations liberated from the shackles of regulations and taxation; and managers liberated from the excessive rule-bound rationalism of Weber's bureaucracy. Adam Smith's public welfare springing from private self-interested behaviour can be allowed to operate, as the entrepreneurial element of managers flourishes. In managerialism there is a set of components to rival Weber's rationalistic bureaucracy. Where Weber saw the bureau as a machine, managerialists see firms as organisms. New managerialism sees management as centred around people where each person's contribution is valued as part of the 'team'. Secondly, it sees itself as customer-oriented with customers viewed as people. Here the idea is generated that the market and customers-as-people have a symbiotic relationship with market demands revealing the wants and desires of people. The aim of the firm is to satisfy those wants and desires. Thirdly, new managerialism suggests that the firm must develop a corporate culture to which the team members, still as people, subsume their own individual aims. Note the sociological flavour of this approach to human behaviour, far removed from the economic assumptions of rational self-interest of the public–choice models. By allowing each member of the team to have their own creative identity and to develop their own schemes, the team is held together by the same vision of the corporate culture. Whereas traditional bureaucratic structures were rule-bound and controlled by corporate regulations, the new management structure is open and changeable but cemented by shared aims and the same corporate culture. Clarke and Newman (1992: 9) write:

> There are very strong connections between the views of the relationship between human nature and work in the new managerialism and the relationship between human nature and economic activity in neo-liberal economics. Both identify the self as essentially enterprising and regret the imposition of restraint or control which inhibits the full expression of enterprise. Both also articulate a homology between the self, the corporation and the national economy, such that 'over-regulation' inhibits enterprise in all three domains and the desire for 'free enterprise' involves a unity of interest between the individual, corporation and nation.

The problem with this vision of the civil service is that, legally, the constraints under which servants of the state operate cannot be lifted in the manner desired by the new managerialist ideology. Civil servants are necessarily rule-bound by the legislation which requires them to provide services. This has been described as 'custodial management' because it involves the civil servant, as a custodian of the values of the nation embodied in its legislation, providing a service expected as customary (Ackroyd *et al.* 1989). Whilst some discretion is permissible with regard to certain elements of the job, even then discretion may go too far. For example, Common *et al.* (1992: 106) describe the decision taken by a new manager of the Radio Vehicle Licensing Division at the DTI to stop writing to local authorities to check for objections to any company getting a licence. The manager took this decision because this step caused long delays and, as no objection had been lodged for ten years, it seemed a perfectly reasonable one. However, given the political relationship between central and local governments, the practice of not allowing local authorities to object to the issuing of such licences seems to be a policy decision which should be taken by ministers.

New managerialism has to be put into the context of the economic restructuring which occurred from the mid-1970s onwards. The so-called 'flexible specialization' of the 'post-Fordist' age came about as declining profits stimulated firms to restructure their manufacturing processes and cut labour costs. New technologies reduced reliance on a permanent skilled workforce, allowing a 'casualization', with a core of labour around which there was a periphery of casual workers, part-time workers, female workers (on lower wages) and new systems of control; and as a necessary corollary of all this, cutting union power and de-unionizing where possible.

As Clarke and Newman (1992: 16) point out:

Nonetheless, there are problems about taking the new managerialism too seriously. It has certainly provided a legitimating discourse for a variety of organizational transformations and may indeed have been practised in some of those changes. But, despite its visibility, it is by no means the only version of managerialism. It may be practised rhetorically even though forms of control being exercised change superficially or do not change at all. In some settings the new management may extend no further than the introduction of customer care training for front line staff or issuing mission statements. It is more likely that many organizations are relatively untouched by the new managerialism, even though they are exercising the manager's 'right to manage' in other ways: extending working conditions, exercising greater power over hiring and firing, changing working conditions, creating new contractual arrangements and finding other ways of exploiting the 'flexibility' of labour.

Indeed, most of the claims under the heading of the 'right to manage' look just like old managerialism, what managers through the ages have wanted the discretion to do, what the welfare state sought to curb, and what the Whitley principles of good conduct for the public sector as a model employer sought to overcome as an image for the immorality of the private sector (Bercusson 1978; Beaumont 1981).

The Thatcher government was clear that the entrepreneurial spirit of risk-taking and innovation it believed existed in the private sector needed transferring to the civil service. A Cabinet Office document states 'We now need more managers of budgets and more team leaders; more risk takers and innovators' (Cabinet Office 1986: 14). This is an extraordinary statement in some ways. What sorts of risk does the Cabinet Office want civil servants to take? The very nature of risk-taking determines that we will have more failure if budget-holders take greater risks, even if we also have greater success. The very nature of entrepreneurial activity determines that we cannot identify successful entrepreneurs in advance. Whilst market activity can help us to pick out the successful entrepreneurs in terms of their profit margins, it is harder to spot successful entrepreneurs in the public sector even after the event, and, what is worse, harder to register failures. This is simply a failure to understand that allowing managers greater discretion in order to achieve greater productive efficiencies is not on a par with the innovations which create new products in the marketplace (Parsons 1988). It confuses good management with dynamic capitalism. In order to correctly allow innovation yet allow bureaucrats to operate as cogs-in-a-machine, we need to distinguish (a) routine tasks versus those allowing innovation, (b) top and lower levels of management, (c) when rewards are too great and create perverse incentives, (d) private versus public goods and services.

The move to create greater latitude within bureaucratic structures has developed in order to overcome some of the paranoias of large organizations where it seems very difficult to change what all concerned admit to be anomalous outcomes. By allowing greater discretion to managers within the organization, such obvious anomalies can be overcome more quickly. The problem for such a discretionary approach is that universal principles hold for the service aspects of the state. Discretion is still largely constrained by the rules laid down by law. Discretion gives greater power to managers and thus enables them to do good. But power also allows managers to do more wrong. It should not be forgotten that the reason why formalized non-discretionary rules developed in the British civil service from the last century was to overcome the problem of corruption, which was endemic.

Table 5.2 Managerial decision-making

	Public sector	Private sector
1	Statutory and parliamentary regulation; codes of conduct	Aims of company created by directors
2	Framework of national economic planning	Marketplace
3	Parliamentary accountability	Commercial confidentiality
4	Public/government interest	Shareholder interest
5	Multiple, competing goals	Profit maximizing
6	Primary resource base: coerced taxation.	Primary resource base: operational returns, borrowing
7	Parliamentary accountability	Marketplace, profit margins
8	Strategic concerns dependent upon time horizon of General Election	Strategic concerns dependent upon nature of shareholder base
9	Complex performance indicators.	Quantitative financial measures

Table 5.2 suggests that the roles of the private-sector and the public-sector manager are different in important respects. Public managers have a greater set of competing goals and regulatory frameworks in

which to manage and thus require a complex set of performance indicators. It is much easier to judge the performance of private-sector managers, for the market itself provides a ready way of measuring it simply in terms of market success and the company's (or division's) relative profitability. The judge of the success of the private-sector managers is their shareholders, whereas that of the public-sector managers is the elected government and parliament.

There are also dangers inherent in the new managerialism as applied to the public sector. New managerialism is largely about the devolution of responsibility to the lower levels of management. Higher levels of management still have the responsibility of ensuring that the lower levels are living up to these new responsibilities and of providing the direction and performance expected of them. Their output needs to be measured in some way. As we have seen, whilst cost measurements can be quite easy to determine, there are many other sorts of managerial activity which are harder to assess. When the general objective of the company is the output of products there is always some sort of measurement available, whether it is sales figures, targets on noise emission, success of advertising activity, personnel recruitment or whatever. In some departments these measures are harder to find, but the number of departments to which this applies is much lower in the private sector for the simple reason that at the end of the day the final reckoning derives from profitability. When this seems to suffer in some way – relative to last year, say, or relative to one's competitors – the efficiency of each department and at each level can be considered. Often devolving responsibility means that one has to create a system of checking that each person is doing their job properly. These problems of measuring output are much greater in the public sector and there is the great danger, already perceived in some quarters, that the new managerialism is all about checking up that individuals are doing their jobs in the most efficient manner. This is most intensely felt by professionals who often believe that the measures by which their performance is assessed are not appropriate to the job they think they are doing, because they feel that these measures are devised by managers who have little understanding of the professional's job. The condemnation of 'efficiency-related' pay for doctors and nurses by their professional organizations is just one example.

The major problem with new managerialism, particularly in the public sector, is that it can soon become a paper exercise where performance is measured by ensuring that the forms by which one's performance is measured are correctly filled in. Whilst new managerialism is supposed to be a panacea for rampant bureaucracy, in practice it can add to it. Introducing market procedures in the National Health Service saw a 315 per cent increase in managers (from 4,350 to 14,290) whilst the number of nurses and midwives fell by 6 per cent (from 383,150 to 361,270), and hospital admissions rose by 4 per cent (7.4 million to 7.7 million). The internal health market has increased bureaucracy and not decreased it. It has done so by giving bureaucrats greater control over their own units, allowing them to increase their core budgets, managerial staff, working conditions and salaries, directing health care reform in which doctors and nurses suggest they have little expertise. We can expect the same situation to develop in the agencies whether they remain in public or private hands.

In their study of the first five agencies to be set up, Common *et al.* (1992) discovered that some had been more successful than others. There were a number of reasons for this. First, they had different roles to play. Some were more commercially oriented than others and so commercial tactics were more appropriate. Some have tasks which are more easily measurable and so the framework agreements were clearer over the objectives of the organization. But Common *et al.* obviously felt that the people at the highest levels of the organization were important. They particularly picked out two organizations (not specified) whose senior managers did not seem very amenable to any kind of criticism and refused to accept that any of their practices might be improved upon. We can extend this to the new managerialism overall – its success in Britain relies very heavily on the calibre of the top managers. Looking at the quality in both the private and public sectors does not inspire confidence that new managerialism is going to be a long-term success.

FINANCIAL RECTITUDE

With the agency process and the creation of extra governmental organizations, health service trusts and more flexible contractual arrangements for policy-making Whitehall mandarins, the role of financial rewards is receiving more scrutiny. Ironically, the marketization process creates more opportunities for senior management to maximize their personal rewards, for, in fact, there is no real market for top managers. Rather, contractual negotiations more closely resemble bilateral bargaining than perfectly competitive market relations. There has been a great deal of debate in the financial and business press in the United States about the rewards paid to chief executives in major US corporations. Certainly the figures suggest that chief executive officers (CEDs) have rewarded themselves handsomely during the 1980s. Those in the 365 largest publicly held US corporations had total remunerative rises of 212 per cent. This was four times the growth in pay of the average factory worker and three times that of the average engineer, whilst earnings per share in those companies rose by just 78 per cent. The average salary and bonus for CEOs reached $1.2 million plus a further $0.75 million in other benefits such as long-term share offers (Milgrom and Roberts 1992: ch. 13).

Figures for chief executives are harder to calculate in Britain, but similar rises can be found. Critics of these inflated rewards argue that they bear little relationship to the true incentive structures for top executives and that a benefit system has been captured by top executives for their own reward. The board of directors is supposed to represent the interests of shareholders in companies, but there are serious doubts about whether directors truly take these into account when considering their own incentive schemes. The system of outside directors is supposed to form some sort of check and balance, but there is some intermingling across boards in major companies, with outside directors being nominated by CEOs who in turn nominate CEOs as outside directors of their own companies, so that there is a real danger of collective action in directors' own interests. Others suggest that whilst the sums may seem vast, they create a real incentive system for CEOs. If senior executives need to be motivated to maximize the market value of the company, then tying their remuneration to that market valuation should provide the right incentive system. Jensen and Murphy estimated CEOs' remuneration as a linear function of the change in shareholder wealth (dividends paid and increase in share value) and estimated that, under the most generous estimates, each extra $1,000 of shareholder wealth brought an average of $3.25 for CEOs. They suggest that these figures indicate that remuneration is too low, and greater rewards for success will provide greater incentive effects (Jensen and Murphy 1990a, 1990b).

Indeed, not only is the market for top executives more like a bilateral bargain than a competitive market, but also in Britain it is more like an old-boy network or a cultural closed shop, with a multiplicity of multiple directorships and the rewards of office being handed out by those with the offices. Most major companies have remuneration committees, but only 50 of the top 100 companies reveal the membership of these committees in their annual reports. The independent directors of these companies are also executive directors of other companies, hiring as their independent directors other executive directors. Over 70 per cent of independent directors are recruited because they are personally known to the chairman, around 15 per cent recommended by shareholders and 15 per cent independently sourced (Rodgers 1991). This is the accountability conspiracy in another guise.

This excursion into the incentive structures of senior executives in private companies is pertinent to the civil service, given the increasingly made argument that chief executives of the new agencies have to be paid salaries equivalent to those paid in the private sector for similar work. Are these methods better than the reviews currently held in the public sector and will they keep top pay down, or is the private sector less efficient in this regard? Furthermore, even if these inflated figures paid to senior executives in the private sector are justified, how are we to create similar incentive systems in the public sector?

COMPETITION IN THE MANAGERIAL MARKET

Niskanen's model of bureaucracy illustrates the greater incentives for managers in the competitive market for productive efficiency. If profits constitute 5 per cent of costs, then a 5 per cent increase in productivity produces a doubling of profits. If salaries are related to productivity, then that constitutes a powerful incentive to be productive and efficient. The problem for the model, however, is: (a) profits are geared far more to other aspects of the market than the firm's own productivity, such as the relative productivity of other firms, the state of the economy, and so on; and (b) that incentives are generally not structured in that way.

If the salaries of higher executives in the private sector are geared to profits – as they often are – then the presumption is that they have an incentive to create higher profits for their companies. This seems to be a reasonable presumption. The stick to back up this carrot is that if they are not successful, they face some sort of sanction such as the sack. The problem with this system in practice is that the carrots are not tied closely enough to performance and that the stick often looks much like a carrot too: the penalties of failure all too often look more like rewards. When Sir Ralph Halpern took Burton's to the top with his high-risk high-street strategy, his salary and perks also shot up. When that high-risk strategy faltered (as, statistically, high-risk strategies are apt to do), he was sacked, albeit with £1.5 million handshake. There are few people who would mind failing for such a reward, which is not to say that it was in Halpern's interest to fail or that he tried to do so, but when the costs of failure are so low, then it becomes rational for top executives to take greater risks. Among other such payoffs in the private sector are Robert Horton (£1.5 million when forced out as chairman of BP), Stephen Brown (£1 million on leaving Tate and Lyle after only a year), and Ernest Mario (£3 million when forced out from Glaxo). In fact, so great has been the concern over such payoffs that the BT and Post Office pension fund, Postel, has pressed for executives to be given one-year rolling contracts to stop the 'golden handshakes'.

Is this accountability conspiracy likely to occur in the agency structure? It appears so, though the payments are much lower: John Bowman received £130,000 to quit the National Rivers Authority two years into his five-year contract after wasting £1 million in a £2.65 million office relocation (Hencke 1992a); the Welsh Development Agency paid £250,000 to Mike Price to buy his silence about fraud and mismanagement (Hencke 1992b; Beckett 1994); John Hoare received a severance payment of £111,940 following £20 million wasted on a failed computer system for the Wessex Regional Health Authority; James Ackers resigned just prior to an investigation into the West Midlands Regional Health Authority receiving a £10,000 'golden handshake'; Christopher Watney was paid £81,387 redundancy and £6,462 pension also from the same authority, the Public Accounts Committee suggesting he should have been dismissed for appointing consultants without following rules (Hencke 1994b). The list can be extended, the sticks are orange and crunchy if not quite as tasty as the carrots.

Should the state be encouraging risk-taking in areas now in the public sector? Should risks be taken which are as great as in the competitive market? The failure rate of new firms is around 33 per cent in their first three years of operation (Stanworth and Grey 1991; Sedgwick 1992: ch. 2). Do we want a third of the agencies to be bailed out by government during their first three years? Will the government admit to these failures? Are there any incentives for chief executives to point out to policy-makers that their policies cannot be implemented, or will the CEOs be rewarded more by taking the money and running? Certainly within the health service the idea of becoming a chief executive with the risk of creating either a highly profitable hospital or a disastrous one and walking away with three or five years' worth of high salary regardless of what has been achieved seems a great temptation.

The major problem at the highest managerial levels both in the private and the public sector is that there is just not the structure for a fully competitive market. Managers may compete for the jobs; but once they have them, they are in a monopoly position which enables them to salt away enough so they need not fear failure. Other top executives do not have the incentive to stop this process, for the only way of doing so is to reward success less highly in order to make the sanctions for failure real. But doing so would damage their own interests. There is an accountability conspiracy.[4]

The Niskanen model of bureaucracy with its co-incident model of firms in the competitive market shows that the analogy does not work. Rewards to top managers do not reflect the dangers to their companies. The idea of Niskanen's rationality of businessmen is that if the company is not successful, then it does not survive, with consequent losses to the managers. It is true to say that if a chief executive proves to be unsuccessful, then he does not survive. But how great a loss is this and will it affect his future job prospects? Will it stop the CEO from moving into a lucrative job in the private sector? Probably not, for even if the private sector is wary of his managerial skills – unlikely, on past record – they will still value his contacts as a former civil servant; and there will always be a lobbying job available. The Next Steps reforms have not brought about the perfectly competitive-market rationality that is hoped for.

PRODUCTIVE EFFICIENCY GAINS

It is interesting to speculate on the real reasons for the advances made in productive efficiency both within the public and private sectors during the 1980s. Two major studies of privatization, using different methods, have reached the same conclusions (Vickers and Yarrow 1988; Bishop and Kay 1992): productive efficiency gains cannot be explained by privatization. Bishop and Kay discovered that it was the most efficient public-sector organizations which were privatized, not that the privatized became the most efficient, whilst Vickers and Yarrow argue that organizations throughout the nation became more pro-ductively efficient. Private companies which remained private, public-sector organizations which were privatized and ones which were not (at the time of their study) all became more productively efficient. Certainly the biggest efficiency gains seem to have been made prior to privatization rather than after it. This may lead us to suspect that privatization has little to do with productive efficiency, but that conclusion might be premature. Managers had great incentives for turning around public-sector organizations preparatory to privatization in order to make them easier to sell off. This demonstrates that organizations do not have to be in the private sector to become more productively efficient – though private-sector incentives may have been the key to the public-sector improvements pre-privatization.

There are other factors in the efficiency arguments. The fact that the private sector also became more productively efficient should not be ignored. It does seem that a new enterprise culture at the managerial level was created. In part this is due to new ideas about managerialism and a definite drive from government to encourage this enterprise, not least through its trade-union reforms which weakened organized labour in both the private and public sector. The privatization process was also a part of this new culture and its major effect upon the economy as a whole may be the quick and easy profits created for financiers and industrialists and the confidence this helped to create. Privatization was thus important to the productive efficiency gains of the 1980s, not because efficiency gains are only possible in the private sector but because they were a part of the new spirit of strong and determined management – part of the new managerialism.

The idea behind the agency process is to introduce the sort of incentives into the running of the civil service which exist in the private sector. We have seen that if bureaucrats adopt the same type of self-interested motivation as managers in the competitive market, the outcomes in the public as opposed to the private sector are very different. But then again new managerialism in the private sector found many of the same problems in large-scale industry in competitive markets as has been found in large-scale public bureaucracies.

In many of their roles, civil servants are not required to be innovative. Civil servants at the Benefits Agency should correctly calculate the rate of someone's benefit rather than produce an innovative calculation, though we may want them to be innovative when they are working out what sort of benefits we are entitled to. There are always routine tasks to be carried out in any business, and one of the traditional justifications for the hierarchical structure of the civil service is that the major tasks of most civil servants are routinized. That is, legislation is laid down and the job of the civil servant is to see that that legislation is carried out. So, for example, the tax burden of each taxpayer is established according to their level of income and the allowances they are entitled to, and the job of the tax office is to ensure that the correct tax code is applied to each person and that their tax forms (if they have them) are correctly filled in. The job is routinized. Indeed, the job is so routinized in the Inland Revenue that it is very unusual to receive a letter from a real person rather than a computer-generated one. Similarly most of the work of the Benefits Agency is routinized. Individuals have rights to certain benefits at a certain level, and the job of the civil servant here is to work out the correct level of benefit for each person. There is little room for innovation in this job. But there is room for creativity in other ways. Are the clients satisfied with the service they receive? The Benefits Agency discovered, for example, that whilst people did want a fast service and nicely painted buildings, what they want most of all are cubicles for privacy when explaining their needs. The agency also discovered that it is worthwhile to have relatively experienced rather than junior people on the front desk so that the early advice can be quick and effective. These improvements came about by asking people, by looking afresh at the service provided. It is certainly true that there was no need to create an agency to discover these things. So what difference does the agency make?

Perhaps the different management initiatives, including Next Steps, do not themselves bring about innovative changes and better service. What these constant initiatives do bring is a continual reminder to civil servants to aspire to more effective and efficient working practices and a better service. It is the constancy of the revolution which is important rather than the principles of each one.

HAS NEXT STEPS BEEN SUCCESSFUL?

The speed at which the civil service has been reformed has been remarkable. With the exception of wartime, never has the civil service changed so rapidly. Within three years of the start of Next Steps over 50 per cent of civil servants had moved into agencies and by the end of 1994 nearly 62 per cent of civil servants had done so with a further 17 per cent in jobs which are likely candidates for agency status (Cm 2750, 1994: 1–2). The Treasury and Civil Service Committee suggested that 'if agencies had not been introduced so rapidly, the initial impetus for reform might well have been dissipated' (HC 496, 1990–91: vii). Without the dynamic, forceful and revolutionary persuasion of the Cabinet Office and Peter Kemp being backed by both Margaret Thatcher and John Major, the civil service might have slowed and diluted the reform, as it has done with previous attempts to change its nature.

Indeed one of the most remarkable features of Next Steps is how enthusiastically, in the main, civil servants regard the changes. Certainly the chief executives of the newly formed agencies prefer to feel that they are their own bosses, that they have new responsibilities and are able to direct and shape the organizations for which they are responsible. The only complaint from chief executives, heard fairly early on in the process, was of excessive interference from the parent departments, which attempted to monitor the performance of the agencies too closely. The advantage of the agencies, according to the chief executives, is that they encourage individual initiative to re-examine the purposes of the services provided. Academics have been far more sceptical about these aspects of the agencies than those working in them, but there may be truth on both sides. Elizabeth Mellon suggests that 'The delegations accompanying Agency status were minor principle, have been gained without becoming an Agency' (HC 496, 1990–91: 108).

The key phrase here is 'in principle'. Certainly delegation within hierarchies is possible. Certainly enthusiasm for one's work, the promotion of individual initiative and the re-examination of the services provided could all have been attained without radical change. But the nature of the counteractual statement 'could all have been attained' merits close examination. What this means is that it is possible that these goals could have been attained, not that they would have been attained or that they could have been attained so easily or so well. One of the success factors of Next Steps is that the process is a new and radical departure and that the senior civil servants involved feel that they are making major changes for the better. This feeling of 'making a difference' and taking part in a bold new adventure may, on its own, explain the success of Next Steps. More junior workers in the agencies are not so enthusiastic about the agency process. They feel that their job security has been lowered, the level of work they are expected to do has risen and there has not been any compensating pay rise. Many junior staff feel that the civil service is in crisis, as they are barely able, (and in some cases, such as the Child Support Agency, unable) to keep up with their workload.

One factor of the 'feel good' aspect of the Next Steps changes should be noted. It may be true that senior civil servants, particularly those in the agencies, feel that Next Steps is a success purely because it is a radical and bold departure from previous practices, and this is what underpins their enthusiasm and commitment. What will happen when the agencies are an established feature of the public-sector landscape? Will this enthusiasm subside and the tired old facade of the civil servant's lot re-emerge? Is constant revolution required in order to keep the service providers on their toes, or will Next Steps provide the long-term solution?

Following on from Next Steps is the market-testing process, which looks at what elements of departments and agencies can be tendered to the private sector to see whether the private sector can make lower bids for work presently done by civil servants. Civil servants can bid for the work, and some private-sector bids involve taking on civil servants in a new private-sector capacity. There seems to be no theoretical underpinning of the reason why some areas of civil-service work have been market-tested rather than others; but the degree to which work is put out to tender seems to rely upon the enthusiasm of each minister and permanent secretary: the programme target in 1994 ranging from £2 million in the Department for Education to £130 million for Social

Security (Hencke 1994b). Advice on the £1.5 billion market-testing programme from independent consultants cost £508 million in 1983, of which £65 million was wasted according to the Efficiency Unit (Hencke 1994a). With work being put out to tender, some information once available to scrutiny by parliament is now being withheld on the grounds of 'commercial confidentiality' – exactly the opposite of Niskanen's (1979) justification of competition between bureaux as leading to greater openness. Further doubts have been expressed that the marketization programme is leading to lower ethical standards and greater opportunities for impropriety and moral malfeasance. These issues are taken up in Chapter 6.

6 Policy-making

Civil servants in the crossfire

INTRODUCTION

Whilst most civil servants execute policies, more attention is devoted to those who help formulate policy. As policy advisers they are in very powerful positions to influence or indeed create policy. How powerful they are is a moot point, but their central role makes them the major target of organized pressure groups attempting to influence policy. Senior mandarins have recently felt under greater pressures from their political masters as their policy-making role is increasingly threatened with suggestions of outside political advisers taking on a much more major role (Cm 2627, 1994). Civil servants have also complained that ministers are ignoring their advice and findings if they do not fit in with predetermined plans and that the way to get on is to become 'yes men'. The powers enjoyed by civil servants and the pressures experienced by them is the subject of this chapter.

THE FOUR MODELS OF THE STATE

The constitutional representative government model sees the civil servant as an adviser to and an implementer of elected officials' policies. Like Weber's ideal-typical bureaucrats, top civil servants are underlings of elected politicians but are more than merely cogs in a machine. The collector and collator of evidence and the purveyor of ideas, their role is to advise and aid ministers in the formulation of policies. Civil servants are not meant to be political actors when carrying out this role, but are supposed to be politically neutral. 'Neutrality' here means that civil servants are willing and able to serve differing administrations with equal effectiveness. It means treating equally the incumbent party no matter what its ideology. Weber suggests in his political writings, however, that this ideal-typical form is unlikely to be attained. He recognizes that the bureaucracy is an independent force in society since it has an inherent tendency to overstep its proper function as a technical instrument of politicians. Bureaucrats as a particular social group are unable to divorce their behaviour from their interests. Bureaucracy tends to exceed its proper function because its membership comes from a particular social class. Weber argues that it is unrealistic to expect the bureaucracy fully to accomplish its role as a neutral machine set up to do the will of the elected government. The civil service would have class interests of its own. Various studies over the years have borne this out, showing how many senior mandarins come from public schools and Oxbridge. There is also the under-representation of women at the highest levels. The class and gender bias was not redressed during the 1980s, even if a new breed of senior civil servant emerged. The under-representation of ethnic minorities in the senior civil service has not even been addressed.

The idea that the civil service can be a neutral device, at the heart of the constitutional representative government model, is also open to more fundamental criticisms. First, we can question whether such neutrality is technically possible; secondly, whether it is in fact desirable. In as much as social class backgrounds do not reflect society as a whole, and that this affects civil servants' attitudes and behaviour with regard to policy-making, strict neutrality may be impossible. However, without making the bureaucracy a perfect microcosm of society, necessarily such social-class bias may be claimed. Ellis (1989: 87) writes:

> the theoretical possibility of an administration whose agenda would be affected by an independently pursued policy vitiates the capacity of the bureaucracy to serve any incumbent with an equal degree of effectiveness. Equally, patterns of recruitment, career management or internal organization which impede or promote, however inadvertently, the policies of possible incumbents are impediments to political neutrality.

It appears that the civil service cannot be politically neutral, for it is a matter of fact that parties in government are always better served than parties out of government. The civil service must advise the party of government about the presentation of policies, help ministers avoid attacks during question times and debates and under the 'Osmotherly Rules' only selectively provide information to select committees of the House. These rules, the *Memorandum of Guidance for Officials Appearing before Select Committees*, were drawn up by E.B.C. Osmotherly in response to the setting up of the new Select Committees of the House of Commons in 1980. The document advises that information should only be withheld in the interests of 'good government' – this is deemed to include all discussions of interdepartmental exchanges, civil service advice to ministers, the level at which decisions are taken and anything 'in the field of political controversy'. In other words, this means virtually all information that elected MPs would want to hear.

Even when the civil service sticks to its rules over the presentation of information for use on 'party political' occasions, the duty of civil servants to be loyal to the government cannot ensure neutrality between the parties. When the pendulum swings regularly between the two major parties in a two-party system, this may not matter much. But if a dominant-party system emerges, then the myth of neutrality becomes dangerous. This is compounded by the preference-shaping which ensues when radical institutional change occurs. If they are to speak at all, one cannot but expect chief executives of the new agencies to defend the Next Steps process: that is now part of their responsibility. Given the role of senior mandarins in shaping Next Steps, one cannot but expect them to defend it, no matter what the political consequences. Senior civil servants have also been closely associated with privatization policies, again a highly politicized area.

This supposed neutrality or impartiality is an aspect of constitutional double-speak. Ministers want, and have always wanted, partiality. They want the information which best bolsters the policy positions they favour. 'Impartiality', as used by the commentators, is simply the assumption that civil servants are prepared to be partial to whichever party forms a government. Whilst we may wish civil servants to serve governments of any political persuasion equally, it is not a good description to call this 'impartiality' or 'neutrality'. Rather what we require of our civil servants is objectivity. They are there to provide the best information that they possibly can for ministers no matter what party those ministers belong to. Ultimately ministers will decide policies based on their own judgement and their own partiality, but civil servants should provide the information that enables ministers to decide. Of course, civil servants will be swayed by their own prejudices, but normatively we should expect as much objectivity as possible in providing answers to the questions ministers ask them to address. Whether it follows that civil servants should be as unhelpful to parliament as they are is a question addressed in Chapter 8.

Despite the idea that civil servants are neutral, even the constitutional representative government model acknowledges the fact that senior civil servants are powerful. Advisers are frequently powerful and the civil service has traditionally operated as the ministers' window on the world, providing factual, professional and expert information as well as conveying to ministers the views of interested and affected parties in any given policy area. This element of information-collecting is an important aspect of the pluralist account of the state. Pluralists essentially believe that all legitimate groups should have access to the political process and be in a position to make their views known and thereby *potentially* affect the policies eventually adopted. As long as this process is legitimate and not corrupt, it can be seen as pluralistic, even though some groups are much more powerful than others.

In the past, left-wing commentators, including former ministers saw senior civil servants in some form of 'conspiracy' conservatively holding back radical policies. The New Right views civil servants as having interests of their own, particularly concerned with their own roles and departments and also with their private plans. A crude but telling example of mandarin self-interest emerged with the plan to free Horse Guards Parade of parked cars and traffic and to open it up to pedestrians and tourists. Proposed by the Royal Parks Review, the plan was backed by the Department of National Heritage and MI5, as it would lessen security risks. But the proposal was rapidly quashed. Horse Guards Parade serves as a car park for 800 senior Whitehall mandarins. Rarely has the civil service reacted so quickly or in such uniform fashion against a policy proposal!

The autonomy of the state model suggests that this type of self-interest means that civil servants and elected politicians only accede to the wishes of pressure groups, as in the pluralist model, when they already agree with them or are relatively indifferent to their proposals (Nordlinger 1981). It may appear that groups affect the policies of departments, but often they carry out their policies regardless of what organizations tell them. Those organizations which tell the department what it wants to hear will appear to be influential but this is simply happenstance. Departments are only led by group pressures on this model, when they have no clear policy preferences.

All the models recognize that civil servants are powerful and influential figures, and the view which sees them as ministers' lackeys is consistent with models which see the state as largely autonomous of the desires of society as represented through various organized channels. This view argues that the state does largely as it wants, and only when the views of organized factions are consistent with those of the state does it appear to carry out a representative function. State autonomy was developed in opposition to the dominant view of the democratic state as by-and-large pluralist with government swayed by the competing demands of organized pressures. This is the process which the New Right calls rent-seeking.

Notwithstanding the civil servants' self-interest and the state autonomy models, it has become clear that civil servants have not been able to hold back the radical right-wing policies of the Thatcher and Major Conservative administrations. It has also become clear that ministers have grown accustomed to ignoring the policy advice of their civil servants. Rather than admiring and promoting those who provide tough and uncommitted advice, the government has rewarded those who have not tried to find fault with policies prior to implementation but have got on with trying to put them into practice. Many senior mandarins now privately acknowledge that *Yes, Minister* has lost its irony and genuinely is yes, minister. Whether the new regime is closer than the old to the constitutional-representative government and to the pluralist or state-autonomy models is open to question.

POLICY NETWORKS

All commentators now recognize that the relationship between organized pressure groups and civil servants varies across policy domains. In some the relationship is close. Groups and civil servants meet regularly to discuss policy proposals and information is passed from one to the other. Often groups outside government are vital to the successful implementation of policy. When John Patten was Secretary of State for Education, he discovered to his cost that his plans for a national curriculum and regular national testing could not be implemented in their initial form because he did not have the support of the major teaching unions. Over time the national curriculum and the process of testing were modified in order to win the support of teachers. Similarly whilst health-care reforms have been pressed on a largely reluctant profession of doctors and nurses, the reality and the rhetoric of reform have been far apart (Wistow 1992a, 1992b; Smith 1993: ch 7).

Marsh and Rhodes (1992) suggest that the 'implementation gap' has been a major problem for the Thatcher and, it may be added, the Major governments. They argue that in addition to the problems of insufficient information and limited resources which bedevil all governments, the Thatcher government's 'rejection of consultations and negotiation almost inevitably led to implementation problems, because those groups/agencies affected by the policy, and who were not consulted, failed to co-operate, or comply, with the administration of policy' (Marsh and Rhodes 1992: 181). It is undoubtedly true that the Conservative administrations have attempted to negotiate less than previous administrations with certain types of pressure groups. But whilst the pretence of corporatist-style negotiations with unions and business lobbies is over, the administrations have been unable to resist pressures in many areas. Policy failure in some areas is certainly due to this lack of willingness to negotiate, whilst policy compromise, particularly over privatization (Marsh 1991), has been as extensive as ever it was in the past. Indeed the power of the business lobby and the close links between ministers, senior policy-making civil servants and businessmen gives increasing cause for concern.

Departments and the policy process

Whosoever makes decisions, decisions about policy are made within departments. Whilst cabinet committees co-ordinate policy and agreements over interdepartmental policy may emerge there, most of the major decisions about government policy are made within departments. Only on the grand issues such as important aspects of foreign relations and the economy does the prime minister have a continual role, and rarely, even under Thatcher, does the prime minister intervene directly in policy-making. Yet, despite the many books about policy-making, there are few that deal with departmental policy-making (Smith *et al.* 1993). It is often claimed that different departments have different cultures which lead them to favour different policy styles or types of policy. However, it is difficult to explain policy outcomes by pointing to different cultures within departments, since then what is to be explained (the policy) looks too similar to what is supposed to be the explanation (the culture). It is true that different departments seem to favour different *types* of solution, but we can look to institutional factors and inertia to explain this.

The Department of Trade and Industry has interventionist instincts, whereas the Treasury has always been less keen to get involved in helping industry. But the *raison d'être* of a department looking after the interests of trade and industry is intervention. If British businesses are simply to be ignored and help and advice – on EC policy, on trade abroad, to small firms and so on – not given, there is little point in having a Department of Trade and Industry. A similar argument may explain the defence of continued agricultural subsidies within the Ministry of Agriculture, Food and Fisheries. Without denying the power of the National Farmers' Union, the interests of civil servants suggests that continued support for agriculture justifies their very existence. The Foreign and Commonwealth Office is closely linked with a pro-EC stance which can be explained in terms of increasing the power within Whitehall of the FCO.

Other departments are known to have taken a policy stance over a number of years. The Department of Transport is noted for its single-minded pursuit of road as opposed to rail transport and the Home Office for its 'liberal' culture. Here the self-interest of civil servants is less closely connected to the policies they pursue, and other explanations may be sought. In the case of Transport, the plans for an integrated road network were developed in the post-war years, looking towards expected growth over the century. At that time, it was not realized quite what the plans for continued road use (up to 40 million cars on the road at present-day estimates) would actually mean. The health and environmental problems caused by car pollution have not been factored in to plans. Only in 1994 has the chief scientist at the Department of Environment placed the blame for rising air pollution and health problems on excessive car use and 'the burden of deregulation co-ordination' (Lean 1994). Here policy inertia can go a long way towards explaining the 'car culture' of the Department of Transport. Rather than changing policy direction, the department has tended to respond to road chaos with road-widening schemes and new roads, often running parallel with old roads to ease congestion. It has developed techniques to predict road use which it continues to employ despite evidence that better techniques exist, and it continues to take expert advice from those who accept the overall car strategy. Simplistic cost-benefit analysis which assumes a monetary gain for shortening a road journey by a given time multiplied by expected car use allows the department to produce a largely spurious calculation about the benefits of a new road to put against the costs of building it. Ironically, given that the value of land declines once development possibilities decrease, the Department of Transport favours building on areas of outstanding beauty or Sites of Special Scientific Interest, since their value is depressed by development restrictions, thus altering the cost-benefit calculations in favour of road building.

The department has long promoted a programme of road growth by stealth which has helped develop its siege mentality. Local communities always favour major road developments somewhere other than in their own backyard, environmentalists oppose road building in areas of natural beauty, and so on. Wherever a road is built, some pressure group will be dissatisfied. This leads to the attitude that if you cannot satisfy everyone, then you just have to plough on regardless of protest. The department has also promoted a secret strategy of gaining support for building major trunk roads by building 'bypasses' around towns and villages, gaining support from inhabitants of those communities and then linking the bypasses in order to create a major new road. This often seems puzzling to those in the affected communities who cannot understand why the department insists on building a bypass to the east when most people prefer the bypass to the west. The puzzle is explained by its secret strategy, in which the bypass to the west makes their road linkage plan easier. The 'culture' of secrecy and of car use is explained here by institutional factors and rational self-interest. There are costs involved in radical change in policy stance which make inertia easier and change in long-range plans more difficult (Dowding 1991: ch. 7). It also explains why the department, despite consulting widely with groups of all sorts of policy interest, seems to follow the advice of road-user groups far more often than environmental or pro-rail lobbies.

The 'liberal' attitudes of the Home Office may be similarly explained. Here the culture has been generated by decades of research findings from Home Office officials and from funded external research. Despite the general public's desire that criminals should receive long gaol sentences and murderers should be executed, deriving from the felt need for retributive justice, the Home Office considers gaol in terms of deterrence and rehabilitation. Research suggests that the death sentence does not deter murder, that longer gaol sentences do not deter criminal activity, indeed rehabilitation decreases with longer sentences. The point here is not that the Home Office is right and the public wrong, but that the type of calculation is different. Though again, certain groups such as the Radical Alternative to Prison reform group are given less access to policy-makers than other less radical groups, since their plans are so obviously out of kilter with current policy and with what the public would accept (Jordan and Richardson 1987: 190). Culture and favoured policy are explained by rational decision-making, given the underlying principles which exist. Why those principles are there may need further, historical, explanation, but rational administrative inertia can help to explain their continued dominance.

The ways in which different departments make policy can largely be explained, therefore, in terms of the policy objectives by which departments define themselves and in terms of the self-interest of civil servants. Departments tend to 'consult' very widely in the sense that on any particular topic they will have a consultation list. This list will reflect a judgement by the civil servant concerned with the policy issue within a given division, but he will generate it by consulting other officials in his department and possibly other departments too. Jordan *et al.* (1992: 19) report that consultation processes in the Ministry of Agriculture involve approximately five hundred groups for food labelling issues, and over a thousand consultees for nutrition-labelling. This seems to be a wide consultation but does not reveal the true extent and nature of consultation. Many organizations will not respond (some on the list may no longer even be in existence) and the responses received will not all receive the same consideration. If some important organizations do not respond – regarding food-labelling, the National Consumers Council, for example – the civil servant will try to stimulate a reply. The number of replies varies, but the figure supplied by Jordan *et al.* (1992) suggests a reply rate of about four to twenty per cent depending on the nature of the issue.

Is such consultation 'token' or is it genuine? One civil servant said to Jordan *et al.* (1992: 23) 'Better to consult too many than too few . . . There are no rules against joining a list. Any discrimination is at the comment stage. Now those determined to interpret the process to suit their prior prejudice will claim that this means that consultation is meaningless.' And of course, others determined to interpret the process to suit *their* prior prejudices will claim that this means that consultation is significant. A better way of trying to judge the process is by looking at outcomes, seeing how these fit in with interests of affected groups and historically with the direction of policy from the department. As Jordan *et al.* demonstrate, seeing who was 'consulted' first does not enable judgement. In fact, they (1992: 23) go further and argue that consulting more widely is advantageous since 'it allows civil servants to present an image of wide participation and over-consultation, rather than under consultation'. Richardson *et al.* (1992) suggest that the government was forced to establish an environmental regulator against the wishes of the Regional Water Authorities during the privatization of water process because they failed to consult all the relevant interests. Cosmetic consultation thus enables departments to avoid taking notice of groups as much as it enables them to take their interests into account. For example, some people have claimed that the Department of Industry selected Sir Monty Finiston to head the inquiry into the engineering profession in the mid-1970s in the belief that he would produce proposals so radical as to lack credibility. Jordan (1992: 94) suggests that this may be too Machiavellian an interpretation, but 'it cannot be assumed that because Whitehall set up an inquiry it was convinced there was a problem to solve: "the problem" may have been the calls for an inquiry'.

According to pluralist writers, policy is the result of negotiation and bargaining between sets of pressure groups and civil servants within departments. The relative power of outside interests varies across policy domain within departments and across departments. Different types of policy networks exist; some are readily open to outside influences, others are relatively closed (Marsh and Rhodes 1992a). According to state autonomists, the degree to which outside interests seem to be influential depends upon the relative strength of preference within departments. Thus if a department does not have any particular preference within some policy area it may be quite open to outside influence. Where it has a policy agenda, such as the Department of Transport with regard to road-building or the Home Office on prison policy, it is not open to outside influence. State autonomists argue that, whilst the road lobby may appear strong, it is equally plausible to argue that it only appears so because the road lobby is pushing a policy which fits with the long-term plans of the Department of Transport.

In an attempt to assess state autonomy models and pluralism, Christiansen and Dowding (1994) conducted a study of the influence of Amnesty International (British Section) in two policy arenas: human rights abroad with the FCO and human rights in Britain at the Home Office. It was found that whilst Amnesty enjoyed close and regular consultation with the FCO, its relations with the Home Office were distant. Whereas Amnesty was regularly consulted by the FCO, which initiated contact with Amnesty more often than Amnesty initiated contact with the FCO, contact at the Home Office was at 'arm's length', and one civil servant who had worked at the Refugee Unit at the Home Office said he could not recall a single occasion upon which Home Office officials had requested to speak to Amnesty (Christiansen and Dowding 1994: 22). This may appear to support the state autonomy model, with the FCO using Amnesty in order to attack foreign governments on their human rights records when expedient, but ignoring Amnesty when it comes to home policy on similar issues. In fact, the problem is more complex. The way in which pluralism has been defined makes it hard empirically to distinguish between pluralism and state autonomy. For the purposes of this chapter, however, we can see that civil servants tend to use groups when they are useful and ignore them (as far as they can) when they are not. It would be surprising to find anything else.

The relative powers of different groups and organizations in society, the degree of consultation and the extent to which it is real as opposed to cosmetic are exceedingly complex issues on which it is hard to provide final confirmatory evidence. Different researchers reach contrary conclusions using much the same evidence. However, virtually everyone agrees that some departments consult more widely than others, that some issues are more open to competing interests than others, and that departments have stronger policy preferences in some areas than in others. Also, of course, departments are made up of divisions and divisions of sections, and sections are operated by people. In the same way that departments may fight each other, so may divisions within departments, sections within divisions and even individuals within sections. When we write of a 'departmental view' we are simplifying, but it is a useful simplification for understanding the nature of policy-making. The effects of the European Community are further complicating these issues. Most organizations now recognize that Brussels is at least as important a player in many policy arenas as Whitehall, and the more powerful organizations and most professional Whitehall lobbyists have opened offices in Brussels. In agriculture, food and health, for example, Brussels has been the leading policy-maker for many years. Brussels has brought closer links between departments and organized groups as Whitehall and UKRep advise organizations on current commission plans and how to go about lobbying in Europe. In this way departments and lobby organizations use each other against the European Union to their own mutual advantage.

The apparent consistency in departmental approaches to issues, which survive outside pressures and changes in elected governments, may in part be seen as policy inertia and the desire of civil servants to continue down paths which, if not widely perceived as successful in solving problems, may at least be seen by the department as containing them. Change may be less of policy than of nomenclature, for example, the abolition of specially assisted areas and the creation of enterprise zones (Jordan 1984). Ideologically driven solutions to problems often do not seem to be solutions to those who have examined the evidence. The poll tax was introduced despite a welter of academic advice and warnings from civil servants in the Department of Environment that it would not be implemented and would be politically disastrous. William Waldegrave persuaded Margaret Thatcher that the replacement of the rates with the poll tax was a good idea, and once convinced Thatcher was tenacious in its defence (Butler *et al.* 1994). One reason why governments of different party colours reach similar policy conclusions despite ideological differences is that incoming governments do not see the working papers of their predecessors. Similar solutions may thus be promoted by the civil servants.

The dominance of the Treasury

At the centre of policy-making in Britain is the Treasury. One of the smallest departments in budgetary and personnel terms – with just under 2,000 staff in 1993, 70 per cent in Whitehall, around 300 at principal level and above – it is also one of the most important in all areas of policy-making. Each year the spending departments have to agree their forthcoming budget with the Treasury. This involves a scrutiny of all spending in departments, and therefore entails analysis of the expenditure implementing current policies and the expected expenditure on policies being developed within the department. The process of deciding public expenditure is almost continuous, peaking in early autumn before the Autumn Statement, though in future this and the budget are to be combined in November, pushing back decision-time. Decisions are taken by a small community of decision-makers. Thain and Wright (1992) suggest that the circulation list for the *Survey Guidelines* is about two hundred ministers and senior officials in spending departments, though around five hundred more will be involved in preparing materials. In the Treasury around a hundred officials working for the Chief Secretary for the Treasury will be involved. These exercises consider a three-year period – though estimates for years 2 and 3 are often very inaccurate – and the process gives the Treasury greater bargaining power when years 2 and 3 become year 1.

The Treasury thus indirectly influences policy-making. It also has an effective veto over plans which seem too expensive and its support in some policy initiatives can be vital. The Treasury was always opposed to the setting up of the Civil Service Department in 1968 and was a key actor in its abolition in 1981, four governments later (Greenaway *et al.* 1992: ch. 7). The Treasury has two great sources of power, money and knowledge. As the purse of all other departments, its views on the policies of other departments cannot be ignored. Treasury officials often deny that they have policy priorities within the ambit of other departments. The principal in charge of spending on housing said in 1984:

> I don't think the Treasury necessarily has a housing policy. It will have a housing aspect of a general public expenditure policy, and if there are general policy objectives, such as keeping the level of expenditure down, then that will influence the attitude that one takes to policy issues that come up in housing. But I don't think it has a free-standing housing policy as such.
>
> (Young and Sloman 1984: 44)

Keeping down expenditure could, perhaps, be described as *the* Treasury policy. A rather different story is told by Tony Benn who suggests that the Treasury influence is all-powerful and has been since the Second World War:

> When I had my officials in to look at energy forecasting, they gave me the forecast and there was this great energy gap. It was intended

to be filled by nuclear power, but they didn't want to tell me that and so I said 'Well, let's look at the assumptions'. When I asked for them I found all hell broke loose in my department because my officials had been forced to put in assumptions about rates of growth and inflation and so on, which had come from the Treasury and which they didn't necessarily agree with. I then realized that the Treasury had written our entire energy forecast.

(Young and Sloman, 1984: 114)

The Treasury's control of the purse-strings should not be exaggerated: spending overshot the Treasury's planning total in 8 out of 11 years from 1980 (Thain and Wright, 1992b: 206). Thain and Wright also suggest that spending departments get around a third to a half of the extra money they bid for (1992a: 20), figures similar to past estimates. One recent attempt to change this has been the introduction of a cabinet committee to produce a 'control total' to be agreed by full cabinet early in the annual spending round. Each department then defends its plans before a scrutiny conducted by the Chief Secretary (the 'prosecutor') in a cabinet committee (EDX) chaired by the Chancellor (the 'judge') who is the Chief Secretary's departmental boss. This allows the Treasury to affect other departments' policy priorities discussing their plans in detail in EDX.

The bargaining over expenditure, however, also involves the Treasury in policy discussions across other departments. In this sense it knows more about each department than other departments do about each other. Thus the Treasury is, as much as the Cabinet Office, the department which co-ordinates policy. This means that the Treasury only knows what other departments are doing by what those departments tell them; though it is not true that it only knows what other departments choose to tell them. It gains its knowledge through asking intelligent questions (Young and Sloman 1984: 47). According to Douglas Wass, one-time Permanent Secretary at the Treasury and Head of the Civil Service, when Treasury officials move to other departments, their knowledge of the Treasury helps them in this bargaining game (Young and Sloman 1984: 63). This movement also helps the Treasury, or at least so mythology suggests. Crossman (1975: 615) claims that all his officials were 'imbued with a prior loyalty to the Treasury and felt it necessary to spy on me and report my doings to the Treasury'; and Joel Barnett (1982: 188) confirms that when he was at the Treasury, he heard from his officials what his cabinet colleagues were up to. Jim Callaghan is said to have suffered 'information deprivation' when he moved from Chancellor to Home Secretary.

The Treasury is very much a small community of people with very fixed ideas (Heclo and Wildavsky 1974). Contemporary reports support Sam Brittan's statement of a generation ago:

> it is a small organization of highly intelligent and sensitive individuals. As in most such organizations, members tend to be intensely loyal to each other and they will not question too deeply reports or recommendations which emanate from among their number, but have an instinctive reluctance to take seriously contributions from outside.
>
> (Brittan 1969: 26; cf. Young and Sloman 1984;
> Hennessy 1990; Grant 1993)

It was partly in response to this long-perceived problem that in 1991 the chancellor established a panel of independent forecasters. The Treasury has also started to commission outside teams to examine and revamp aspects of its model of the economy, starting with those aspects concerned with consumer borrowing and spending. The government's desire to obtain more advice from outside the civil service will also encourage this movement.

The Treasury is the most secretive department (apart from the secret service) in a very secretive civil service. The great responsibility felt by Treasury officials for the economic well-being of the nation, the secret nature of their business and the feeling that they are an elite group create community spirit and an insular attitude.

Some deny that the Treasury has a monolithic view (Thain 1984; Browning 1986). The micro-analysis of dispute between divisions and sections within the Treasury and the concentration on dispute over detail or more radical disagreement across policy documents does suggest that there are variations and diversities of opinion. This does not disprove the thesis of the monolithic viewpoint, however, since variety over detail and broader disagreement, which is discussed but never acted upon, are compatible with the more standard monolithic view of the Treasury. Examining variation amongst the trees does not alter the shape of the forest.

The role of pressure groups in relation to the Treasury is one area of change since 1979. The previous Labour government felt great pressures on its economic policies from trade unionists, businessmen, financiers, international bankers and other international organizations, and other governments. The Conservative government maintained an economic strategy which was also subject to pressures in the early years of its administration but felt able to resist many, though not all, of them. Pressure still exists, of course, but the mainstream thinking of Treasury officials fits more closely with that of the international financiers than did the previous Keynesian and neo-Keynesian orthodoxy. Leading up to the budget, the pressure on the Treasury increases, though much of this is of a routine nature, with the Treasury well aware of the desires of the leading pressure groups without having to be told.

The Treasury shares with the Bank of England the control it tries to exercise over financial markets. This includes its intervention in foreign exchange markets to support the pound, intervention to affect the level of interest rates throughout the economy and the terms on which it borrows money. These have been the key tasks of economic policy since the mid-1970s. The Bank is now as important as the Treasury in some regards; it has a closer link with financial interests and a closer understanding of their needs, though a lesser understanding of the needs of productive capital. Whilst the Treasury has the legal right to issue instructions to the Bank, it never does so; rather discussions between the Bank and the Treasury occur regularly, both informally and in a monthly forum.

The nature of Treasury officials over the past twenty years has changed more than in other departments. Whilst the generalist 'amateur' ethic with a humanities degree has been changing throughout the civil service, it has done so more rapidly and thoroughly in the Treasury where professional economists from a wider social-class background have reached and dominated at the top. The high intellectual calibre of Treasury officials is often remarked upon (Healey 1989: 376), though Sam Brittan's description of them as clever as 'dons at an Oxbridge High Table' may perhaps indicate the simplest explanation of Britain's relative economic decline.

The internationalization of economic and therefore other policy matters is also demonstrated within the structure of the Treasury. An international finance group deals with matters pertaining to the International Monetary Fund (IMF) and other international economic organizations, and the Treasury has officials located in the British Embassy in Washington and on secondment to the IMF and the World Bank. Its European Community group is very important and is split into three divisions concerned with EC financial and economic policy issues, the EC budget and international trade policy.

DECISION-MAKING

It is a mistake to think that it is easy to measure the relative power of ministers, civil servants and outside pressures. Even those on the inside are hard put to identify relative powers, as the late Lord Crowther-Hunt explains:

> In our seamless web of government, it is never easy to identify the moment and place at which crucial decisions are taken, let alone who takes them. Take devolution, for example. This was the problem I came into government to handle as Harold Wilson's Constitutional Adviser in March 1974, after serving for four years as a member of the Commission on the Constitution, which produced a whole series of devolution recommendations in 1973. In September 1974 the Labour Government produced a White Paper committing itself to a broad but quite specific scheme of devolution for Scotland and Wales. In November 1975 in a second White Paper, it elaborated those schemes in much more detail. During the whole period I was present at virtually all the ministerial discussion on devolution; and up to September 1974 I was at virtually all the civil service inter-departmental discussions as well. But out of this whole range of meetings and discussions, some formal and some informal, it is impossible for me to point to a particular meeting and say that *there* the crucial decision or decisions were taken. Indeed, there are only two generalizations I can make with confidence. The first is that the two meetings of the cabinet which approved the September and November White Papers were certainly *not* the occasions when crucial decisions about devolution were taken. For the most part, they were merely rubber-stamping meetings for all that had gone before. The second is that most civil servants were fundamentally opposed to devolution, and so, for that matter, were most ministers. The point is that when it is so difficult to be certain when and where crucial decisions are taken, it makes it even more difficult to decide whether ministers or civil servants have the more powerful voice.
>
> (Kellner and Crowther-Hunt 1980: 210)

It seems clear from this evidence that the decision to go ahead with devolution was not a policy preference of non-elected state officials and that it was not really the preference of the elected state officials either. Outside pressure groups were influential in those difficult times of a minority Labour government. The detail of that policy was hammered out over time, and it is difficult even for one of the participants to identify who was behind which detailed provision. In the end this policy failed as indeed did the government, this case demonstrating that ultimately parliament does have the final say. But this is an instructive instance of how it is often hard to pin down who was influential and whose interest triumphed.

A declining influence?

The power and influence of civil servants over their ministers have diminished during the last decade. Two reasons may be put forward to explain this. The first is the radical and determined nature of the Thatcher government which set a precedent for the ministers serving under Major. The second is the sheer length of time of the Conservative administration. Thatcher was renowned for her 'is he one of us?' question. When asked of a civil servant it was not a question about ideological predilections but about attitudes towards policy proposals. Thatcher admired senior civil servants who looked to solving problems with policy proposals rather than finding them. She promoted men who did not try to find fault with radical plans but instead went ahead and executed them (Young 1989; Ranelagh 1992). At first this may have breathed fresh life into the higher reaches of the civil service, but over a period of time such attitudes promote the 'yes men' who may be just as feeble as the policy-conservatives Thatcher despised (Plowden 1994). When two experienced officials at the Department for Education were moved sideways after pointing out problems that would emerge with the planned reform of teacher training (Hugill 1994), one civil servant complained, 'They did their bloody job and got carpeted for it.'

The changed relationship between ministers and civil servants has many causes. In part it is a result of a radical government determined to make radical changes. Partly it is a result of one party being in power for a long time. A ratchet effect starts to work, where tasks which once civil servants would have refused to do over time become standard. One example is press officers in departments responding to press inquiries about the policy proposals of opposition spokespeople or about criticisms of government policy without consulting the minister. These may be minor examples of blurring boundaries of what is deemed appropriate for 'neutral' civil servants to do, but the ratchet effect suggests that once crumbling, the boundary will continue to disappear. Senior and former civil servants complain that the pressures to work on party political issues has increased. In evidence to the Treasury and Civil Service Select Committee in 1993, Elizabeth Symons, general secretary of the civil service trade union, The First Division Association, said that two officials had complained that they had been instructed to work on what were effectively party political speeches (HC 390-II, 1992–93: para 231). One had done so and the other had refused. The National Health Service (NHS) chief executive Sir Duncan Nichol was criticised for his defence of Conservative party policy during the 1992 election campaign, stating that Labour was wrong on the NHS. The Prime

Minister did not rebuke him but stated that he was entirely justified in making such public statements. This demonstrates the impossibility of neutrality for senior mandarins when they are in the public eye. One can hardly expect the chief executive of the NHS to do other than defend its current form when speaking publicly but given the political nature of reform, this draws such figures into taking what appear to be party political stances. All that can be expected is objectivity, and that can only reasonably be checked upon by an independent assessor, parliament, which suggests more direct accountability than exists at present.

Certainly, ministers appear much more willing to ignore policy advice than they once were. At the Home Office relations between the Home Secretary Michael Howard and his senior civil servants were placed under great strain as official criminal justice reports which contradicted his policy plans were systematically shelved. Similarly advice over the police and criminal justice bills was ignored; they were then heavily amended in the Lords following scornful attacks by former home secretaries. So great has been the anger amongst civil servants that in July 1994 the Association of First Division Civil Servants sent a detailed complaint to the head of the Home Civil Service, Sir Robin Butler, about the attitude of Charles Wardle, minister for immigration. This followed his rejection of a report by the Home Office research unit which disproved his belief that most asylum-seekers were generally economic rather than political migrants. It was not until 1983 that the research unit had to seek ministerial approval for its research plans, and reports were automatically published until 1988. At least these stories demonstrate that ministers are getting forthright advice from their civil servants even if they browbeat them for giving it. More disturbing evidence suggests that these kinds of ministerial attitude are leading civil servants to give less candid advice. With government increasingly looking to outside advisers, there is an increasing crisis of confidence amongst civil servants. One civil servant told William Plowden (1994: 104) that 'The government knows what it wants and needs no advice', whilst another said 'What's new is the number of Ministers who won't listen to advice'. A third story is more disturbing still:

> A Grade 3 . . . told of a meeting with a senior Minister at which only he was from another department. When the Minister asked for frank comments on his current policy proposals all 8 or 9 of his officials, led by the permanent secretary expressed approval. Only the outsider dissented. Was this, he wondered later, because his future alone did not depend on a good mark from that permanent secretary? (The policy was a fiasco.)

PANTOUFLAGE AND THE REVOLVING DOOR

Of even more concern in recent years are the close links that exist between many senior civil servants and business interests. Whilst pluralism is a model of democracy, too close links between policy-makers and pressure lobbies suggest that certain groups will have an unfair advantage and the danger of malfeasance will exist. There are three separate but related causes of concern. The first is that civil servants, or more often government advisers, have links to business which makes their advice suspect, since they may have ulterior motives. A majority of the government's advisers on food receive money from food and drug companies (31 out of 59 on all committees), as shareholders, or employees, as fees for consultancy work or in the form of research money. Three of the nine members of the Medical Aspects of Food Policy Committee in 1992 were supported by food and drug companies. The most blatant clash of interests was exemplified by R. A. Hendry who sat on the working group on weaning diet and was a full-time employee of Nestlé, the world's largest producer of infant formula milk (Erlichman 1992). Among the many recent examples of potential impropriety is Peter Pink, one-time deputy inspector-general of the Insolvency Service, who was seconded back to the disqualification unit of the service whilst running a company which offers confidential advice to companies in financial difficulties on how to handle visits from inspectors (Hencke 1994c).

Also of concern is the practice of civil servants taking up lucrative posts in companies with which they had dealings when they were civil servants. This is called *pantouflage* meaning 'putting on one's slippers' signifying a nice retirement. Companies often open their doors to retiring civil servants valuing their knowledge of Whitehall and their expertise in given policy areas. Whilst this practice has long caused some disquiet, privatization and a greater willingness to allow retiring civil servants to take up any post offered to them have led to growing concern. Officials in the top three grades of the service have to receive permission from the Cabinet Office to take outside jobs within two years of leaving the service. Lower ranks must also receive permission to take jobs with firms with which they have had official dealings or if they have had access to commercially sensitive information about their prospective employers' competitors. In the top two ranks the Prime Minister's advisory committee have to take decisions. In 1981, the Commons Treasury and Civil Service Committee concluded that the arrangement (HC 236-I, II, III 1981–82 : 19) 'tilted too much in the direction of freedom of movement and too little in the direction of removing the suspicion of impropriety', whilst the Commons Defence Committee concluded in 1989: 'We do not say that impropriety exists. We do say that the Government has been unwilling to demonstrate to us, either publicly or privately, that impropriety does not exist.' Between 1985 and 1990, 114 individuals asked permission to take up 191 appointments, 39 of them from the Ministry of Defence. Senior mandarins who have recently left the service to take up business appointments include: Lord Armstrong, Cabinet Secretary 1979–87, who took directorships at BAT, RTZ, Shell, Lucas, NM Rothschild and Inchcape; Sir Michael Palliser, Head of the Diplomatic Service 1975–82, who took directorships at BAT Industries, Shell Transport and Trading Group PLC, Eagle Star, United Biscuits and Booker PLC; Sir Frank Cooper, Permanent Secretary at the Ministry of Defence 1976–82, who took directorships at Westland Helicopters, Babcock International, Morgan Crucible, NM Rothschild, United Scientific Holdings and High Integrity Systems; Sir Peter Middleton, who left his post as Permanent Secretary at the Treasury (1983–91) early to take up a post as director and deputy chair at Barclays Bank, and Chair at Barclays de Zoete Wedd Group; Sir Geoffrey Littler, Second Permanent Secretary at the Treasury 1983–88 became a director at National Westminster Investment Bank, director of County Natwest Group Ltd and Natwest Bank PLC and of Maritime Transport Services Ltd; Sir Brian Hayes, Permanent Secretary at Trade and Industry 1985–89, became a director at Guardian Royal Exchange, Tate & Lyle and Unilever; Sir Michael Franklin, Permanent Secretary at MAFF 1983–87, became a director at Agricultural Mortgage Corporation, Barclays Bank, Barclays PLC; and Sir Jack Rampton, Permanent Secretary at Department of Energy 1974–80 joined London Atlantic Investment Trust, ENO Company as director, and become a deputy chair at Sheerness Steel Company 1985–87, a director at Flextech PLC and special adviser to Sun Exploration and Development Co, North Sea Sun Oil Co and director of the Magnet Group 1981–84; Sir Duncan Nichol former chief executive at the NHS who became a diretor of BUPA, the private health care company. The list goes on.

The revolving door syndrome is even more alarming to some people. This involves business people coming into the civil service and then returning to business in policy areas in which they worked as civil servants. The situation at the Ministry of Defence causes most concern. Sir James Blyth was general manager at Lucas Aerospace 1977–81, becoming head of MoD defence sales 1981–85, then managing director of Plessy Electronic Systems in 1985; whilst Sir Colin Chandler who was group marketing director at British Aerospace 1983–85, became head of the MoD export service 1985–89, then moved on to become managing director and then chief executive at another defence company, Vickers. In fact, in 1990, 373 MoD officials and officers in the armed forces left to take jobs in industry, most with defence contractors. Whilst conditions were placed on 50 of them, no moves were stopped. One former mandarin said that the interests of the MoD's procurement programme and those of large defence companies were identical (Pallister and Norton-Taylor 1992). There is another side to this situation. Lack of such interchange was an area of criticism of the civil service in the 1960s, and the Fulton Report suggested that more businessmen should be seconded to the civil service and that civil servants should have a spell in the private sector. A case may be made that defence sales and the defence industry do have similar interests, which do not clash with the public interest, but given repeated criticism from the National Audit Office, the Public Accounts Committee and the Defence Select Committee about excessive profits in the defence industry from MoD procurement, the 'revolving door' does not instil confidence in civil service neutrality.

It is the possibility of malfeasance that causes concern. Whilst it may seem perfectly reasonable for companies to want on their boards civil servants who can advise them on how best to negotiate with government and on likely governmental responses to world events, it does not seem unreasonable that certain businesses should be advantaged by their links or that civil servants after retirement should join companies with which they had dealings whilst civil servants. The suspicion here is that such companies may reward civil servants who helped them, thus compromising decisions made by departments. Where genuine interests coincide, then a case can be made for the revolving door, otherwise civil servants and seconded business people should be used in separate policy areas. The main problem is not that the institutions for ensuring propriety do not exist, it is that over the last fifteen years they have not been used successfully. A government which believes that the state is evil and business good is unlikely to be disturbed by the revolving door. Others with different ideological predilections may be more concerned.

7 European Union

New opportunities[1]

INTRODUCTION

Britain entered the European Economic Community (EEC) after an eleven-year battle on 1 January 1973. The EEC was later renamed the European Community (EC) and now has two names depending upon which institutions and policy area is involved. In this chapter the term 'European Community' is used to refer to matters concerned with the supranational pillar, that is, matters developing from Commission-led legislation and harmonization, and 'European Union' (EU) refers to matters specific to the two intergovernmental pillars – foreign policy and security, justice and home affairs – or to all three pillars collectively. Most of this chapter is concerned with how the British home civil service is affected by EC matters.

Since 1973 successive British governments have maintained a relatively stable policy towards Europe. Despite inter- and intra-party battles, the outward rhetoric of Heath's committed enthusiasm, Wilson's and Callaghan's careful acceptance and the Thatcher/Major 'us versus them' stance, Britain has sailed a consistent course in her relations with the EC. British governments have accepted the fact of the EC and committed themselves to maintaining and furthering their links, without ever taking too engaged a stance or a leading role. This stable policy stance is in no small measure because of the fact that day-to-day relations as well as more mundane policy questions are largely handled by the civil service. Its attitude towards the EU has not changed much, though the attitude of civil servants varies across departments, the Foreign and Commonwealth Office (FCO) being consistently the most enthusiastic and the Treasury the least.

Initially the entry negotiations and early relations with the other member states and the EC bureaucracy itself were handled by the FCO and the Cabinet Office. On entry the Cabinet Office set up a European

Secretariat to co-ordinate British responses to European initiatives across all departments. Some departments have developed closer relations with Europe than others and have set up their own EC divisions. Now all departments must keep a close eye upon developments in Europe, for even policy initiatives which prima facie have little to do with the EC may in fact contradict European Law or European Directives. Thus the EC is fully integrated with the workings of the British bureaucracy. I will begin by briefly describing the way in which the EC operates and how its major bureaucratic wing, the European Commission, works. I will then concentrate on what the EU actually entails for the civil service in Britain and suggest the ways in which this is likely to develop in the coming years.

ORGANIZATION OF THE EU

The basic structures of the EC were laid down by the founding treaties; they have subsequently been amended to change institutional rules and add policy powers, most notably by the Maastricht Treaty of 1991. Furthermore, conventions and practices have evolved which have strengthened some community powers.

The major decision-making institution of the EU is the Council of Ministers. This brings together political representatives of the member states both to negotiate and to legislate. Each country is represented at these meetings by the minister most appropriate for the issue under discussion. Thus for agricultural issues the agriculture ministers will meet, for finance the finance ministers and so on. The Council of Ministers can be seen as acting much like cabinet committees in Britain, where the relevant politicians thrash out policy, serviced by bureaucrats. Member states take it in turns to preside at the council meetings, which are serviced by the Council Secretariat in Brussels. In addition to the meetings of the Council of Ministers on specific issues, foreign ministers meet regularly once a month or more. As well as discussing affairs foreign to the whole union, they act as a co-ordinating body for everything else which has been decided. This helps make the FCO much more influential in British government as a whole than was so before Britain's entry.

Before ministerial meetings, many months of negotiating will have taken place to try to smooth the path, and on many issues the Council of Ministers will be rubber-stamping agreements made by the bureaucrats. Tony Benn complained that when he was a minister at the departments of Energy and Industry 'There were one or two officials in Brussels all the time, and I have some links with them, who would go in for package deals. They would then come and tell you about a package deal when it was too late to unpick it' (Young and Sloman 1982: 74). Civil servants tell a rather different story. Whilst a number of issues are sorted out by civil servants in official committees in Whitehall and meetings in Brussels, these would be 'the technical, the non-political stuff'; whilst the issues which have 'political dimensions, the sorts of thing you get in the news' would be made within the policy guidelines or referred to the minister. One possible explanation of these divergent views recognizes that these are different conceptions of what counts as 'political' and therefore what implications may be drawn from the 'technical stuff' for future policy options. Radicals such as Tony Benn tend to define the 'political' much more widely than 'middle-of-the-road' thought suggests. Civil servants may believe that their decisions are technical, but radical politicians like Benn or Thatcher see them as emanating from a dominant 'consensus' ideology or culture. Either way, Young and Sloman's conclusion is probably right:

> Brussels is not a mandarin's playground in the sense of letting civil servants off the leash of the Constitution and giving them enormous untrammelled power. On the contrary, the opposite is truer: that in this area of government activity . . . the lines of political control are drawn tight.
>
> (Young and Sloman 1982: 79)

Such is the nature of bargaining and negotiation within the EC's decision-making structure that we should expect 'package deals' to be the norm rather than the exception. The political controls over British civil servants are well-established; but the very nature of EU decision-making does allow scope for mandarin manoeuvring and departmental enhancement and entails greater difficulties for parliamentary control of the executive.

Most issues these days are taken on the basis of a majority vote, though on some issues the vote is weighted with larger nations having more votes than smaller ones. Until 1995 Britain, France, Germany and Italy had ten votes, Spain eight, Belgium, Greece, the Netherlands and Portugal five, Denmark and Ireland three and Luxembourg two. To approve a proposal of the Commission, the Council requires 54 of the 76 votes, although unanimity is required to amend the Commission's proposal. A blocking minority of 23 votes is required, thus ensuring that the big five of Germany, France, Spain, Italy and the UK cannot muster enough votes to force through any proposal but require the support of at least two other nations. Thus no proposal can be carried without the support at least seven of the twelve. New voting rights, fought by Britain have now been agreed. When the EU is enlarged with the entry of Austria, Norway, Sweden and Finland, those countries will get between 3 and 5 votes each. From 1995 a blocking coalition of 30 votes out of 90 will be required. This will not change the nature of the bargaining game, but overall Britain's voting power has been reduced.

The complexity of the bargaining game with its weighted voting is compounded by the member states' different interpretations of the 'Luxembourg Compromise'. The Luxembourg Compromise developed during 1965–66 when General de Gaulle insisted whenever 'very important national interests' were involved that unanimity was required. The other five nations never formally accepted the French proposal but did not vote de Gaulle down at any time in the subsequent three years of his presidency. However, when Britain, Denmark and Ireland joined the EC in 1973 they all espoused the principles of the Luxembourg Compromise. It appears that the countries which now subscribe to the Luxembourg Compromise are Britain (10 votes), France (10 votes), Greece (5 votes), Portugal (5 votes) and Denmark (3 votes). Both Ireland (3 votes) and Spain (8 votes) might be described as moderate supporters (Butler 1986). At times, particularly, for example, during the annual Common Agricultural Policy (CAP) price review, the Luxembourg Compromise may be invoked by one of these nations trying to secure the support of the other nations which accept it. This does not always work. The UK attempted to invoke the compromise during the 1982–83 CAP price review but France, Britain's major ally on the compromise, voted with the majority, whilst Denmark and Greece abstained. Here Britain invoked the compromise as part of its negotiations over the budget rebate it wanted. France argued that the indirect nature of the claim of national interests was against the spirit of the compromise, thereby justifying its voting with the majority (Swinbank 1989).

The Council of Ministers is serviced by the Committee of Permanent Representatives (COREPER), consisting of the ambassador and other civil servants from each country. It works closely with bureaucrats from both the commission and the respective civil services. There are about forty British civil servants working in COREPER of which about half come from the FCO and the rest from other departments. The number goes up slightly when Britain holds the presidency.

The European Commission is the other main wing of the EU and the central pillar of the EC. Despite the frequent allegations about the EC's overwhelming bureaucracy, the numbers of civil servants in the commission are small in comparison to that in Whitehall. In part that is because of the founding father Jean Monnet's wishes to have a small, non-hierarchical and supranational bureaucracy (Mazey 1992). It has remained supranational and small, though it has become more hierarchical, perhaps a necessary development of its increasing scope and size.

Its role is to prepare legislation, initiate legal action against member states which have infringed community laws, administer community funds, and prepare the budget. It does not implement legislation; that is for member countries to do. It is led by the seventeen-strong College of Commissioners, two each from Britain, Germany, Italy, France and Spain and one each from the other nations. With enlargement and new institutional reforms the numbers and nationalities of commissioners will be adjusted. They are appointed by their respective governments to serve renewable four-year terms. They are supposed to serve the community as a whole and not the particular nation which appointed them, and by and large this is the case. Both Lord Cockfield and Leon Brittan were appointed by Margaret Thatcher in the hope that their, at best, ambiguous attitudes towards the EC would ensure they put Britain first. However, both soon 'went native'. The two commissioners are supposed to reflect differing elements of the politics of the nation – as the appointment in 1995 of the former Labour leader Neil Kinnock as Britain's second commissioner demonstrates. This is rather alien to Britain's adversarial political system and reflects the more consensual heritage of much of continental Europe. Each commissioner is in charge of a particular policy area, though the commission as a whole is collectively responsible for all policy. Each commissioner has a private office known as a 'cabinet' which includes both administrative staff and a political office.

Within the commission as a whole there is a staff of over 12,000 civil servants distributed amongst twenty-three Directorates-General (DGs) or 'departments'. There are also various other units, such as the Euratom Supply Agency, the Legal Service and the 'Spokesman's Group' (or Press Office) which helps service the DGs and other aspects of community business. There are four grades of staff within the commission: A – administration, B – executive, C – clerical and D – others. Each DG is divided into directorates which are themselves sub-divided into divisions. At the head of each DG is a director general at A1 grade, a post roughly equivalent to deputy secretary; the directorates are headed by directors at A2 grade (approximately under-secretary level); and heading divisions are A3 grade personnel (equivalent to assistant secretary). The majority of the British national 'Eurocrats' have come from Whitehall, though some have entered the service from outside government altogether. These Eurocrats work closely with civil servants from the member states and serve as the main focus of pressure group activity and outside professional advice.

EC legislation is drawn up on the basis of treaty provisions. Regulations are directly binding on member states. Directives set the framework and objectives that each member state is supposed to implement in national laws. Other sorts of agreement are advisory. British courts have never formally incorporated themselves into EC law but in practice do not contradict decisions of the European Court of Justice and accept the precedents. The European Court of Justice develops EC jurisprudence by case law and by interpretation for national courts. It also operates as the final court of appeal for cases from national courts in which any EC law or directives can be held to be binding. It also hears cases brought by member states against each other or by EC institutions, such as the commission, against member states. Its decisions are political in the sense that they are politically accepted (or not) by British governments and therefore accepted by British courts.

British courts take on board political decisions of the British government even if they seem to go against the rulings of the European Court of Justice, for example, on the Prevention of Terrorism Act. They also refer cases to the European Court of Justice for decision, for example, the case of Marshall v. Southampton and South West Hampshire Area Health Authority.[2] The Health Authority dismissed Miss Marshall because of her age and sex. It operated a general policy that employees would normally retire at the age at which state pension becomes payable, though it had a discretion to waive this in individual cases and did so for Miss Marshall for two years. She complained to an industrial tribunal about unlawful discrimination contrary to the Sex Discrimination Act 1975 and article 5(1) of Directive 76/207. The tribunal held that (i) the claim was excluded by section 6(4) of the Sex Discrimination Act which specifically exempts provision over retirement but decided that (ii) the policy of requiring someone to retire at sixty violated Directive 76/207. The appeal tribunal upheld the first decision but not the second because 'even if the compulsory retirement policy was contrary to the Directive, an individual could not rely on the Directive before a national court' (Bates 1986: 538). The Court of Appeal referred two questions to the European Court of Justice for a preliminary ruling under article 177 of the EEC Treaty, which states that the court has jurisdiction to give preliminary rulings about: (a) the interpretation of the treaty; (b) the validity of acts of the institutions of the community; (c) the interpretation of the statutes of bodies established by acts of the council, where those statutes so provide. Article 177 further states:

> Where such a question is raised before any court or tribunal of a Member State, that court or tribunal may, if it considers that a decision on the question is necessary to enable it to give a judgement, request the Court of Justice to give a ruling thereon.

The two questions put to the European Court were:

1 Whether the [authority's] dismissal of [Miss Marshall] after she had passed her sixtieth birthday pursuant to the [authority's retirement age] policy and on the grounds only that she was a woman who had passed the normal retiring age applicable to women was an act of discrimination prohibited by [Directive 76/207].

2 If the answer to (1) above is in the affirmative, whether or not [Directive 76/207] can be relied upon by [Miss Marshall] in the circumstances of the present case in national courts or tribunals notwithstanding the inconsistency (if any) between the Directive and section 6(4) of the Sex Discrimination Act [1975].

(Quoted from Bates 1986: 538)

The European Court of Justice answered both questions in the affirmative, but made it clear that it did so only because the claim was made against the state in the form of the Area Health Authority. In another case, also involving sex discrimination and retirement which was referred to the European Court of Justice but in which the plaintiff was unsuccessful, the Attorney General observed that the plaintiff would not have been able to enforce a successful decision since the UK had failed to implement Directive 76/207.

Those decisions reflect the somewhat odd status of European Directives and the legal relationship between Britain and the EC. The directive had not been implemented at the times of either plaintiff's enforced retirement. Since the first case was against an agent of the state – Southampton and South West Hampshire Area Health Authority – and the state had agreed the directive by its presence at the Council of Ministers, the plaintiff's case was upheld. In the second case the private body – Tate and Lyle Industries Ltd – was not bound by the European Directive until it had been passed into British law by an act of parliament. EC power over the British citizen and other private bodies is mediated through the British parliament but more directly affects the actions of the British government itself, including its failure to implement such directives.

The final institution of the EU is the European Parliament which, since 1979, is a directly elected body. It is not very powerful despite having its powers increased in 1986 and again by the Maastricht Treaty of 1991. Before the 1986 change the European Parliament had no legislative powers, even though MEPs were consulted over legislation and had some powers over spending and officially the right to dismiss the College of Commissioners en masse. The Single European Act introduced a new 'co-operation procedure' which grants the European Parliament the right to a second reading of all community legislation over the internal market, social and economic cohesion, technological research and development and certain aspects of EC social and regional policies. It gives the MEPs the opportunity to propose amendments to the position taken by the Council of Ministers, which can be over-turned only by a unanimous decision of the council. During the period July 1987 to November 1990, 1,052 parliamentary amendments were accepted by the commission (out of 1,724 put forward by parliament) of which 719 were adopted by the Council of Ministers (Mazey and Richardson 1993: 11). Nevertheless, the parliament is weak, having no rights to initiate legislation nor to override decisions by the Council of Ministers. It has no sovereign powers apart from dismissing the College of Commissioners and only limited influence.

WHITEHALL'S RESPONSE TO THE EC

Whitehall's workload has increased considerably with the advent of the EC. Ministers and Whitehall bureaucrats participate regularly and directly in the running of the EC. Many Whitehall civil servants cross the Channel regularly to negotiate and consult with their counterparts in the commission, to negotiate at COREPER or to accompany their minister at the council. The Council of Ministers meets eighty or more times a year with some ministers such as Agriculture meeting perhaps twenty times, whilst foreign ministers meet at least twelve times a year. Ministers also meet at fringe bodies such as the Standing Committee on Employment, whilst the Prime Minister attends the bi-annual Heads of State meetings. These days many civil servants from numerous Whitehall departments spend much of their time in Brussels: flying to Brussels towards the end of the week to meet members of the 'Office of the United Kingdom's Permanent Representative to the European Communities' (better known as UKRep) and other EC civil servants. Similarly UKRep staff will fly to Whitehall on a Monday to brief civil servants and ministers there. Much business is done by telephone and FAX as well of course. A measure of how much activity takes place is that the weekday flight between London and Brussels is in airmiles the most expensive in the world!

UKRep is divided into 10 sections: Agriculture; Economic Affairs, Finance and Taxation; External Affairs; Legal; Press and Information; Industry, Energy and the Internal Market; European Parliament and Economic and Social Committee; Chancery and Institutions; Industry, Energy and the Internal Market; and Administration. Each of the forty or so members of UKRep takes on a particular area, though their small number leads to overlapping responsibilities and the ability to take on others' briefs when necessary.

The EC affected the power struggle in Whitehall by increasing the power of the FCO and the Cabinet Office enormously, though this may become less marked as the EC becomes ever more ubiquitous. Figure 7.1 maps the organization of the FCO within EC affairs.

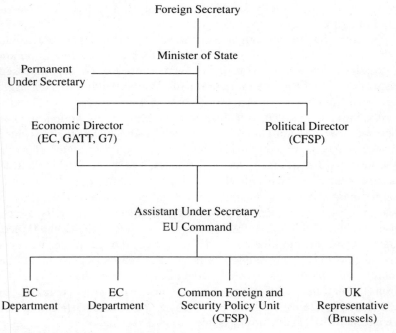

Figure 7.1 Co-ordination of EU policies

The FCO was involved at every stage in the decade-long negotiations for entry and has since played, with the European Secretariat in the Cabinet Office, an important co-ordinating role. Roy Hattersley suggested in 1981 that:

The Foreign Office has been transformed by our membership of the EEC. It now interferes in and is concerned with subjects which were not its proper province ten years ago. Foreign civil servants are interfering in agricultural prices; they're interfering in economic policy; they're interfering in energy policy. Naturally enough the Foreign Office has an enthusiasm for continuing an institution that gives them this very substantial increased power. . . .

(Young and Sloman 1982: 81)

Indeed in 1987 when relations between the FCO and Thatcher were at one of their lowest ebbs, partly over EC policy, she considered hiving off EC policy into a separate department (Hennessy 1990: 405) because she felt that the FCO was too sympathetic towards the EC. She was persuaded by the Cabinet Office that it could handle the FCO. But as more and more departments set up their own internal EC divisions and take more care over the policy implications of EC directives, overweening Foreign Office influence may start to wane.

EC entry has made a greater difference to some departments than others. With the great importance, or rather cost, of the Common Agricultural Policy, the Ministry of Agriculture has greatly increased its workload and become more powerful. Whilst Britain, by and large, has lost autonomy over agricultural policy, being forced, often reluctantly, into policies against its instincts, the Ministry of Agriculture has become more autonomous (Smith 1990: ch 7). Other departments whose workload has increased considerably include the departments of Trade and Industry, Environment and the Treasury. The 'trade side' at the DTI is now centred almost entirely on Brussels, whilst over half of the Department of the Environment's effort on the environment in 1992–3 was spent negotiating and implementing European Community directives (Burnham and Maor 1994). Departments such as the Home Office, Health and Education have been less affected, though all departments are increasingly being brought into the EC sphere of influence. The number of departments affected by the EC has doubled during the 1980s from the first decade of membership as the area of competence of the EC expands almost exponentially. Even the Home Office and the Department of Health now assume some direct negotiating responsibilities. Some policies affect several departments which are then drawn into negotiations with the FCO, with the Treasury overseeing the financial side of the process.

In the mid-1980s the Treasury introduced new controls to stem the enthusiasm of other departments for EC spending. These controls called EUROPES (pronounced 'EuroPez') involve a trade-off for a department of its overall budget, given any EC spending on programmes under its control. For example, if the Council of Ministers decides to spend the equivalent of, say, £30 million on youth-training schemes throughout Europe, Britain could negotiate for, say, £6 million to be spent in Britain. Under EUROPES the department which manages this expenditure in Britain, the Department of Employment, will have to cut £6 million from its own budget. Under matching agreements, it would be illegal for the Department of Employment to find those cuts from money that it would have spent on youth training in the absence of the EC money, so the department would have to cut other schemes or find savings in its core budget. EUROPES means that the first consideration of any British department is to try to keep the costs of EC programmes down, thereby doing the Treasury's job in Europe. Secondly, it has decreased Whitehall enthusiasm for the EC, given that civil servants' own pet schemes may have to be casualties of the commissioners' pet schemes. Thirdly, it means that sometimes no department wishes to be the 'lead' department on issues which do not obviously come under its own sphere of influence. Rather than departments squabbling to be 'lead' departments in order to empire-build, they fight shy of new initiatives. Thus in 1994 no department wanted to be the lead department for the EC's 'Youth in Europe' initiative and negotiate on Britain's behalf.

The speed with which proposals are being created and implemented has increased enormously over the past few years. This is partly because of the commission under President Jacques Delors speeding up the process towards a more unified EC. There has also developed an unhealthy competition between member states when they take over the reins of the presidency for six months each in turn. In the mid-1980s around ten to fifteen single-market measures would be adopted within each six-month cycle; this rose to twenty or more with the Dutch Presidency in early 1986; and the UK Presidency doubled this to forty-eight in the second half of 1986. Now the going rate is more than sixty per six-monthly cycle which leads to a rush of measures at the end of each six-month period (Bender 1991: 14). Each country seems to think that there is a prize to be awarded to the nation which can come up with the most original, or controversial, bi-annual meeting and so create objectives to be reached within the specified time of their presidency. That, taken together with Jacques Delors's burning desire to go down in the annals of history as the founder of a new Europe, means that the EC has rushed from initiative to initiative with no real consideration of the implications; and few people fully understanding what is happening. The Maastricht Treaty furthered this process of expansion of EC competence.

The often complex and detailed negotiations which take place between Whitehall and Brussels have given civil servants some extra discretion over many matters, though British civil servants work to a more tightly co-ordinated set of policies than most of their European counterparts. It is a far more frequent occurrence for British civil servants to break off negotiations to consult Whitehall than for bureaucrats from other member states; indeed this is something of a joke amongst regular negotiators. Britain gives far less discretion to individual departments than do other EC states. Here the Cabinet Office European Secretariat along with the FCO is the key player.

THE EUROPEAN SECRETARIAT

Because no special 'Department of European Affairs' was created this has helped ensure that no champion of Europe or target of discontent could be set up – though the FCO has been criticised for encroaching upon domestic affairs. The co-ordination of European affairs has been carried out through the normal inter-departmental channels using the services of the Cabinet Office. In this way the collective responsibility of government for EC affairs has been assured.

The European Secretariat acts like the other five secretariats within the Cabinet Office, providing the main civil service back-up for cabinet committees on matters within their competence: in this case for matters pertaining to the European Union. The European Secretariat selects the issues to be discussed – whether at ministerial or official (i.e. civil servant) levels – provides the agenda and chairs meetings at the official level. It has around twenty-two members of staff in total. The Cabinet Office chairs about two hundred meetings of officials annually and circulates over three hundred papers (Bender 1991: 16).

This business falls into three main categories. First, there is the consideration of new proposals emanating from the commission which require a British response consistent with the overall policies and objectives of the British government. Secondly, there is the overall look at some current issue, for example, recent EC environmental directives. Thirdly, there are meetings to fine-tune policy and decide negotiating tactics for some forthcoming meeting, for example, a meeting of the Council of Ministers. These meetings of the secretariat generally involve only civil servants, with departmental representatives bringing their departments' views, while the Cabinet Office provides an overview from the government as a whole. The Cabinet Office is very initiatory and tries to ensure that a consistent line is being pursued in Europe by all departments.

The European Secretariat is thus more than a body merely reviewing initiatives emanating from the commission and other parts of Whitehall. It convenes meetings where it believes co-ordination is necessary. It tries to ensure that departments are aware of the implications of their negotiations and of decisions being taken in other parts of the civil service. Three bureaucratic aspects of this central co-ordination role are important: (1) that the United Kingdom has a policy on all EC matters; (2) that these policies remain consistent with the broader objectives of the government; and that (3) these policies are implemented in practice. The second of these bureaucratic objectives hints at the important political aspect of the European Secretariat's role: ensuring that the Prime Minister remains the key actor. Without the European Secretariat at the centre, the FCO would have powers well beyond those of any other department, with the exception of the Treasury, and the Foreign Minister's would be the most important job apart from the Prime Minister's. However, not all matters are referred to the European Secretariat, and some agreements over the details of packages agreed in Brussels do not need to go to the Cabinet as long as they conform to previously agreed guidelines.

Figure 7.2 shows there is a complex co-ordination procedure between departments, Brussels and the Cabinet Office, with the latter at the

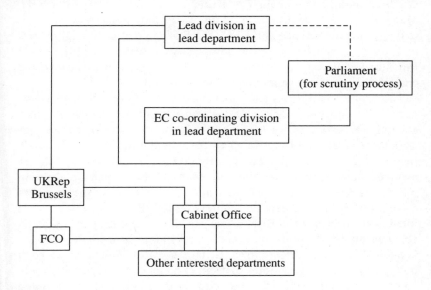

Figure 7.2 Co-ordination of EU legislation
Source: Bender (1991: 18)

centre. The European Secretariat within the Cabinet Office ultimately brings in all the interested actors and ensures that a common line is pursued within each policy area. Whilst the FCO is always involved, since it generally deals with UKRep, members of UKRep are often directly involved in Cabinet or official committees in Whitehall and regular meetings at the Cabinet Office at which tactics for any forthcoming negotiations will be hammered out. Bender says:

> Between the Cabinet Office, FCO and UKRep Brussels there is accordingly a sort of troika on policy formulation. All three tend to approach problems not just in isolation but as part of a wider policy and negotiating context. Acting together they can exert strong influence on the overall Whitehall view.
>
> (Bender 1991: 18)

It is widely recognized throughout Whitehall that Britain tends to formulate a coherent position on current issues faster than most of the other nations. Britain is recognized to be adept at lobbying the commission very early on in the formative stages of policy formation. Britain also forms mini-alliances of common concern with other nations and often uses its policy networks to bring in lobby groups at these early stages. The networks of lobbying groups operating around Whitehall are often mobilized on behalf of British government within Brussels. Many important lobbyists have set up offices in Brussels as they begin to realize the importance of the EU. The British government has always had a strong central co-ordination – largely because of the Prime Minister overseeing the business of the Cabinet in pursuance of the convention of collective ministerial responsibility.

The strong co-ordinating mechanisms within Whitehall bring advantages to Britain but they also bring some disadvantages. First, their counterparts expect British representatives to develop their strategies at home and then to bring them to the negotiating table in Brussels rather than to work out what is best for Europe at Brussels. All the member states look at the internal effects of EC policies and try to influence decisions in their own self-interest; but because Britain moves earlier, this helps to create the impression that British negotiators are interested only in what Britain can get out of a deal rather than in considering what is in the best interests of Europe as a whole.

Secondly, other states expect Britain to raise objections to each policy proposal. Bender states that 'other member states can often rely on us to have done our homework and will leave us to make the running in raising objections to particular issues' (Bender 1991: 20). But what he and other officials do not seem to recognize is that this gives an advantage to these other states in the bargaining game. Other states, say, the Netherlands, can let Britain raise objections to policies to which the Netherlands is equally opposed, thus allowing Britain to use up its bargaining resources persuading others to support their objections. These bargaining resources include goodwill, reciprocity over other issues, as well as material resources. The nation which speaks last often has a bargaining advantage over the nation which speaks first. Finally, the strong negotiating stance which Britain is able to adopt through its great reliance upon central co-ordination leads to a degree of inflexibility, as British officials have stricter guidelines than most of their EU counterparts. Furthermore, Britain does not have the overarching goals of some of the other member states. Officials brought up in the tradition of British empiricism, as opposed to the grand theory of continental academia, tend to look to present problems and their resolution. They lose sight of longer-term goals or developing a grand strategy under which to operate. This tends to lead to short-termism in government, each problem being dealt with as it arises rather than developing schemes extending beyond the life of any particular government. Some claim that co-ordinating mechanisms within national states are declining in importance (Siedentopf and Ziller 1988: 59–60), but the mechanisms are still significant.

Each nation has a permanent office to represent it in the EC. UKRep has four main functions. First, to participate in and to service the British side of the Council of Ministers at all levels. All meetings of the Council of Ministers need to be prepared for by officials. Only the last stage is carried out by the Committee of Permanent Representatives (COREPER). It meets at least once a week at both ambassadorial and deputy permanent representative levels. It ensures that the council's work is carried forward in the intervals between ministerial meetings. There is a Special Committee on Agriculture (SCA) because over half of the community budget is spent on the Common Agricultural Policy. In 1993 John Gummer, the Minister for Agriculture, stated that 80 per cent of his department's spending is decided in Brussels (Burnham and Maor 1994: 2).

Below these senior levels a large number of more specialized Council Working Groups meets to prepare particular items of business for submission to COREPER and the SCA. They operate much like official committees in Whitehall which prepare business for ministerial decision in cabinet committees. UKRep provides the representation for Britain on COREPER and the SCA. British representation on council working groups may come from Whitehall but will always have assistance and advice from UKRep and usually representatives as well, even if they are junior to the Whitehall officials. Generally speaking UKRep also provides the negotiators for these working groups, for they tend to have the specialized knowledge required for detailed EC negotiations. UKRep keeps in constant contact with Whitehall through the FCO European Community Departments.

The second major function of UKRep is to ensure that contact is always maintained between the commission, the presidency and other permanent representations within the community. By keeping in constant contact with the commission, UKRep tries to influence its policies and ideas. In this way UKRep operates much as a pressure group on the commission. It tries to discover what proposals the commission is likely to take up and to influence its ideas in ways advantageous to Britain. It tries to ensure that where Britain has potentially breached EC law some form of accommodation can be reached without recourse to the European Court. Similarly, the commission will try to discover what policies are likely to emanate from Britain. Part of UKRep's role is to inform the commission about the policy proposals of the British government. UKRep has the major job of trying to discover what is happening in the other nations' Offices of Permanent Representatives to strengthen the bargaining position of Britain. UKRep on behalf of Her Majesty's Government tries to build alliances where possible with the other representatives against the commission.

Thirdly, UKRep provides advice to civil servants back in Whitehall and thereby to government ministers. Policy is officially formulated and co-ordinated in Whitehall, but UKRep can influence decisions through its expertise on matters pertaining to Europe. It will be aware of what is and is not possible within community regulations and have a good idea of what is likely to be non-negotiable with other member nations. Officials from UKRep regularly attend meetings in Whitehall, as many Whitehall officials regularly attend meetings in Brussels.

Fourthly, UKRep is the centre of a network of pressure groups trying to influence British policy and EU policy. The relationship between these groups and the civil service is often close and both sides use the other to their own advantage. Lobbying in Britain is rather different from other EU nations, since Britain is a far more centralized state in which the bureaucracy is the key actor. Brussels has a more complex institutional structure and thus for lobbyists poses strategic problems similar to those faced in other EU nations.

This causes some difficulties for British pressure groups used to the simpler symbiotic relationship which exists in Britain. As a result UKRep has become the European key for many British pressure groups – a source of both information and of hope. UKRep has special facilities for helping British firms make the best of opportunities under EC programmes. This strengthens the hand of British civil servants and allows them to play the 'British interests' card in much the manner they please, sometimes advising British pressure groups on tactics. How long this behaviour can be maintained is open to doubt, as Mazey and Richardson suggest, 'everyone is on a learning curve as the EC develops' (Mazey and Richardson 1990: 24).

UKRep is made up of officials from many Whitehall departments. Almost fifty per cent originated from the FCO but increasingly it has been necessary to recruit from other specialties within Whitehall. Most of the officials come from generalist backgrounds within Whitehall, the official line being that that is what is required. Indeed the EC may have strengthened the generalist position in Whitehall. It is not clear why UKRep prefers to have so many non-FCO people. Officially this is because the expertise in more fields within the EC negotiating structure is required, though given the nature of the bargaining and the possibility of expertise coming over from Whitehall when required (as indeed it often does), this may not be the only reason. UKRep may like to have representatives from other Whitehall departments in order to forge closer personal links. This is advantageous in bargaining with those departments, and will allow, in the long run, some colonization of those departments with people who have absorbed the basic culture of UKRep.

Parliamentary scrutiny of EC business is difficult given its sheer weight and complexity. However, all documents published by the EC are presented to parliament for scrutiny by MPs and Peers. Whitehall departments prepare explanatory memoranda to accompany all proposed changes in EC laws, and the government publishes a White Paper every six months outlining recent and forthcoming EC developments. Six days are set aside each session for debate on the White Papers and EC business. A Ministerial Statement is read in the House following each meeting of the Council of Ministers, and European Union affairs has a regular slot in the Question Time rota of business. There are no procedures within community arrangements for national parliaments to participate directly in producing community law. Nevertheless, conventional procedures allow time for the Commons Select Committee on European Legislation and the Lords Select Committee on the European Community to examine all proposed legislation. Indeed successive British governments have agreed that ministers will not approve proposals in the Council of Ministers until they have passed through the scrutiny process at Westminster, though ministers may take no notice of the views expressed in the House and proposals may change in many regards from those scrutinized by parliament. The Commons Select Committee has the terms of reference set out in Standing Order No 127:

> There shall be a select committee to consider draft proposals by the Commission of the European Communities for legislation and other documents published for submission to the Council of Ministers or to the European Council whether or not such documents originate from the Commission, and to report its opinion as to whether such proposal or other documents raise questions of legal or political importance, to give its reasons for its opinion, to report what matters of principle or policy may be affected thereby, and to what extent they may affect the law of the United Kingdom, and to make recommendations for the further consideration of such proposals and other documents by the House.

The committee has taken on the role of bringing controversial proposals to the attention of the House. The earlier undertakings of successive governments not to agree to European instruments selected by the House for debate was enshrined in a Resolution of the House on 30 October 1980 which states:

> In the opinion of this House, no Minister of the Crown should give agreement in the Council of Ministers to any proposal for European legislation which has been recommended by the Select Committee on European Legislation, etc. for consideration by the House before the House has given it that consideration unless – (a) that Committee has indicated that agreement need not be withheld, or (b) the Minister concerned should, at the first opportunity thereafter, explain the reasons for his decision to the House.

> (HC Deb. vol 991, col 843)

British representatives at the Council of Ministers have often held back agreement on the basis that the matter has not yet been through the scrutiny process, but increasingly the government has agreed to adoptions before scrutiny (in about one-fifth of cases). The minister concerned then, in time-honoured fashion, proves his or her account-ability to the House by explaining that he has done so. The government has justified adoption before parliamentary scrutiny in a Memorandum to the European Legislation Committee Special Report in 1984 (HC 527, 126-iv, (Session 1983–4)). It gives four categories of agreements which it will adopt before scrutiny:

1 confidential documents (e.g. anti-dumping measures);
2 transfers of appropriations;

3 extensions of existing arrangements (usually to preserve legal continuity); and
4 other.

The final category gives the executive all the powers it could possibly want, and is the one under which most agreements occur. However, few have caused much controversy. The government has been much more reluctant to come to agreements with European partners before parliamentary debate if the Scrutiny Committee decides the matter should be debated in the House.

Bender claims that 'a system has been developed, which the Cabinet Office supervises, whereby parliament is informed immediately of any commission proposals with an indication of the government's position' (Bender 1991: 19). However, the term 'immediate' here is a civil servant's 'immediately' which is not as immediate as most people's and certainly not always as fast as committee members would like. Perhaps Bender means by 'immediate' that the proposals and the government's response are given to committee members before being given to anyone else – that is, with no intervening medium – without thereby implying that any great haste is given to the process. One of the ways in which information is slowed down is by the preparation of accompanying Explanatory Memoranda. However, the staff of the committee do have a good working relationship with personnel in the Cabinet Office, and parliamentary scrutiny is as thorough as it ever is: in effect, often not very thorough or only after the event.

About one-sixth of items coming before the Select Committee are referred to the House for consideration, but pressures of the parliamentary timetable mean that often they are not debated or are taken in obscure standing committees or late at night. Since much EC legislation is about obscure technical details, they only rarely provoke parliamentary or public interest apart from the occasional statement read out by some MP prepared by some lobby group opposed to the new regulations. Few MPs specialize in EC affairs. It has yet to prove a route to public or party prominence.

The Select Committee on European Legislation takes evidence from British ministers and civil servants but not from European Commissioners who are barred from giving evidence to national parliaments. The Lords Select Committee on the European Community is divided into a number of subcommittees which examine specific subject areas. By common consent the Lords Select Committee, which has more time at its disposal and is more willing to make political judgements about the merits and problems of EC proposals, is the more effective scrutiny body. Some commentators have noted that for that reason civil servants tend to be less forthcoming to their Lordships than to Honourable Members.

In recent years the moves towards even closer financial and political union have increased debate over the question of parliamentary sovereignty. In fact much of the controversy is just huff and puff. The EC has changed nothing with regard to the sovereignty of parliament. Parliament can still do as it likes and decide to confirm or reject anything the government has decided within or without EC competence. The fact that parliament long ago gave up any actual control over the executive, making this sovereign power merely a logical possibility, does not make it any less a sovereign power. John Biffen made this point to the Select Committee on European Secondary Legislation:

> I think we have a situation where, of course, Parliament ultimately controls the executive, the executive draws its life blood from Parliament, but the truth is that in the day to day exercise of authority the executive really runs without too much constraint from Parliament and in the circumstances of our relationship with the European Community government has retained its sphere of authority, I believe, more effectively than has Parliament.[3]

The extension of the powers of the EC parliament reduces the sovereignty of the British parliament in as far as it reduces the power of Crown Ministers within the Council of Ministers. But then, the strong party system and the three-line whip render de facto power of parliament over ministers minimal. The sovereignty of parliament is lost only when the sovereignty of the British government is rendered subservient to EC decision-making processes; and, after all, while the British armed forces stay loyal to the British government, that sovereignty is only lost when the government allows it to be so. The real check on parliamentary action is how hard it would be to roll back the powers of the EC, but then, again, this is the case in many areas of international affairs, from GATT to the exchanging of ambassadors. The political or economic difficulties of asserting parliamentary sovereignty do not demonstrate the absence of that sovereignty, though the assertion of sovereignty without force of arms to defend it is as valueless as a contract without a sword, which indeed without a loyal standing army is what it would be.

British civil servants working in Brussels have to get used to different institutional processes, cultures and policy styles. They are used to working under great constraints where policy is largely formulated at the highest levels, and constitutionally they are supposed to be carrying out their ministers' wishes and not their own. To a greater or lesser extent, the constitutional position is a fiction but a fiction which partly determines attitudes and ways of administrative behaviour. Continental civil servants do not feel the same sorts of constraints. In part this is because the cultures of other member states do not allow for the same degree of ministerial responsibility, but more often it is because of the nature of coalition government with which civil servants are used to working. Coalition government with ministers from different and competing parties may confuse the lines of accountability and give greater operational fluidity to senior civil servants. Civil servants from other member states are much more apt to make policy on the hoof, and are by no means all considered to be politically neutral.

The commission is different again. Here civil servants feel much greater allegiance to the European ideal than to individual member states, and do not have the same constraints of democratic accountability or collective responsibility. The College of Commissioners does not form a cabinet with a *primus inter pares* to anything like the degree of *primus* apparent in the British Cabinet, and hence individual commissioners and their civil servants have much greater autonomy. This leads to a mish-mash of policies which do not always cohere nor have strategic sense. David Williamson, the EC Secretary-General under Delors, has tried to create a more co-ordinated commission with a far greater number of interdepartmental committees and greater emphasis on monitoring policy initiatives. Williamson's strategy is based on the Whitehall model (Ludlow 1991). The commission also has the mission, constitutionally, to initiate policy and lead the charge towards a united Europe. This constitutional function is often ignored by those who criticize Jacques Delors and other commissioners for their forward planning. To some extent the drive towards a united Europe is in their job specifications.

The commission is politicized to a much greater extent than is Whitehall. Again it is much more like the different ministries under coalition governments where senior civil servants are political appointees. Different directorates-general are inhabited by socialists or liberals or whatever, and there is no pretence or embarrassment about this fact. It is not unknown for civil servants to have framed photographs of opposition leaders on the walls of their offices (Christoph 1992: 11).

The British system is, despite current reforms, hierarchical and ordered. Decisions are made in writing and passed on to all relevant officials. The process of administration is seen to be as important as the outcomes themselves. This is not nearly as important in the continental tradition. Far more business is done by telephone, informally and much less is written down; whatever is written down is taken to be a binding commitment. This rather lax culture, for example, in answering letters has spread to British officials working permanently in Brussels.

The most pertinent difference between working in Brussels and working in Whitehall, is the degree of openness. Secrecy is the byword in Whitehall, though it is true to say that leaks spring from Whitehall far more frequently than once was the case. The greater openness to a wider variety of pressure groups, in part explained by the use made of these groups by the different national governments, entails the process of decision-making and is more open to public and media scrutiny. It is not possible, for example, for the British government to hide its negotiating stance once it has taken it up in Brussels. The line pursued by each member state is known to journalists as soon as the closed meetings end.

The EC route is now a possible career-enhancing road for civil servants from many departments. Whilst the British government's stance with the EC remains ambiguous, too enthusiastic an attitude towards the EC is probably not a good idea; but becoming known as an expert on the EC side of the department is a good career move. About a hundred civil servants are on secondment to the commission each year, and there is about a 20 per cent turnaround annually. The members in UKRep, the cabinets of the directors-general and the regular commission staff plus the EC divisions within Whitehall give a sizable number of civil servants, plus all the civil servants in domestic divisions whose work is affected by the EU.

CONCLUSIONS

The EU has provided both an opportunity and a threat to the civil service. It offers the opportunity for individual civil servants and Whitehall departments to use the authority and power of the EC to expand their own sphere of influence. Dealing with Brussels is time consuming and complex and broadens the policy network in which civil servants operate. It is difficult for politicians, both ministers and other parliamentarians, to oversee this work, though the opportunity for autonomous action should not be overstated. The tradition of the British civil service is for bureaucrats to work within the political constraints and policy decisions made at the highest levels. Civil servants from Britain tend to consult with their political masters far more often than their counterparts from other EC nations. Nevertheless, the EC has provided a big opportunity for departments to alter the map of influence in Whitehall. The biggest gainers have been the FCO, MAFF and the Cabinet Office, though in the future the DTI may also be able to utilize its opportunities to a greater extent than was possible under the Thatcherite free-market ideology at odds with commission-directed interventionism.

Paradoxically, the EC has also allowed the centre to rein in some departmental power, as the Cabinet Office is the centre of the Whitehall network and the source of all EC co-ordination. Setting up the European Secretariat on entry was a deliberate move to limit the power of the FCO. The setting up of European divisions in all Whitehall departments has altered the geography of Whitehall slightly; more importantly these divisions take on key roles in all departments since any policy initiative now has to be checked against the complex welter of European legislation. The 'European expert' route is increasingly one which ambitious individual civil servants cannot ignore.

The threat to civil servants is that the commission presents another source of bureaucratic authority which may threaten that of the British civil service. To this extent, the 'discovery' of the idea of subsidiarity by the British government during its presidential tenure allows the British civil service to shape the area of national competence and ensure greater control in some policy arenas.

The biggest difficulty for British civil servants in their dealings with the EC is the different bureaucratic culture. Officials on their first 'tour of duty' find the informality of their European colleagues bemusing and the constraints imposed by the greater centralization of British policy a 'negotiating neckbrace'. This greater centralization and more careful scrutiny of commission proposals is seen as an advantage by many officials at the highest levels. But it allows other nations to 'free-ride' on Britain. Other member states let Britain object to commission proposals which is one reason why Britain has the reputation for being the reluctant European. It is claimed, moreover, that many directives are happily accepted by other nations but never implemented. Even where they are formally ratified by national parliaments, the procedures to ensure that the policies are carried out are not put into place. In Britain, civil servants assert directives which are quickly ratified and the measures required properly to implement them are set in motion. Only where directives are difficult to implement in the British case does Britain fail or ask for special dispensation. Other nations, argue the civil servants, just pass the necessary laws and then wait for their public to demand proper implementation. Because other publics, particularly in southern Europe, do not have such high expectations as the British public (and pressure groups), Britain appears – though, in fact it is not

– a worse European. In response European bureaucrats suggest that their British counterparts, in their enthusiasm to implement directives, add unnecessary interpretations, making guidelines stricter than requisite. The truth of these competing claims is hard to judge and goes beyond the bounds of this book, but the different cultures of implementation do much to explain the major source of irritation felt by home-based British civil servants to the EC.

8 Accountability
Myths and empirical evidence

A myth is a traditional narrative usually involving supernatural or imaginary persons and embodying popular ideas on natural or social phenomena (*Concise Oxford Dictionary* 1990). The British constitution is largely mythical. It is a narrative peopled with civil servants, politicians and judges blessed with a nature not typically human and a set of statements about 'conventional behaviour' which does not describe how people typically act. This chapter considers the nature of accountability of the civil service whose 'chain of loyalty binds civil servants to Ministers, and Ministers to Parliament (constitutionally to the Crown in Parliament, but in terms of political reality to the House of Commons)' (HC 92, 1985–86: para. 3.7). It examines the traditional narrative and explores the reality of accountability.

ACCOUNTABILITY IN THEORY

The government is accountable through ministers to parliament; that much is clear. There are more expansive paths: the government is held to account through the electoral process, through its own party and through the scrutiny of the mass media. It is also held to account through the legal process. Chapter 6 touched on the more direct accountability to the public, while this chapter concentrates on parliament and the courts; for these are the means by which civil servants are most likely to be held to account, even if their misdemeanours are first publicly aired in the press.

The expression of accountability through ministers to parliament makes theoretical sense, as shown in the hierarchical model encountered in Chapter 2. At the pinnacle of the hierarchy are government ministers, collectively and individually accountable to parliament. Collective responsibility developed to ensure cohesive government and became entrenched as strong party organizations grew up within parliament. Collective responsibility also creates a challenge for accountability, certainly for departments and can be used as a cover to prevent scrutiny of policy decisions. Parliamentary scrutiny of the civil service depends almost exclusively on the doctrine of individual ministerial responsibility.

The minister must answer for the actions of his or her department (given the definitional problems encountered in Chapter 2, it is best defined here – albeit with some circularity – simply as the institution for which the minister gives account). The minister accounts for the policy of the department, its reactions to any contemporary crisis, the implementation and the administration of policy. He or she must explain failures and errors, suffer the recriminations of the House and explain how the situation will be retrieved. Civil servants are accountable to their superiors up to and including the minister, who will decide what action, if any, should be taken against individual civil servants for error. Civil servants are accountable to the courts for illegal actions, most obviously corruption, as, for example, in the case of Gordon Foxley, former director of the Ministry of Defence's munition procurement department. Foxley corruptly received over £2 million between 1979 and 1984 for awarding contracts to overseas arms producers.

How deep accountability runs, according to the traditional model, is open to question. Nevil Johnson suggests that ministerial accountability is 'fundamentally a doctrine about the manner in which public powers are to be established and located: it defines who is responsible for what rather than who is responsible to whom' (Johnson 1977: 85, cf. Jones 1987). In this sense then ministerial responsibility is formally recognized merely in so far as governmental responsibilities are organized into departments on behalf of which a named person – the minister – speaks in parliament. Ministerial responsibility is therefore seen in action on any occasion when the minister speaks in parliament or to MPs on matters pertaining to his or her department. These matters include the various occasions for debate, answering questions at regular question times, ministerial statements, private-notice questions, replies to letters from MPs (which are always signed by the minister), plus the occasions when evidence is given by the minister at select committees. In this sense there is no retributive quality in the doctrine of individual ministerial responsibility. The Cabinet Secretary Sir Robin Butler, favours this interpretation, telling the Scott Inquiry (see below) that he preferred the term 'accountability' to 'responsibility' because it was 'blame free'.

There are two problems with this view. The first is that it seems to be empirically false. Ministers and their civil servants have faced retribution from parliament following ministerial statements to the House. Secondly, if the thread of accountability is slender enough with blame attached, it is vanishingly slight without it. The only inducement ministers have to answer questions honestly and abide by Johnson's version of accountability is fear of parliament. That is a fragile thread upon which to hang responsibility and is stretched further the longer one party is in power. Without accountability in the retributive sense, there can be no guarantee of accountability in Johnson's sense either.

Academics have catalogued five senses of accountability (Marshall and Moodie 1959; Woodhouse 1994, cf. Marshall 1978, 1990, 1991; Turpin 1990): redirecting, reporting, explaining or justifying, amending and sacrificial or punitive responsibility.

Redirecting responsibility occurs when the minister redirects MPs' questions to an appropriate person or body. This mode has become of greater moment with the proliferation of agencies under Next Steps, and of 'quangos' or EGOs (extragovernmental organizations) more generally. The major concern is that responses from EGOs and 'quangos' are not published as ministerial answers are but rather are personal replies. Moreover, one Labour backbench MP complained to the author that the chief executive of an opted-out hospital refused to give any information about a complaint from one of the MP's constituents on 'operational grounds', while the Health Minister also refused to become involved, saying it was an issue concerning the hospital. The MP claims such responses were unthinkable only a few years ago.[1] Answers from the chief executives of Next Steps agencies are published in *Hansard*, which seems to reaffirm ministers overall responsibility for the agencies.

Reporting responsibility is the type to which Johnson and Butler want to restrict all ministerial accountability, simply relating what goes on in the department. However, if fault is to be found, ministers rarely get away with merely reporting it. They have also to explain it, which is the third category. As Woodhouse (1994: 30) says, 'The extent to which a minister is constitutionally required to explain to Parliament is not clear, although politically it will be the minimum the House will accept.' Unfortunately this statement does not tell us much. The minimum the House will accept might be the minimum ministers are prepared to tell the House, if they are secure in their position with their own party; it may be more than ministers are willing to give if they are not secure. We find out when it happens. The practicalities and bargaining strengths of the various competing interests within and between the parties in the House decide the issue.

Amendatory responsibility occurs when the minister feels obliged to make amends in some way. He may order an independent inquiry, discipline civil servants, change organizational procedures or even introduce policy change. The Next Steps process should increase the opportunities for amendatory responsibility, for the separate reporting of agency action admits greater scope for recommendations for organizational or personnel change; and the greater distance between the minister and the agency may allow greater willingness for ministers to promulgate change, as will be discussed further in this chapter.

The final category is *sacrificial or punitive responsibility*. This mode is the requirement of ministerial resignation. Certainly this responsibility is the type that receives most press attention, and without this ultimate sanction the other types could not be sustained.

The reason the constitutional position on accountability is not clear is that there is no constitutional position. The constitution is mythical; all that really exists are the political practicalities of the day.

THE OSMOTHERLY PROTECTION

The path of accountability from civil servant through minister to parliament is definite and clear cut. Civil servants are not allowed to answer any questions put to them by parliamentarians except in the manner which would be approved by their minister. This ruling has been established by various documents setting out their responsibilities. The most famous is the Osmotherly Rules, which state:

> Officials appearing before Select Committees do so on behalf of their Ministers. It is customary, therefore, for Ministers to decide which officials (including members of the Armed Services) should appear to give evidence. Select Committees have in the past generally accepted this position. Should a Committee invite a named official to appear, the Minister concerned, if he did not wish that official to represent him, might suggest that another official could more appropriately do so, or that he himself should give evidence to the Committee. If a Committee insisted on a particular official appearing before them they could issue a formal order for his attendance. In such an event the official would have to appear before the Committee. He would remain subject to Ministerial instructions as to how he should answer questions.

The importance of this document was made clear during the Westland Affair (Hennessy 1986; Dunleavy 1990). A letter was leaked from the Attorney General to the Trade and Industry Secretary, Leon Brittan, about the actions of another cabinet minister, the Defence Secretary Michael Heseltine. It was never established whether the leaking was cleared by Bernard Ingham, press secretary and close confidant of Margaret Thatcher. He denies that he gave clearance but admits a confused conversation with Colette Bowe, the civil servant who leaked the letter (Ingham 1991). The Defence Select Committee was unable to call the civil servants it wished to speak to. The government argued that since the civil servants would not be allowed to answer the questions the Committee wished to ask them there was no point in their appearing before it. The committee never spoke to either Bowe or Ingham but had to make do with the Cabinet Secretary, Robert Armstrong, who carried out an investigation of the affair: hence it was never made clear what really happened.[2]

Armstrong himself, in his other guise as Head of the Home Civil Service, drew up *The Duties and Responsibilities of Civil Servants in Relation to Ministers* following Clive Ponting's acquittal of breaking the Official Secrets Act in passing documents to an Opposition back-bencher. This document states:

> Civil Servants are servants of the Crown. For all practical purposes the Crown in this context means and is represented by the Government of the day. . . . The Civil Service as such has no constitutional personality or responsibility separate from the duly elected Government of the day.
>
> (Armstrong 1989: 140)

The civil service is accountable through the minister, though the rules as drawn up make it very difficult for parliament to call ministers to account. The Osmotherly Rules and the Armstrong Memorandum protect ministers as much as they protect civil servants. If ministers blame civil servants, the civil servants have little rejoinder under these rules. The Scott Inquiry has revealed the blurred relationship which exists between civil servants and ministers. As I write, it has not published its findings, but it is worth considering what we have learned about ministerial–servant relationships.

THE MATRIX CHURCHILL AFFAIR[3]

The Scott Inquiry into the Matrix Churchill Affair 'slowly undressed Whitehall, exposing dissembling, dishonesty, a patronizing approach to parliament, and – perhaps worst of all – unacceptable interference in a criminal prosecution' (Norton Taylor 1994: 2). It erupted as three directors of the machine tool company Matrix Churchill were being tried for selling machine tools with military uses to Iraq during an arms embargo. The trial collapsed when Alan Clark, trade minister during

1989, admitted in court that he did not care whether the equipment exported to Iraq could be used to make weapons. The judge later suggested that it would have collapsed anyway because of the weight of evidence showing the government's complicity in selling arms-related equipment. This evidence would have appeared when the judge refused to accept (most of) the public immunity certificates signed by five ministers representing four departments (Foreign and Common-wealth Office, Defence, DTI and Home Office). These certificates stopped the defence from calling documents which proved that the government had relaxed the guidelines for selling arms-related equipment to Iraq without informing parliament.[4] Three issues in the Matrix Churchill Affair concern us. (1) Should the government have changed the rules governing arms without informing parliament? (2) How was the decision reached and what does this process tell us about core executive decision-making? (3) Did the ministers have the right to refuse to sign the public immunity certificates?

Table 8.1 The Matrix Churchill Affair

Date	Events
Oct 1980	Iran/Iraq war begins
Jan 1981	Cabinet decides to exploit Iraq arms market
Oct 1985	Restrictive export guideline announced to parliament
Nov 1987	Intelligence reports that UK machinery being used for arms production in Iraq
Jan 1988	Ministers approve first set of Matrix Churchill exports, knowing military uses
Aug 1988	Iran/Iraq ceasefire
Dec 1988	Ministers secretly agree to relax export guidelines
Feb 1989	Ministers approve second set of Matrix Churchill exports, knowing military uses
Jul 1989	Cabinet stops sale of Hawk aircraft to Iraq
Nov 1989	Ministers approve third set of Matrix Churchill exports, knowing military uses
Jul 1990	Ministers approve fourth set of Matrix Churchill exports, knowing military uses
Aug 1990	Iraq invades Kuwait
Feb 1991	19th Matrix Churchill directors charged 24th British troops involved in Gulf War
Nov 1992	Matrix Churchill trial collapses, Major announces Scott Inquiry

(1) During 1988, MI6 had persuaded DTI officials to give export certificates to equipment from Matrix Churchill on the grounds that information about Iraq was being supplied by directors of the company through their contacts. A year later it is less certain the Matrix Churchill information was as useful to the intelligence services. If ministers had since argued their own policy had been breached but that parliament had not been told for security reasons, then perhaps less could be made of this breach. However, the breach in regulations continued long beyond justification for security reasons. Ministers and civil servants have argued that the change was not a change in policy but a 'flexibility of interpretation'. Eric Beston, head of export controls at the DTI during the 1980s, told the Inquiry that many ministers including Prime Minister Margaret Thatcher had misled parliament by supplying answers drafted by civil servants at the DTI. He stated that answers to MPs' questions were treated by civil servants as more of 'an art form than a means of communication' and that 'the avoidance of controversy was not an uncommon concern in the presentation of, or in this case, the non-presentation of policy' (cf. Kellner and Crowther-Hunt 1980; Chester 1981). Beston also admitted to having 'forgotten' to tell Lord Trefgarne, minister in charge of defence procurement, about an MI6 warning about the use Iraq was making of British machine tools. To complete the intrigue, Beston was to be a prosecution witness at the trial.

It emerged that not only was parliament misled by ministers but some ministers were misled by civil servants. The Cabinet Secretary, Sir Robin Butler, had told the Prime Minister, John Major, in November 1991 he could deny that the government was aware that Matrix Churchill machine tools were used in Iraqi arms production. Senior officials at the DTI were aware that this statement was, in the words of one of them, 'simply wrong', but the Cabinet Office decided not to correct the advice given to the Prime Minister. This decision was taken by Sonia Phippard, Sir Robin's private secretary. In the words of one memorandum by Michael Coolican, an official at the DTI, the disclosure would be 'extraordinarily embarrassing'.

With such systematic misleading of parliament, and indeed at times ministers, well beyond the bounds of national security (which may have been justified during 1988), accountability even in Johnson's limited sense had been broken: not only in the line of ministers to parliament but at times in the line from civil servants to ministers. It was feared, it appears, again in the words of Coolican, that if the full affair became public it would make the DTI 'look like a bunch of bungling amateurs'.

(2) The decision to breach government regulations was reached in a chaotic and incoherent manner. This case illustrates the difficulties of

seeing all policies as a departmental rather than an interdepartmental matters. The DTI (and Alan Clark) were involved as the giver of export certificates, the defence department (and Lord Trefgarne) over a defence procurement issue, the Foreign Office (and William Walde-grave) over security aspects and intelligence on Iraq. Both Thatcher and Major, PM and Foreign Minister at the crucial time, denied they were informed of the decisions. At the Inquiry it emerged that Clark had told Waldegrave 'whatever is agreed between us will require the Prime Minister's approval', and civil servants had said in December 1988 that a decision to revise the guidelines would need 'to be cleared with the Prime Minister'. Yet Thatcher stated to the Inquiry that the new interpretation 'was not formally put to me'. She further stated she had not appreciated the significance of a mention of the revised guidelines in a document she was sent by one of the private secretaries. John Major, who during the affair held relevant positions as Foreign Secretary and Prime Minister, claimed to be unaware of the changing interpretations until 13 November 1992. This shows that ministers and civil servants made policy on the hoof, with little or no regard to parliament whatsoever and, worse, later lied about it.

(3) The final issue concerns whether or not ministers had the right to refuse to sign the public immunity certificates.[5] This issue has assumed prominence since many ministers have tried to avoid public outrage at their willingness to sign documents vital to the defendants' defence by hiding behind the advice of the Attorney General that they 'had a duty to sign' which 'could not be waived'. The question is: a duty to whom? To the courts? This view is argued on the grounds that the court itself may suggest that the public interest and justice is not served by the exemption of certain issues from discussion in the court. Once the immunity certificates have been signed, the court may then decide to over-rule them, as in the Matrix Churchill case. But none of this imposes on ministers a duty to sign simply because their legal officers, even the Attorney General, have told them to do so. The law may be above a minister, but that is to be decided in a court of law, not by the government's legal officers. Legal officers advise ministers, but ministers must be their own judges of their duties. If not, there can be no clear accountability of departments through ministers. If ministers are the final arbiters of departments, they must judge whether public immunity certificates should be signed for areas within their responsibility. If they are not, the legal officers and the Attorney General must in the end answer to parliament.

The relations between law and the duties of ministers highlighted by

British constitution. Ministers' duties are laid down by constitutional convention, but there is no supreme body to give authoritative opinion on the composition of these conventions. We must now turn to the nature of the constitution.

THE 'CONSTITUTION' AND ACCOUNTABILITY

The doctrine of ministerial responsibility is a constitutional convention (Marshall 1984; Waldron 1990: 62–4) which is not written into any statute with known penalties to be extracted if a given minister fails to abide by it; rather it is an expectation of behaviour. In any law there is an amalgam of the prescriptive and the descriptive, the normative and the positive. Laws tell us how we ought not to behave, what we ought not to do. They prescribe limits for behaviour rather than describing it. They are also descriptive or positive in the sense that they state what will happen (if the law is enforced) if our behaviour does not conform to those prescriptions. Written law is a description of how the state will react if we do not conform within the limits laid down. Constitutional conventions, however, are not established by statute even if they fill out statutes and are set limits by statutes. They are understood in terms of how people have tended to behave. Nor have sanctions been prescribed that the state will enforce if the convention is not maintained.

One standard definition of a constitutional convention is provided by Sir Kenneth Wheare (1966: 179): 'a rule of behaviour accepted as obligatory by those concerned in the working of the constitution'. Now as Waldron points out, conventions cannot just be moral rules, for there are many moral rules which we do not consider to be constitutional conventions. They are moral rules which are accepted 'by those concerned' in the working of central government, expectations engendered by past behaviour which provide prescriptions for present and future behaviour. Waldron (1990: 63–4) writes:

> They are not merely habits or regularities of behaviour; they enter into people's consciousness and become the subject-matter of reflection and of a sense of obligation. But they are not merely subjective views about morality either. They have a social reality, inasmuch as they capture a way in which people interact, a way in which people make demands on one another, and form attitudes and expectations about a common practice with standards that they are all living up to.

The prescriptive and the descriptive mix of laws is well caught in Waldron's description of conventions, as is the oddness of this mixture.

A convention is a moral rule which describes how, with ministerial responsibility, the minister ought to behave. It is based on how ministers have usually behaved in the past under the standards which as Waldron says 'all are living up to'. But what if all are not living up to them? F.F. Ridley (1988: 356) puts the dilemma rather neatly:

> How does one distinguish supposedly binding rules that are not enforceable in law from other patterns of behaviour? If such a rule is broken does it mean that there has been a breach of conventions, that the convention has changed, or that it was not a convention after all? As soon as one analyses what is meant by a rule in this context, the idea of conventions dissolves into a mixture of practices and precepts one expects to be followed, but may not be, and more less widely held beliefs that are subject to change – all distinguished from other practices, precepts and beliefs simply because a particular label is attached to them.

One of the problems with the nature of constitutional conventions is that what is taken to be conventional behaviour, what commentators claim to be the convention, is not sustained by empirical analysis of the way in which ministers have behaved in the past. Essentially the problem is that Britain does not have a constitution, or, perhaps more precisely, the scope of the constitution does not cover important areas at the very heart of the state.

Many commentators argue that Britain does have a constitution, albeit not codified. This view is false. For there to be an object, we have to know by what principles we can identify it, or as Quine pithily remarks, 'no entity without identity'. Britain does not have any such means of identification. For a nation to have a constitution there has to be an authoritative statement of its content. Ordinarily this statement is provided by a codified written constitution and, more importantly, an authoritative interpretation of that document. With a codified written document called 'The Constitution', one has the set of rules laid out. This document will be open to numerous, competing interpretations. Actions by government will be open to question as to whether they are constitutional, and can be referred to some other body, a supreme or superior court, for an authoritative decision. Thus the Supreme Court interprets the US Constitution. Its interpretation is authoritative, though still open to question and debate, and, the Court may change its interpretation on some future occasion. There is a Constitution (which includes the written document and the authoritative interpretation of that document) and various (non-authoritative) interpretations of it.

Ontologically speaking, the constitution and the various competing interpretations are separate.

In Britain parliament can, in theory, do what it wants, limited only by what it finds physically possible. There are no legal limits on its action. Whilst there are authoritative interpretations of particular constitutional matters, from the Law Lords to the Speaker of the House of Commons, there is no constitution. Nor is there any arbiter, despite lame claims that the head of the Home Civil Service is the supreme judge of whether constitutional conventions have been broken (HC 390, 1992–93 para. 116: 25–6). It might be claimed that the authoritative interpretation is evidenced through the actions of previous relevant actors. The constitution is maintained through conventional behaviour, and examination of past behaviour will provide the objective conditions of what the constitution entails. This may be so. The next section examines the behaviour of ministers to see if we can capture the essence of one aspect of the British constitution: when should ministers resign? Even here, such 'constitutional conventions' provide no authoritative interpretation, for often there is little agreement over the circumstances of ministerial action. Competing interpretations of why one minister behaved in a particular manner do not provide an authoritative guide as to how another minister should behave in similar circumstances.

SACRIFICIAL RESPONSIBILITY[6]

When should a minister resign? Backbench MPs and newspaper columnists are clear that personal error and departmental blunder afford prime examples of sacrificial responsibility. Most political scientists are more sceptical, noting that rarely do ministers resign when their departments have bungled. There are, at most, a couple of examples when a minister has resigned after departmental error. When any high-profile case emerges, the press and academics judge the behaviour of the minister concerned by comparison with previous cases (Fry 1969–70, 1976; Baker 1972; Ganz 1980; Pyper 1983; Hennessy 1986; Oliver and Austin 1987; Doig 1989, 1993; Phythian and Little 1993). Surprisingly little empirical evidence of the nature of ministerial responsibility is ever offered. Most discussions of ministerial responsibility revolve around a particular case and the author's interpretation of that case in relation to one or two earlier cases discussed in the literature. The most famous to which repeated reference is made is the Crichel Down Affair (Wheare 1975; Nicholson 1986) where the minister concerned, Dugdale, resigned after finding his civil servants were at fault not through corruption or illegality but merely through 'errors of judgement'. More general articles on ministerial resignations have been written, most famously by Finer (1956), with recent pieces tending to concentrate on resignations during the Thatcher years (Doherty 1988; Woodhouse 1993, 1994). Again little systematic evidence of the practice of ministers and the reasons why they resign is offered in these more general pieces. Finer's is still the most systematic study of ministerial resignations over a long period of time, but is now out of date.

All the discussions of ministerial resignations (with the exception of Woodhouse 1994) suffer from one fatal methodological flaw. They examine why ministers resign in order to uncover the doctrine of ministerial responsibility about resignation issues and to establish whether conventions are changing. However, it is not enough only to examine those cases when ministers resign. One needs to study the cases where they *do not resign*. One cannot claim that ministers resign under such-and-such conditions if one has examined only cases where ministers have resigned when those conditions obtain. There may be an equal or greater number of cases where ministers have not resigned despite those conditions obtaining.

Data have been collected on 'resignation issues', defined simply as any issue over which the press or MPs in the House have suggested that the minister should resign, or, in the case of known policy disagreements in the cabinet, over which a minister did resign. All ministerial changes (cabinet ministers, ministers of cabinet rank, junior ministers and government whips) have been coded according to the following categories: (a) personal error, (b) departmental error, (c) sexual scandal, (d) financial scandal, (e) policy disagreement, (f) personality clash, (g) performance, (h) 'other controversy' (i) retirement, alternative appointment or reshuffled.[7] This analysis has allowed a full survey of conventional behaviour over resignation issues. The results pertinent to the question of the relationship between ministers and civil servants – that is the issue of individual ministerial responsibility – are presented below.

Excluding ministers who retired with no associated contemporary scandal or criticism or who moved to alternative appointments or were reshuffled by the PM, there were 69 resignations during 1945–91.[8] Of these resignations, 26 were in protest at government policy, and we may ascribe them to the doctrine of collective responsibility. That leaves 43 ministers who resigned on grounds of individual responsibility. During the same period there have been 123 'non-resignations'. Ignoring 'protest resignations': it depends on whether the minister publicly announces his serious disagreement with the government and votes against it in the House, or just goes quietly) and personality clash, there is a total of 21 resignations and 86 non-resignations.

Table 8.2 Ministerial resignations and non-resignations 1945–91

	Personal error	Department error	Sexual/ financial scandal	Perform-ance	Other contro-versy	Total
Non-resignation	27	22	2	24	11	86
Resignation	8	4	7	0	2	21
Total	35	26	9	24	13	107

Table 8.2 shows that 57 per cent of ministerial resignations result from personal or departmental errors, whilst 43 per cent from sexual or financial scandal or other controversies. The two cases under the latter heading are Patrick Gordon Walker and Jeremy Bray. Gordon Walker resigned as Foreign Secretary in January 1965, having been appointed despite losing his seat at the General Election, and subsequently losing the theoretically safe seat of Leyton in a by-election. Bray wanted to write a book on the machinery of government and was forced out by Harold Wilson in May 1969. The resignations over sexual and financial scandals include: (sexual) Harvey, November 1958; Profumo, June 1963; Lambton and Jellicoe, May 1973; and Parkinson, October 1983; (financial) Maudling, July 1972; and Brayley, September 1979.

The Profumo, Lambton and Jellicoe resignations were sexual scandals but had implications for national security; the Harvey, and Parkinson scandals were matters of personal impropriety (Harvey involving charges of gross indecency, Parkinson simply ruffling moral feathers). All involved personal and not departmental faults. The Maudling case is more complicated and demonstrates the care that must be taken when interpreting bare statistics. He has been codified as primarily resigning because of 'financial scandal' because of his dealings with John Poulson who was involved in local government corruption. Maudling resigned from the Home Ofice 'under the misapprehension that he was in charge of the police force' (Marshal 1988: 128). The nature of (what he thought) his departmental responsibilities were led to his resignation as much as the scandal itself.

That two-thirds of resignations arise from personal or departmental error might indicate the strength of the doctrine of individual ministerial responsibility. A comparison with the 'non-resignations', however, suggests otherwise. Far more frequently ministers did not resign following personal or departmental error. On the other hand, only two ministers have avoided having to resign after sexual or financial scandal (Short in May 1974 and Fairburn in December 1981). Ministers have resigned 78 per cent of the time when there has been sexual or financial scandal, but only 22 per cent and 15 per cent for personal and departmental errors. In the category of 'other controversies' half of the time ministers have resigned.

A closer look at these cases shows the bare statistics are more generous towards the doctrine of individual responsibility than even these figures suggest, since the figures are for ministers and not occasions. The four instances of ministers resigning over 'departmental error' represent only two cases: the Crichel Down Affair when Dugdale went following error by his civil servants (Wheare 1975; Nicholson 1986; Chester 1989), and the resignation of Carrington and his junior ministers, Luce and Atkins, over the Argentine invasion of the Falklands (Pyper 1983; Jordan 1983; Woodhouse 1994: 87–106). Even in these cases there is some doubt over whether 'departmental error' is the correct category. Carrington resigned as the minister responsible when Thatcher chaired the Cabinet Committee which reviewed the evidence from the Foreign Office about Argentine intentions. Had Carrington (or perhaps the Defence Minister John Nott) not resigned, then the Prime Minister herself would have been forced to go. Indeed, had Labour's Michael Foot turned in a less incoherent performance in the House of Commons during the emergency debate, she might have had to go anyway. Even the Dugdale case is not as straightforward as many seem to believe, for there is some merit in George Jones's (1987: 89) comment: '[Dugdale] resigned not because of mistakes by his civil servants but because he lost the political support of his backbenchers. His agricultural policies were disliked by a major part of his party.'

In only two other cases where a minister resigned, Galbraith in 1962 and Fairburn in 1982, had departmental error been coded as a secondary reason for resigning. In both cases personal fault was seen to be paramount, and Fairburn had also used up political capital only a month earlier in a sexual scandal when a former House of Commons secretary, with whom the self-confessed womanizer Fairburn was friendly, attempted to commit suicide by hanging herself from a lamp post outside his London flat. On the other hand, there are 22 cases of ministers not resigning when the primary reason has been coded as errors made by their departments – for example, Kenneth Baker who did not resign after the two IRA suspects escaped from Brixton prison (this example is discussed below). A further 9 non-resignations occurred where departmental error was seen as a secondary reason in the resignation issue. For example, Heseltine did not resign when the Appeal Court ruled that he had acted unlawfully in cutting the rate failing to listen to the representations of the councils. In all the cases of non-resignation, political capital may help explain their survival.[9]

If a constitutional convention is 'a rule of behaviour accepted by those concerned in the working of the constitution' (Wheare 1966: 179), then the rule for resignation is simple: do not resign when your civil servants make a mistake. At most, since 1945, less than one-fifth of ministers have done so; it could be argued that none has. In fact, reviewing all the evidence, the constitutional convention seems to be: 'use all strategies available to avoid resigning; only resign when you have to'. We can see this rule by looking at better reasons for the causes of resignation.

An examination of the reactions of the public (through the eyes of the media), opposition parties, the minister's own backbenchers and the Prime Minister reveals more about the true causes for a resignation than any consideration of similarities in the issues. The following tables show the reactions of these groups to the cases of cabinet-level ministerial resignation/non-resignation for the categories of personal and departmental error (45 cases) and sexual or financial scandal (4 cases). There is no table recounting the PM's reaction to possible resignation. Apart from the cases of Dalton and Jellicoe whose resignations happened very quickly, in all the cases which appear in these tables the PM defended the minister concerned. The prime minister was always publicly against the resignation in these cases, though often accepting advice that the minister must resign, or even pressurizing him (through advisors) to go.

The two 'Not Applicable' situations apply to Jellicoe and Dalton who resigned before any criticism could be levelled at them. In both cases many believed that resignation was the right thing to do. Jellicoe was a clear case of sexual scandal with national defence implications. Dalton resigned after inadvertently telling a reporter details of his forthcoming budget, which were then made public before his budget speech. His economic policies were detested by the Conservative Opposition who were gleeful at his resignation and publicly applauded his resignation as the honourable action. However, many also stated privately that it was not strictly necessary. It could be said that censure that would have resulted, especially in the case of Jellicoe, less so in the case of Dalton, led to their resignations. These could be thought of as cases of anticipated reactions.

Table 8.3 Attitudes towards ministerial resignation – own party

	For resignation	Against resignation	Mixed	N/A	Total
Non-resignation	1	27	8	0	36
Resignation	2	1	4	2	9

Table 8.4 Attitudes towards ministerial resignation – opposition parties

	For resignation	Against resignation	Mixed	N/A	Total
Non-resignation	28	2	6	0	36
Resignation	6	1	0	2	9

Table 8.5 Attitudes towards ministerial resignation – public/media

	For resignation	Against resignation	Mixed	N/A	Total
Non-resignation	3	0	33	0	36
Resignation	2	0	5	2	9

Tables 8.3 to 8.5 demonstrate what most commentators have long recognized. Ministers resign when they lose the support of their own backbenchers. Only once has a minister held on to his portfolio when his own backbenchers have been against him: Lord Young during the 1988 Barlow Clowes Affair. Even here, the reaction could be described as mixed but has been coded as 'his own party against' since the first, and most critical, comments came from his own side. However, as he was in the unusual situation in modern times of being a cabinet minister in the Lords (and where backbenchers do not enjoy the prestige of those in the Commons), his survival may have been because he was unelected. He was also severely criticized in his absence in the Commons and faced a hostile reaction from the backbench Conservative 1922 Committee. Moreover, as Woodhouse (1994: 143) points out, this and the other two major cases involving Lord Young at the DTI were not finally resolved during his period as minister there – and so his could be the case of the 'timely reshuffle'. In 22 per cent of non-resignation cases there has been criticism of the minister by his own backbenchers, and they have received support 75 per cent of the time. When ministers have resigned, their own party has almost unanimously demanded their resignation 22 per cent of the time, and given a mixed reaction 44 per

cent of the time. Only once has a minister resigned without a call for resignation from his own backbenchers (indeed in this case, that of Reginald Maudling, no MP called for his resignation).

Opposition parties call for resignation 78 per cent of the time when ministers do not resign, and 66 per cent of the time when they have resigned. This latter figure is rather misleading as there are only nine cases, and for two of them, Dalton and Jellicoe, the opposition did not have the chance to so demand.

The situation is less clear cut with the general public, as revealed through the media. With many newspapers of all shades of opinion reflecting and leading a similar combination in public opinion, the largest category is a mixed reaction, some papers calling for resignation and some not – 92 per cent of the time. On only three occasions have there been near universal calls for the minister to resign. When ministers have gone, 22 per cent of the papers universally agreed, and 56 per cent have mixed opinions. Again the cases of Dalton and Jellicoe are coded as 'Not Applicable' though in both cases there was near universal agreement that they were right to resign.

The message is clear. To repeat, ministers resign when they lose the support of their own backbenchers, and the reaction of the opposition and the public is only causal to the extent that they can persuade the minister's own party that someone has to go. One recent example, though outside the time-frame of the statistics, is that of David Mellor. Mellor hung on to his post for three months during 1992 following newspaper revelations about a love affair and a libel action brought by a family friend against *The People* newspaper. Despite support from the PM (he offered to go almost immediately) and initial support from his own backbenchers, so tenacious was the press assault (and perhaps his own handling of the affair) that eventually his party felt he had to go, and the Prime Minister accepted his resignation (Doig 1993; Woodhouse 1994: 77–86).

The evidence of this study destroys the Crichel Down Affair as the key example of ministerial responsibility. The true convention regarding ministerial resignations is hang on for as long as you can. How long a minister can hang on depends upon his or her stock of political capital.

To bolster this statistical analysis we shall examine three similar cases involving prison breakouts. In each case there were calls for the minister concerned (in two cases the Home Secretary, in the other the Secretary of State for Northern Ireland) to resign, though none did resign. All seem to accord with Finer's (1956: 381) affirmation:

Ministers do not have to defend subordinates who defy instructions or who act reprehensibly in circumstances of which the Minister could not have become aware. It is equally clear that ministers have defended themselves by blaming their officials and firing them. And it is also true that the House does not censure the Minister who can show that the delinquency was against his express instructions, or that he could not physically have known of it – provided he makes it clear, by speech or action, that the offender has been dealt with and that therefore the delinquency is unlikely to recur.

Roy Jenkins, Home Secretary, following the escape of George Blake from Wormwood Scrubs on 22 October 1966

George Blake was a very important prisoner. A great deal had been made of the capture of this arch-traitor who had betrayed an estimated forty British agents. Blake's perceived danger to British security was reflected in the severity of his sentence on conviction in May 1961: forty-two years, the longest sentence imposed by a British court this century. Yet just five months later in October 1961 he was removed from the 'escape list' by the Prisons Department.

When the escape was discussed in parliament, the opposition Conservative front bench called for an immediate inquiry. Jenkins declined to make the Blake escape the subject of a special inquiry but said that it would come within the terms of the Mountbatten Inquiry into prison security which was already under way.

The Mountbatten Inquiry reported in December 1966, finding that 'there is no really secure prison in existence in this country'. This conclusion was reached in the light not only of the escape of Blake but also of the train robbers, Charles Wilson (1964) and Ronnie Biggs (1965). Mountbatten recommended an extensive building programme, including the construction of a high security prison on the Isle of Wight, and a restructuring of the Prison Department. The Inquiry noted severe security defects at Wormwood Scrubs where Blake was held and cited four instances when he should have been moved elsewhere.

The Mountbatten Inquiry revealed that the governor of Wormwood Scrubs had recommended Blake be transferred in January 1966, but the Prison Department had not acted on this recommendation. Mountbatten concluded that more serious consideration should have been given to the governor's warning and it should have been brought to the attention of more senior officials, though not necessarily to that of ministers.

James Prior, Secretary of State for Northern Ireland, and his junior minister, Nicholas Scott, following the Maze Prison breakout on 25 September 1983.

Unionists demanded that Nicholas Scott, the minister responsible for the province's prisons should resign following the breakout of 38 prisoners from the Maze Prison. Prior made it clear in public that if Scott resigned he would resign too.

An inquiry headed by Sir James Hennessy was set up to investigate the escape, including how five handguns were smuggled into the prison. The Hennessy Inquiry reported in January 1984 and criticized the security arrangements at the Maze, saying they arose from a general malaise in the prison service. The blame was put on the governor of the Maze who resigned as soon as the report was published. An unnamed official in the Northern Ireland Office was also criticized. Prior argued that responsibility for the escape lay with officials and prison staff and could not be blamed on ministers. Critics (including the *Sunday Telegraph*) argued that the 'general malaise' in the prison service was surely the responsibility of ministers, particularly of Scott who had special responsibility for prisons in the province. Those who called for Prior's resignation included Dennis Concannon, a former Labour Northern Ireland Minister, Julian Amery, a former Conservative minister, Enoch Powell and Unionist MPs. *The Economist* thought Prior was dodging responsibility by blaming operational errors. It argued the policy of maintaining good relations with prisoners following the hunger strike had led to reduced vigilance, and to argue this error was operational without policy implications was simply passing the buck.

Kenneth Baker, Home Secretary, following the escape of two IRA suspects from Brixton Prison on 7 June 1991.

Baker said he had considered resigning after the escape but changed his mind after Judge Tumin's report into the incident, published on 5 August, which blamed prison staff rather than departmental policy. Opposition spokesmen pointed out that Tumin had recommended the previous August that category A prisoners should not be housed at Brixton.

In the inquiry into the escape, Tumin found that metal detectors which had been provided were not being used by prison staff and that the prison authorities, including the governor, had been alerted by the police five months previously of the intention of the two men to escape. The Special Branch had been able to tell the prison authorities the escape plan, including the smuggling in of a gun. Ministers were not made aware of this information, according to the report. The Prison Governor, Reg Withers, went on leave before taking early retirement in October, and Brian Bubbear, head of the Directorate of Custody at the Prison Department, was moved to another post.

These three very similar cases teach much about the doctrine of responsibility and the relationship between ministers and civil servants; and about the relationship between policy, which is the direct responsibility of ministers, and the day-to-day execution of policy, which is the direct responsibility of civil servants.

At the time of the Maze breakout in 1983, Geoffrey Smith, writing in *The Times*, said 'the doctrine of direct ministerial responsibility has become outdated where no vestige of blame attaches to the minister and needs to be replaced by more direct sanctions to those who are in the public service'. Similar sentiments were aired after the Brixton escape in 1991. *The Times* leader argued it was inconceivable that the home secretary should resign every time a prisoner escaped. Such views constitute the practical view of the doctrine of ministerial responsibility.

A purer view of the doctrine was put forward by other observers. The *Sunday Telegraph* argued that James Prior had made prisons the sole responsibility of his junior minister Nicholas Scott. The failure of security at the Maze was the responsibility of the governor and the staff in the first instance but ultimately of Scott and Prior. In the case of the Brixton escape Brian Appleyard in the *Sunday Times* said that Baker was dodging his responsibility by making a false distinction between policy and administration.

In practice the distinction between policy and administration is difficult to define. In the Blake escape the Mountbatten Inquiry found there was a general security problem in Britain's prisons. George Blake, whose escape was hugely embarrassing for Britain, was put in a prison with known security defects after the escape of high-profile prisoners such as Wilson and Biggs and, despite the length of his sentence, was taken off the escape list. The Hennessy Report put the Maze breakout down to particular failures on the part of prison staff, but also to a 'general malaise' in the prison department. Surely the low morale of prison staff would have been of concern to a minister solely charged with the running of Northern Ireland's prisons? Again, in the Brixton escape in 1991 the unsuitability of the prison had been pointed out. The escape was blamed on prison staff; but is not the keeping of category A prisoners in unsuitable prisons a matter of policy?

More important in all these cases than the details of operational and/ or policy failure is that in all three cases ministers had the support of their prime minister and at least a large section of their party. Jenkins faced the least opposition in his determination to stay as home secretary after the Blake escape, and he enjoyed the full support of Harold Wilson and the Parliamentary Labour Party. There were more forceful calls for Scott's and Prior's resignations after the Maze breakout. But Margaret Thatcher felt it would be politically damaging following the resignation of Cecil Parkinson. Although a number of Tories wanted Prior out of the Cabinet, most did not favour using this example as an excuse. Kenneth Baker faced the strongest demands of all to resign, as the Brixton escape followed a number of political errors of judgement on his part, including his failure to act quickly over 'joyriding' and his handling of the dangerous dog legislation. He was seen by many in the party as a liability, and John Major was more low key in his support than Thatcher had been when her ministers had been under attack.

In these three cases ministers have easily sidestepped any responsibility by pinning blame on civil servants or prison staff. It would be ridiculous to expect a minister to resign every time there was an escape, but the doctrine of ministerial responsibility does not demand this. It requires that the minister should acknowledge that mistakes were made, take the blame as though the actions of his subordinates were his own, and then set about putting things right to ensure that the same thing does not recur.

In all these cases the minister refused to take any responsibility, blamed civil servants and set about ensuring that they paid the penalty. Responsibility seems to stop with civil servants rather than flow up and down the hierarchy. These cases reflect the more general finding of the statistical analysis, that the ability of a minister to stay in office depends more upon his or her political standing than his or her personal culpability.

AGENCIES AND THE SEPARATION OF POLICY AND ADMINISTRATION

What difference has Next Steps made to ministerial accountability? Much ink was initially spilled over academics' constitutional worries that the agencies would break the link between minister and departmental responsibilities (Chapman 1988; Fry *et al.* 1988; Jenkins *et al.* 1988; Butcher 1991; Drewry and Butcher 1991; Drewry 1993; see Dowding 1994b for a critical response). In many ways accountability has been enhanced. The chief executive is responsible to the department and thus ultimately to parliament through the minister. The manner in which this responsibility works, and the degree of freedom given the chief executives, varies with the framework agreements. These arrangements offer potential for greater rather than less scrutiny of the executive work of many departments.

The scope of the accountability of ministers may appear to have altered as more direct means of dealing with operational matters, particularly complaints, exist with MPs writing directly to chief executives. This reform has led to a decentralization of routine accountability. To some extent it has advantages for MPs, though some have expressed qualms about the way some issues have been dealt with. Chief executives are regularly called before select committees and operate under the same Osmotherly Rules as other civil servants when answering questions.

The role of agencies has increased the pressure for a distinction between operational matters and policy matters, with ministers accepting less responsibility for operational matters. However, as we saw in the three gaolbreak cases, this distinction is certainly not new and has been maintained for some time. Many are sceptical that such a distinction can be made. It is rather an is-dusk-day-or-night type of problem. Operational matters can be distinguished from policy matters, but the two are intertwined, and at times it may not be immediately obvious whether a problem is simply operational failure or a consequence of policy failure. The whole point of explanatory accountability to parliament and its committees is to try to sort out such matters. Furthermore, whilst it is true that policy and service decisions cannot be neatly divided it does not follow that the division between service and policy divisions will not allow for the links between the two to be made. Chief executives are supposed to be left on their own to run their agencies, but they will still be making regular and frequent reports to both departments and select committees. Indeed the policy input of managers at the front line of services has now been formalized. When asked if his agency could influence policy Mike Fogden, Chief Executive of the Employment Service, said:

> Indeed not only influence but, in fact, the Department look to us for information to enable policy formulation to proceed . . . in our Framework Document there are two key sentences: one is that the Chief Executive is permitted to make proposals for policy changes to the Secretary of State, but equally as important, and perhaps some would argue more important, there is also a sentence which says no policy proposals regarding the work of the Employment Service can be made to the Secretary of State until we have actually been consulted.

(HC 496, 1990–91: 3)

Other chief executives confirmed this with regard to their own inputs into policy formulation.[10] Indeed Sir Angus Fraser, the Prime Minister's adviser on efficiency, claimed that

> it is possible to argue that the setting up of . . . agencies has ensured that if there was a divide between operations and policy that divide has now been bridged because those in charge of operation are much more deliberately being taken into the policy-making process.
>
> (Evidence to HC 496, 1990–91: 55)

The policy impact of service decisions and the service impact of policy decisions will be one of the issues most frequently discussed. It is just not true that the division will mean that policy may be decided at a 'depoliticized' service-delivery level or that policies will be decided without consideration of delivery possibilities. Indeed, creating agencies with more clearly demarcated responsibilities should mean that managers have an interest in pointing out the dangers for service delivery of policy decisions – they will not want to carry the blame if it proves impossible to implement policies to which they are contracted. Next Steps will only entail this result if the incentive structure for managers is correctly specified. There is a great danger that it has not been.

> What is worrying in this separation of policy from agency is the tendency to blame agents for failures of policy and for the mounting costs of services. This disconnection tends to hide the realities of mixed messages and divided allegiances. In what sense can a Vehicle Inspectorate 'please' its customers when its job is to keep those with unsafe vehicles off the road? Can a school or hospital 'compete' for patients or pupils when its mandate includes accessibility to all, especially the disadvantaged and most ill? Why wouldn't such institutions compete in shedding their more costly and intractable customers? These are problems of policy not of distribution, issues of effectiveness not efficiency.
>
> (Charles Hampden-Turner 1992: ix)

Similarly the policy impact of decisions made within the delivery arena will be of great interest to ministers and their policy advisers if they then find themselves accounting for those policies to parliament or to the public through the mass media. There are dangers in the splitting of policy and implementation. These arise where ministers try to depoliticize decisions or distance themselves from decisions within their sphere of competence. When a health minister states that he cannot comment upon the closing of a hospital maternity ward because that is an operational decision of the chief executive of the relevant opted-out hospital, then he is automatically reducing the sphere of his competence.

One reason why creating new incentives for managers in the public sector is more difficult than in the private sector is that there is a greater number of conflicting demands. Public-sector organizations are encouraged to find savings, be efficient, serve the public effectively, police the public, and attain welfare targets set by government.

This aspect of the reforms may also cause the blurring of policy formation and implementation. How far can the government be blamed for the ills of some sector for creating the policies and how far can the providers be blamed for giving a poor service:

> If service users are treated as 'customers' and their satisfaction or dissatisfaction can be interpreted as being a result of the strength or otherwise of the managers' abilities to deliver this can reduce the accountability of politicians. Some of the elements of the Citizen's Charter can achieve this end. For example if passengers are compensated by British Rail for the delayed arrival of trains, it implies that British Rail and its managers are at fault. If the underlying reason for delays is a history of underinvestment in signalling equipment and rolling stock or of staff shortages, this will not be apparent to the passenger in the role of 'customer'. In the role of citizen, the rail user could rightly complain of the government's policy towards transport in general and the funding of the railway in particular. As customers they can only blame management.
>
> (Common *et al.* 1992: 78)

The reasoning of Common *et al.* here is impeccable: to the extent that the Next Steps and the Citizen's Charter turn our attention to the managers of services and the service we receive and away from the fact that government vitally affects these services, the real political accountability for these services may be diminished. However, the underlying implication of their argument is that political accountability is changing with these innovations: the implication that we as citizens are well aware that government is to blame and that under-investment in the railway network is the result of decades of politicians making mistakes but that suddenly when the Citizen's Charter is introduced, we will forget this and turn our ire upon the poor old British Rail staff. This is nonsense. British Rail staff have faced the anger of their passengers for decades. The under-investment in the rail network has been discussed *ad nauseam*. The political accountability of politicians has hardly entered the debate. The implication that the British public is going to forget its role as 'citizen' is faintly ridiculous; or rather it is ridiculous to think (if this is too much like asking whether the public is going to forget to stop beating their spouses) that it will stop blaming the government for many of the ills of the nation. Equally absurd is the implication that all was well with political accountability in parliament till the Conservative government started messing around with it. There is no doubt that the Conservative government has reduced the areas under which it will admit responsibility or liability. That is a policy decision. Mrs Thatcher came to power in 1979 determined to reduce the power of the state and that aim has been maintained under Mr Major. The nature of the 'state' for the Conservatives largely means 'the area where the government will accept responsibility'. When they aim to reduce the regulations that govern, say, worker or consumer rights, they are stating that if some claim is to be made against a firm or management, then that is something in which the state has no role. It is not the concern of the government nor of the courts. Thus the Conservatives have aimed to reduce the sphere of accountability of government. The Next Steps process can be seen as a part of that process. Responsibility for certain decisions will be given to individuals outside government and will not be accepted by ministers.

However, to claim that this abrogation of responsibility has affected the nature of government accountability is to make a number of unjustified assumptions. First, it assumes that ministers used to accept responsibility for operational service decisions. This is palpable nonsense. Secondly, it assumes that the agency process and the government aim to reduce the influence of the state are inseparable. But that is not so. It is possible for a government with no such aims to work within the structure of the civil service set up under Next Steps. If one government chooses to use that structure in a particular way, it does not follow that the structure is to blame for the way it is being used. It is perfectly within the powers of parliamentarians and the media to ensure that government does not get away with altering the nature of accountability in the UK. If parliament chooses not to stop government from changing the nature of accountability, it cannot blame government for doing so – though the structure of the British party system (and hence perhaps of the electoral system) may be the underlying factor in parliamentary impotence.

CONCLUSION

The theory of governmental accountability still relies on the simple Weberian account. The agency process has opened up some procedures to greater public scrutiny. The popular version of individual ministerial responsibility, which has ministers weighing up their own position whenever departmental error occurs, has been empirically demolished. This interpretation is largely the preserve of former ministers and backbench MPs, whose interests rather than their understanding may lead them to push the idea; it is also the preserve of journalists who are looking for controversial copy and, somewhat surprisingly, of constitutional lawyers (for example, Turpin 1990: 353), who seem to base their views on the opinions of dead journalists.[11] In reality there will be no deep-rooted accountability until parliament truly appropriates the sovereignty that in theory it maintains. Until parliament has the power and the will to demand answers from anyone to any question which falls within its responsibility (which may not include aspects of local government which parliament sets up with it own system of accountability), ministers will hide behind civil servants, and civil servants will aid and abet ministers. Government should be accountable to parliament, and the civil service is every bit as much a part of government as are ministers. Civil servants too should be answerable to parliament through the select committee system. The veils of secrecy need to be stripped aside.

Notes

2 HIERARCHY: WEBER AND THE OLD MODEL

1 The idea of women in public service in the mid-nineteenth century was simply inadmissable. Today the civil service is still male-dominated at the higher levels, though more women serve at the lower levels (see Table 2.2 for some figures). I use the term 'men' to reflect this fact of Northcote-Trevelyan.
2 I am indebted to David Beetham's (1985) excellent account for my understanding of Weber. Much of my text is based on Beetham's writing there and elsewhere. Students wishing to follow up the account in this chapter should start with Beetham (1985).
3 All power is based upon the resources available (see Dowding 1991).
4 Following Beetham's (1985: 74) translation, I have changed the original 'service secret' to the more familiar 'official secret'.
5 At the time this was written British Leyland was in public hands.
6 *Eleventh Report from the Expenditure Committee, 1976–77: The Civil Service*, HC 535–1, London: HMSO, 1977, Appendix: Definition of a Civil Servant.
7 See Fry (1993) for a contrary view.
8 From *Civil Service Statistics*, London: HM Treasury, annual.
9 *Civil Service Statistics 1993*, London: HM Treasury.
10 I use the male pronoun deliberately here. At the time of writing there are only two female permanent secretaries and neither one of these in a major department. At the highest levels of the civil service 'he', unfortunately, means he.
11 In large departments there is a second permanent secretary.

3 EFFICIENCY: ITS MEANING AND ABUSE

1 This table assumes that utilities may be linearly added, and therefore interpersonal welfare comparisons may be made. Later in the chapter when the logic of Pareto-comparison is considered, this assumption will take on great importance.

2 However, if voter A represents the 'rich' and B and C are middle- to low-income groups, then the comparison of utilities may be more complex.

3 Interpersonal comparison of utilities is still recognized as problematic (Elster and Roemer 1991).

4 See Stevens (1993: ch. 2) for a good discussion of these or any book on welfare economics such as Boadway and Bruce (1984: ch 3).

5 Such compensation tests are also difficult, for the losers have an incentive to exaggerate their losses. Given that compensation depends on cardinal calculations of losses, it is also very 'unParetian'. Indeed, most attempts to get around the strict conclusions that Pareto reached simply beg the question he was asking.

6 There are more careful uses of the Pareto-principle which involve a two-stage process. First, generate a set of Pareto-efficient allocations; secondly, use a welfare rule (such as that developed by Rawls (1971) to choose the Pareto-efficient allocation which maximizes distributive justice, as embodied in the welfare rule. Moral conflict is thus generated over the different welfare functions available. However, a more complicated version of the objection in the text may be generated to this more complicated use of Pareto comparisons. More pertinently, the crude use of the Pareto-principle discussed in the text underlies the arguments about externally generated bureaucratic inefficiencies.

7 This moral component is brought out in texts on welfare economics such as Boadway and Bruce (1984), though they still claim it is a weaker ethical premise than those underlying other moral principles such as utilitarianism. However, if one moral principle excludes another, it is hard to see how one is 'weaker' than the other. In the public choice tradition, even the simplistic distinction Boadway and Bruce make between normative and positive economics is ignored and such arguments are treated as though they were entirely empirical.

Note that nothing in the text denies that the strong moral viewpoint of Pareto-efficiency cannot be justified. Many attempts to justify libertarianism exist. Hayek (1982) is the best.

8 For a reasonable though flawed discussion of the trade-offs often claimed between equity and efficiency, see LeGrand (1991) especially ch. 3.

9 Only 11 bills failed out of 213 introduced in the 1987–92 parliament, and 6 of the failures were due to the final session ending early for the general election.

10 See the articles in Rush (ed.) (1990) for evidence to the effect that parliament is a target for log-rolling.

11 See McLean (1987), ch. 5; Dunleavy (1991: 154–62) for simple though only partial explanations. See Jackson (1982), ch. 5 for an excellent though slightly more technical account.

12 See Chapters 4 and 5.

13 Probably at a higher price but for other reasons than contained in the equilibrium account.

14 What the reader must keep in mind is that logically possible worlds are being compared. There are rules which allow for proper comparison and do not allow for other types of comparison. For example, if you imagine what the world would be like without trains, you cannot simply assume that everything in the world is the same as it is now but without trains. You either have to explain what happened to them so that they disappeared or

imagine what economies would now be like if trains had not existed. See Elster (1978) for a discussion of this example. Below it is demonstrated that Niskanen's Pareto-efficiency argument breaks the rules of comparison across logically possible worlds.

15 Darwinian natural selection has never been empirically verified in this sense. Evolutionary change has been empirically demonstrated in the laboratory, but it is unproven that the criterion for these is environmental fitness. Nevertheless, there are very good theoretical reasons for supposing that natural selection is the best explanation of evolutionary adaptation (Sober 1993); indeed some claim that it is the only possible explanation of evolutionary change (Dawkins 1991).

4 BUDGET-MAXIMIZING: EVIDENCE OF AND ENDING

1 This is not to say that organizational matters were of no concern to the left – the aims of the Fulton Report can be seen as a part of this critique – but what distinguished the left critique was a concern about the social-class makeup of senior civil servants.

2 See McLean (1987) for a simple introduction to public choice methods and Mueller (1989) for more detail.

3 The self-interest assumption is compatible with a social-class analysis. In so far as class interest is in one's self-interest, this will lead one to act on the grounds of class interest. Most public–choice writers do not take much account of social class as an explanatory force.

4 It is important to note that Niskanen (1971, 1973) argues that bureaucrats both attempt and succeed in maximizing their budget (Blais and Dion 1991). Their attempt to maximize is based upon the behavioural (internal) argument. Why they succeed is based upon the equilibrium (external) argument. The truth of the latter is considered in Chapter 3, the truth of the former here.

5 The time period of consideration for evidence of budget-maximization ends in the mid-1980s before the new modes of service delivery were introduced under the Next Steps process (described later) following the Conservatives' election victory in 1987. This was in order to see whether civil servants in a hierarchical organization budget-maximize.

6 See Mueller (1989: 261–6) for a brief review of evidence from the United States and a useful bibliography. See also Blais and Dion (eds) (1991).

7 This is not the full set of assumptions from Dunsire and Hood. See Dunsire (1991) and the full evidence is found in Dunsire and Hood (1989).

8 Most of the discussion is based on the report of this and the other Jørgensen article in Hood and Dunsire (1989).

9 These are all discussed later in this chapter.

10 See Milgrom and Roberts (1992: ch. 6) for a general discussion of moral hazard in organizations.

11 I take the title for the sceptical view from Hennessey, but the idea of Thatcherism staggering from initiative to initiative is quite widespread and covers many policy arenas.

5 BUREAU-SHAPING: THE NEW MODEL AND THE NEW MANAGER

1 Niskanen (1991) has now acknowledged the need for such budgetary disaggregation but has not attempted to rectify his own model to take this into account.

2 The examples all list the 'core departments' even where the money is transferred to Next Steps agencies.

3 Indeed, it has recently been suggested that 'managerialism' is the new ideology replacing conservatism, capitalism, socialism and liberalism alike, see Entemann (1993).

4 In this respect they resemble dictators in a banana republic. For a hundred years it was the convention in Bolivia for incoming dictators not to execute whatever they had managed to salt away. As each dictatorship had an expected lifespan of under two years, it was in each dictator's interests to keep the convention going.

7 EUROPEAN UNION: NEW OPPORTUNITIES

1 The writing of this chapter was helped by a Nuffield Foundation Grant, no Q9491, which allowed me to visit Brussels and speak to a number of British civil servants. I have also benefited by discussing some of the issues of EC co-ordination with Sonia Mazey.

2 I take all the details of this case from Bates (1986). The reader should also refer to this article for details of the second case mentioned below.

3 *Second Report from the House of Commons Select Committee on European Community Secondary Legislation*, Session 1983–84: 13–14.

8 ACCOUNTABILITY: MYTHS AND EMPIRICAL EVIDENCE

1 Interview July 1992.

2 See Hennessy (1986), Dunleavy (1990) or Woodhouse (1994) for the details of the Westland Affair.

3 This section is based upon contemporary newspaper reports, principally from *The Guardian*, the *Independent*, *The Times*, the *Sunday Times*, and the *Independent on Sunday*.

4 See Tomkins (1993) for an account of the general contents of the three categories of certificate.

5 As a non-lawyer, I find most of the legal debate over the duty to sign public immunity certificates a case of the obtuse discussing the absurd, believing it abstruse. See Tomkins (1993) for the important recent cases and rulings.

6 The data in this section was collected with the financial assistance of The Nuffield Foundation (Grant no SOC/100(302)). I would like to thank my research assistants Helen Cannon and Norman Cooke who did most initial data-collection and coding. Material was collected from *The Times* (the *Daily Telegraph* when *The Times* was on strike), cross-referred to other newspapers and *The Economist*, academic, autobiographical and popular published accounts.

7 All cases were coded for 'primary reason' and then also coded for secondary

reasons. Thus, analysis of all the reasons involved in cases is possible. I have only included analysis in terms of 'primary reasons' for resigning.

8 This includes government whips, junior ministers, ministers of cabinet rank and cabinet ministers.

9 Political capital is a special case of 'social capital'. See Coleman (1990) especially ch. 12 for discussion.

10 See, for example, Mr Michael Bichard HC 496, 1990–91: 32.

11 As Ferdinand Mount (1992: 36) has suggested, our grandly named 'constitutional authorities' consist of an 'assorted band of academics and journalists who have caught the public fancy in their day and survived to be quoted by their successors in search of something to hang an argument on.'

References

Ackroyd, S., Hughes, J. A. and Soothill, K. (1989) 'Public Sector Services and Their Management' *Journal of Management Studies* 26: 603–17.

Albrow, M. (1970) *Bureaucracy* London: Macmillan.

Armstrong, R. (1989) 'The Duties and Responsibilities of Civil Servants in Relation to Ministers' in G. Marshall (ed.) *Ministerial Responsibility* Oxford: Oxford University Press.

Bagehot, W. (1872) *The English Constitution* 2nd edn, London: Kegan Paul, Trench, Trubner and Co.

Baker, R. J. S. (1972) 'The V and G Affair and Ministerial Responsibility' *Political Quarterly* 43: 340–5.

Barnett, J. (1982) *Inside the Treasury* London: Andre Deutsch.

Bates, J. D. N. (1986) 'Sex Discrimination and Retirement: Two Recent Decisions of the European Court of Justice' *Public Law* 537–46.

Beaumont, P. B. (1981) *Government as an Employer Setting an Example?* London: Royal Institute of Public Administration.

Beckett, A. (1994) 'How Clean Was My Valley?' *Independent on Sunday Supplement*, 28 August.

Beetham, D. (1985) *Max Weber and the Theory of Modern Politics* 2nd edn Cambridge: Polity Press.

Bendor, J. (1988) 'Review Article: Formal Models of Bureaucracy' *British Journal of Political Science* 18: 353–95.

Bender, B. G. (1991) 'Governmental Processes: Whitehall, Central Government and 1992' *Public Policy and Administration* 6: 13–29.

Benn, T. (1981) *Arguments for Democracy* (ed. Chris Mullin) Nottingham: Spokesman.

Benn, T. (1987) *Conflicts of Interests: Diaries 1977–1980* (ed. Ruth Wintrobe) London: Hutchinson.

Benn, T. (1988) *Office Without Power: Diaries 1968–72* London: Hutchinson.

Bercussen, B. (1978) *Fair Wages Resolutions* London: Mansell.

Bishop, M. and Kay, J. (1992) *Does Privatization Work? Lessons from the UK* London: London Business School.

Blais, A. and Dion, S. (1991) 'Introduction' in A. Blais and S. Dion (eds) (1991).

Blais, A. and Dion, S. (eds) (1991) *The Budget-Maximizing Bureaucrat: Appraisals and Evidence* Pittsburgh: University of Pittsburgh Press.

Boadway, R. W. and Bruce, N. (1984) *Welfare Economics* Oxford: Blackwell.

Borcherding, T. E. (ed.) (1977) *Budgets and Bureaucrats: The Sources of Government Growth* Durham, NC: Duke University Press.

Bosanquet, N. (1983) *After the New Right* London: Heinemann.

Brittan, S. (1969) *Steering the Economy: The Role of the Treasury* 2nd edn, London: Secker and Warburg.

Brennan, G. and Buchanan, J. M. (1980) *The Power to Tax: Analytical Foundations of a Fiscal Constitution* Cambridge: Cambridge University Press.

Browning, P. (1986) *The Treasury and Economic Policy 1964–1985* London: Longman.

Buchanan, J. M. and Tullock, G. (1962) *The Calculus of Consent* Michigan: University of Michigan Press.

Buchanan, J. M., Tollison, R. D. and Tullock, G. (eds) (1980) *Toward a Theory of the Rent Seeking Society* College Station: Texas A&M Press.

Burnham, J. and Maor, M. (1994) 'Converging Administrative Systems: Recruitment and Training in EC Member States' (working paper) London: The European Institute, LSE.

Butler, D., Adonis, A. and Travers, T. (1994) *Failure in British Government: The Politics of the Poll Tax* Oxford: Oxford University Press.

Butler, M. (1986) *Europe: More than a Continent*, London: Heinemann.

Butler, R. (1993) 'The Evolution of the Civil Service – A Progress Report' *Public Administration* 71: 395–406.

Cabinet Office (1986) *Reforms at Work in the Civil Service*, London: Cabinet Office.

Castle, B. (1980) *The Castle Diaires, 1974–76* London: Weidenfeld & Nicolson.

Castle, B. (1984) *The Castle Diaires, 1964–70* London: Weidenfeld & Nicolson.

Chapman, L. (1978) *Your Disobedient Servant* London: Chatto and Windus.

Chapman, L. (1982) *Waste Away* London: Chatto and Windus.

Chapman, R. A. (1988) '"The Next Steps": A Review' *Public Policy and Administration* 3: 3–10.

Chapman, R. A. (1993) 'Civil Service Recruitment: Fairness or Preferential Advantage?' *Public Policy and Administration* 8: 68–73.

Chapman, R. A. and Greenaway, J. R. (1980) *The Dynamics of Administrative Reform* London: Croom Helm.

Chester, D. N. (1981) 'Parliamentary Questions' in M. Ryle and S. A. Walkland (eds) *The Commons Today* London: Fontana.

Chester, D. N. (1989) 'The Crichel Down Case' in G. Marshall (ed.) *Ministerial Responsibility* Oxford: Oxford University Press.

Christoph, J. B. (1992) 'The Effects of Britons in Brussels: The European Community and the Culture of Whitehall' (paper presented at the Annual Meeting of the Midwest Political Science Association, Chicago, 9–11 April).

Civil Service Department (1980) *Memorandum of Guidance for Officials Appearing Before Select Committees* CSD Gen 80/38.

Clarke, R. (1975) 'The Machinery of Government' in W. Thornhill, (ed.) *The Modernization of British Government* London: Pitman.

Clarke, J. and Newman, J. (1992) 'The Right to Manage: a Second Managerial Revolution?' MS.

Cm 2627 (1994) *The Civil Service: Continuity and Change* London: HMSO.

Cm 2750 (1994) Office of Public Service and Science, *Next Steps Review: 1994* London: HMSO.

Coleman, J. (1990) *Foundations of Social Theory* Cambridge, Mass.: Belknap Press.

Common, R., Flynn, N. and Mellon, E. (1992) *Managing Public Services: Competition and Decentralization* Oxford: Butterworth Heinemann.

Crossman, R. (1975) *The Diaries of a Cabinet Minister* vol 1, London: Hamish Hamilton and Jonathan Cape.

Crossman, R. (1976) *The Diaries of a Cabinet Minister* vol 2, London: Hamish Hamilton and Jonathan Cape.

Dawkins, R. (1991) *The Blind Watchmaker* Harmondsworth: Penguin.

Doherty, M. (1988) 'Prime Ministerial Power and Ministerial Responsibility in the Thatcher Era' *Parliamentary Affairs* 41: 49–67.

Doig, A. (1989) 'The Resignation of Edwina Currie: A Word Too Far' *Parliamentary Affairs* 42: 317–29.

Doig, A. (1993) 'The Double Whammy: The Resignation of David Mellor, MP' *Parliamentary Affairs* 46: 167–78.

Dowding, K. (1991) *Rational Choice and Political Power* Aldershot: Edward Elgar.

Dowding, K. (1994a) 'The Compatibility of Behaviouralism, Rational Choice and the "New Institutionalism"' *Journal of Theoretical Politics* 6: 105–17.

Dowding, K. (1994b) 'Institutional Persistence and Change at the Core of British Government' in H. Kastendiek and R. Stinsdorf (eds) *Changing Conceptions of Constitutional Government* Bochum: Universitatsverlag Dr. N. Brockmeyer.

Dowding, K. (1994c) 'Policy Communities: Don't Stretch a Good Idea Too Far' in P. Dunleavy and J. Stanyer (eds) *Contemporary Political Studies 1994* vol. 1 Belfast: The Political Studies Association of the United Kingdom.

Dowding, K. (1995) 'Model or Metaphor: A Critical Review of the Policy Network Approach' *Political Studies* 43: 136–58.

Dowding, K. and King, D. (1995) 'Introduction' in K. Dowding, and D. King (eds) *Preferences, Institutions and Applied Rational Choice* Oxford: Clarendon.

Downs, A. (1957) *An Economic Theory of Democracy* New York: Harper Row.

Downs, A. (1960) 'Why the Government Budget is too Small in a Democracy' *World Politics* 12: 541–64.

Downs, A. (1967) *Inside Bureaucracy* Boston: Little Brown.

Drewry, G. (1993) 'Parliament' in P. Dunleavy, A. Gamble, G. Peel, and I. Holiday (eds) *Developments in British Politics 4* London: Macmillan.

Drewry, G. and Butcher, T. (1991) *The Civil Service Today* 2nd edn, Oxford: Basil Blackwell.

Dunleavy, P. (1985) 'Bureaucrats, Budgets and the Growth of the State: Reconstructing an Instrumental Model' *British Journal of Political Science* 15: 299–328.

Dunleavy, P. (1986) 'Explaining the Privatization Boom: Public Choice versus Radical Approaches' *Public Administration* 64: 13–34.

Dunleavy, P. (1989a) 'The Architecture of the British State, Part One: Framework for Analysis' *Public Administration* 67: 249–75.

Dunleavy, P. (1989b) 'The Architecture of the British State, Part Two: Empirical Findings' *Public Administration* 68: 3–28.

Dunleavy, P. (1990) 'Reinterpreting the Westland Affair: Theories of the State and Core Executive Decision-Making' *Public Administration* 68: 29–60.

Dunleavy, P. (1991) *Bureaucracy, Democracy and Public Choice* Hemel Hempstead: Harvester Wheatsheaf.

Dunleavy, P. King, D. and Margetts, H. (1994) 'Leviathan Bound: Bureaucrats and Budgeting in the American Federal State' MS, London: LSE.

Dunleavy, P. and O'Leary, B. (1987) *Theories of the State* London: Macmillan.

Dunsire, A. (1991) 'Bureaucrats and Conservative Governments' in A. Blais and S. Dion (eds) (1991).

Dunsire, A. and Hood, C. with Huby, M. (1989) *Cutback Management in Public Bureaucracies: Popular Theories and Observed Outcomes in Whitehall* Cambridge: Cambridge University Press.

Edwards, M. (1984) *Back from the Brink* London: Pan.

Ellis, A. (1989) 'Civil Service Neutrality' in R. Goodin and A. Reeve (eds) *Liberal Neutrality* London: Sage.

Elster, J. (1978) *Logic and Society* London: John Wiley.

Elster, J. and Roemer, J. (eds) (1991) *Interpersonal Comparisons of Well-being* Cambridge: Cambridge University Press.

Enteman, W. F. (1993) *Managerialism: The Emergence of a New Ideology* Madison, Wisconsin: University of Wisconsin Press.

Erlichman, J. (1992) 'Food Advisers' Cash Revealed by Minister' *Guardian* 5 August.

Falkender, M. (1983) *Downing Street in Perspective* London: Weidenfeld & Nicolson.

Finer, S. E. (1956) 'The Individual Responsibility of Ministers' *Public Administration* 34: 377–96, reprinted in abridged form in G. Marshall (ed.) *Ministerial Responsibility* Oxford: Oxford University Press.

Fredman, S. and Gillian M. (1988) 'Civil Servants: A Contract of Employment?' *Public Law*: 58–77.

Freeman, A. (1982) *The Benn Heresy* London: Pluto.

Fry, G. (1969–70) 'Thoughts on the Present State of Ministerial Responsibility' *Parliamentary Affairs* 23: 10–20.

Fry, G. (1983) 'Compromise with the Market: the Megaw Report on Civil Service Pay' *Public Administration* 61: 90–96.

Fry, G. (1988) 'The Thatcher Government, the Financial Management Initiative, and the "New Civil Service"' *Public Administration* 66: 1–20.

Fry, G. (1993) *Reforming the Civil Service: The Fulton Committee on the British Home Civil Service, 1966–68* Edinburgh: Edinburgh University Press.

Fry, G., Flynn, A., Gray, A. and Jenkins, W. (1988) 'Symposium on Improving Management in Government' *Public Administration* 66: 429–45.

Fulton, Lord (1968) *Report of the Committee 1966–68* Cmd 3638 London: HMSO, (Fulton Report).

Ganz, G. (1980) 'Parliamentary Accountability of the Crown Agents' *Public Law* 454–80.

Goodin, R. E. (1982) 'Rational Politicians in Washington and Whitehall' *Public Administration* 62: 23–41.

Grant, W. (1993) *The Politics of Economic Decline* Hemel Hempstead: Harvester Wheatsheaf.

Greenaway, J. Smith, S. and Street, J. (1992) *Deciding Factors in British Politics* London: Routledge.

HC 535–1 (1976–77) *Eleventh Report from the Expenditure Committee, 1976–77: The Civil Service* London: HMSO.

HC 92 (1985–86) *Civil Servants and Ministers: Duties and Responsibilities: Seventh Report from the Treasury and Civil Service Committee* vol. I: Report, London: HMSO.

HC 348 (1988–89) *Treasury and Civil Service Committee, Fifth Report, Civil Service Management Reform: The Next Steps* London: HMSO, July 1989.

HC 481 (1989–90), *Treasury and Civil Service Committee, Eighth Report, Progress in the Next Steps Initiative* London: HMSO, July 1990.

HC 496 (1990–91) *Treasury and Civil Service Committee, Seventh Report: The Next Steps Initiative* London: HMSO, July 1991.

HC 390 (1992–93) *Treasury and Civil Service Committee, Sixth Report: The Role of the Civil Service: Interim Report* London: HMSO, July 1993.

Haines, J. (1977) *The Politics of Power* London: Jonathan Cape.

Hampden-Turner, C. (1992) 'Foreword' in R. Common, N. Flynn and E. Mellon (eds) *Managing Public Services: Competition and Decentralization* Oxford: Butterworth Heinemann.

Hayek, F. A. (1982) *Law, Legislation and Liberty* London: Routledge and Kegan Paul.

Healy, D. (1989) *The Time of My Life* London: Michael Joseph.

Heclo, H, and Wildavsky, A. (1974) *The Private Government of Public Money* London: Macmillan.

Hencke, D. (1992a) 'MPs Attack £130,000 Pay-Off for Executive After £1m Waste' *Guardian*, 21 May.

Hencke, D. (1992b) 'Agency's £1.4m Waste Condemned' *Guardian*, 15 December.

Hencke, D. (1994a) '£65m "lost" on Whitehall Consultants' *Guardian*, 5 August.

Hencke, D. (1994b) 'Lilley and Heseltine Top the League in Payout to Market-test Advisers' *Guardian*, 6 August.

Hencke, D. (1994c) 'Whitehall Chief Offers Firms Advice' *Guardian*, 16 August.

Hencke, D. (1994d) 'MPs Catalogue the Wasted Millions' *Guardian*, 28 August.

Hennessy, P. (1986) 'The Westland Affair' *Journal of Law and Society* 13: 423–32, reprinted in G. Marshall (ed.) *Ministerial Responsibility* Oxford: Oxford Univeristy Press.

Hennessey, P. (1990) *Whitehall* revised edn Glasgow: Fontana.

Heseltine, M. (1987) *Where There's a Will* London: Hutchinson.

Hogwood, B. (1993) 'The Uneven Staircase: Measuring Up to Next Steps' *Strathclyde Papers in Government and Politics* 92 Glasgow: Strathclyde University.

Hood, C. (1992) 'Looking After Number One? Politicians Rewards and the Economics of Politics' *Political Studies* XL: 207–26.

Hood, C., and Dunsire, A. (1981) *Bureaumetrics* Farnborough: Gower.

Hood, C., Dunsire, A. and Thompson, S. (1978) 'So You Think You Know What Government Departments Are?' *Public Administration Bulletin* 27: 20–32.

Hood, C. Dunsire, A. and Huby, M. (1988) 'Bureaucracies in Retrenchment:

Vulnerability Theory and the Case of UK Central Government Departments, 1975–85' *Administration and Society* 20: 275–312.

Hood, C. Huby, M. and Dunsire, A. (1984) 'Bureaucrats and Budgeting Benefits: How do British Central Government Ministries Measure Up?' *Journal of Public Policy* 4: 163–79.

Hood, C. and Peters, B. G. (eds) (1994) *Rewards to Higher Public Officials* London: Sage.

Hugill, B. (1994) 'A Civil Service on its Last Legs' *Observer* 29 May.

Iacocca, L. (1984) *Iacocca: An Autobiography* New York: Bantam.

Iacocca, L. (1988) *Talking Straight* New York: Bantam.

Ingham, B. (1991) *Kill the Messenger* London: HarperCollins.

Jackson, P. M. (1982) *The Political Economy of Bureaucracy* Oxford: Philip Allen.

James, O. (1994) 'Explaining the Next Steps Reorganisation in the Department of Social Security: An Application of the Bureau-Shaping Model' in P. Dunleavy and J. Stanyer (eds) *Contemporary Political Studies, 1994*, vol. 1 Belfast: Political Studies Association of the United Kingdom.

Jenkins, K., Caines, K. and Jackson, A. (1988) *Improving Management in Government: The Next Steps: Report to the Minister* [Ibbs Report] London: HMSO.

Jenkins, W. (1988) 'Symposium on Improving Management in Government' *Public Administration* 66: 429–45.

Jensen, M. C. and Murphy, K. J. (1990a) 'Performance Pay and Top-Management Incentives' *Journal of Political Economy* 98: 225–64,

Jensen, M. C. and Murphy, K. J. (1990b) 'CEO Incentives – It's Not How Much You Pay, But How' *Harvard Business Review* (May–June): 138–53.

Johnson, N. (1977) *In Search of the Constitution* Oxford: Pergamon.

Johnson, N. (1978) 'Politics and Administration as the Art of the Possible' *Political Studies* 26: 267–73.

Jones, G. (1987) 'An Answer: Stand Up for Ministerial Responsibility', *Public Administration* 65: 87–91.

Jordan, G. (1983) 'Individual Ministerial Responsibility: Absolute or Obsolete?' in D. McCrone (ed.) *The Scottish Yearbook* Edinburgh: Edinburgh University Press.

Jordan, G. (1984) 'Enterprise Zones in the UK and USA: Ideologically Acceptable Job Creation?' in J. J. Richardson and R. Hennin, (eds) *Unemployment* London: Sage.

Jordan, G. (1992a) 'Next Steps Agencies: From Managing by Command to Managing by Contract?' *Aberdeen Papers in Accountancy and Management* W6 Aberdeen: Aberdeen University.

Jordan, G. (1992b) *Engineers and Professional Self-Regulation* Oxford: Clarendon Press.

Jordan, G. (ed.) (1991) *The Commercial Lobbyists* Aberdeen: Aberdeen University Press.

Jordan, G. and Richardson, J. J. (1987) *British Politics and the Policy Process* London: Unwin Hyman.

Jordan, G. Maloney, W. A., and McLaughlin, A. M. (1992) 'Policy-Making in Agriculture: "Primary" Policy Community or Specialist Policy Communities?' *British Interest Group Project Working Papers* 5 Aberdeen: Aberdeen University.

Jørgensen, T. B. (1987) 'Financial Management in the Public Sector' in J. Koolman and A. Eliason, (eds) *Managing Public Organizations: Lessons from Contemporary European Experience* London: Sage.

Keliher, L. (1987) 'Policy-Making in Information Technology: A Decisional Analysis of the Alvey Programme' Ph.D. thesis, London: LSE.

Kellner, P. and Crowther-Hunt, Lord (1980) *The Civil Servants: An Inquiry into Britain's Ruling Class* London: MacDonald.

King, D. S. (1987) *The New Right: Politics, Markets and Citizenship* Basingstoke: Macmillan.

Lean, G. (1994) 'Your Policies Cause Pollution Ministers Told' *Independent on Sunday* 31 July.

LeGrand, J. (1991) *Equity and Choice* London: HarperCollins.

Ludlow, P. (1991) 'The European Commission' in R. O. Keohane and S. Hoffman (eds) *The New European Community: Decisionmaking and Institutional Change* Boulder, Col.: Westview Press.

McLean, I. (1987) *Public Choice: An Introduction* Oxford: Blackwell.

Madgwick, P. (1991) *British Government: The Central Executive Territory* Hemel Hempstead: Philip Allen.

Marsh, D. (1991) 'Privatization Under Mrs Thatcher' *Public Administration* 69: 459–80.

Marsh, D. and Rhodes, R. A. W. (1992) 'The Implementation Gap: Explaining Policy Change and Continuity' in D. Marsh and R. A. W. Rhodes (eds) (1992).

Marsh, D. and Rhodes, R. A. W. (eds) (1992a) *Policy Networks in Britain* Oxford: Clarendon Press.

Marsh, D. and Rhodes, R. A. W. (eds) (1992b) *Implementing Thatcherite Policies: Audit of an Era* Buckingham: Open University Press.

Marshall, G. (1978) 'Police Accountability Revisited' in D. Butler and A. H. Halsey, (eds) *Policy and Politics: Essays in Honour of Norman Chester* London: Macmillan.

Marshall, G. (1984) *Constitutional Conventions* Oxford: Clarendon Press.

Marshall, G. (ed.) (1989) *Ministerial Responsibility* Oxford: Oxford University Press.

Marshall, G. (1989a) 'Introduction' in G. Marshall (ed.) (1989).

Marshall, G. (1989b) 'Individual Responsibility: Some Post-War Examples' in Marshall (ed.) *Ministerial Responsibility* Oxford: Oxford University Press.

Marshall, G. (1991) 'Parliamentary Accountability' *Parliamentary Affairs* 44: 460–9.

Marshall, G. and Moodie, G. (1959) *Some Problems of the Constitution* London: Hutchinson.

Mazey, S. (1992) 'The Administration of the High Authority 1952–56: Development of a Supranational Bureaucracy?' in R. Morgan and V. Wright (eds) *The Origins of the European Community* Baden-Baden: Nomos.

Mazey, S. and Richardson, J. (1990) 'British Interest Groups and the European Community: Changing Lobbying Styles' *Department of Government Working Papers* Uxbridge: Brunel University.

Mazey, S. and Richardson, J. (1993) 'Introduction: Transference of Power, Decision Rules, and Rules of the Game' in S. Mazey and J. Richardson (eds) (1993).

Mazey, S. and Richardson, J. (eds) (1993) *Lobbying in the European Community* Oxford: Oxford University Press.

Midwinter, A. and Monaghan, C. (1993) *From Rates to the Poll Tax* Edinburgh: Edinburgh University Press.

Milgrom, P. and Roberts, J. (1992) *Economics, Organization and Management* Englewood Cliffs, NJ: Prentice-Hall.

Mitchell, W. C. (1974) 'Book Review' *American Political Science Review* 68: 1775–7.

Mount, F. (1992) *The British Constitution Now* London: Mandarin.

Mueller, D. C. (1989) *Public Choice II* Cambridge: Cambridge University Press.

Mueller, A. E. (1987) *Working Patterns: A Study Document by the Cabinet Office* (the Mueller Report) London: HMSO.

Nicholson, I. F. (1986) *The Mystery of Crichel Down* Oxford: Oxford University Press.

Niskanen, W. A. (1971) *Bureaucracy and Representative Government* Chicago: Aldine-Atherton.

Niskanen, W. A. (1973) *Bureaucracy: Servant or Master?* London: Institute of Economic Affairs.

Niskanen, W. A. (1979) 'Competition among Government Bureaus' *American Behavioural Scientist* 22: 517–24.

Niskanen, W. A. (1991) 'A Reflection on *Bureaucrats and Representative Government*' in A. Blais and S. Dion (eds) *The Budget-Maximising Bureaucrat: Appraisals and Evidence* Pittsburgh: University of Pittsburgh Press.

Nordlinger, E. (1981) *On the Autonomy of the Democratic State* Cambridge, Mass.: Harvard University Press.

Northcote, S. H. and Trevelyan, C. E. (1853) 'Report on the Organisation of the Permanent Civil Service' (Northcote-Trevelyan Report), in Fulton (1968), Appendix B, 108–18.

Norton-Taylor, R. (1994) 'The Buck Stops Where?' *The Guardian*, 31 March.

Oliver, D. and Austin, R. (1987) 'Political and Constitutional Aspects of the Westland Affair' *Parliamentary Affairs* 40: 20–40.

Pallister, D. and Norton-Taylor, R. (1992) 'Open Arms Welcome Officer Class to Defence Industry' *The Guardian* 10 September.

Pareto, V. (1971) *Manual of Political Economy* trans A. S. Schwier and A. N. Page, London: Macmillan (first pub 1909).

Parkinson, C. Northcote (1958) *Parkinson's Law or the Pursuit of Progress* London: Murray.

Parsons, S. (1988) 'Economic Principles in the Public and Private Sectors' *Policy and Politics* 16: 29–39.

Phythian, M. and Little, W. (1993) 'Parliament and Arms Sales: Lessons of the Matrix Churchill Affair' *Parliamentary Affairs* 46: 293–308.

Pirie, M. (1988) *Micropolitics* London: Wildwood House.

Pitt, D. C. and Smith, B. C. (1981) *Government Departments* London: Routledge.

Pollitt, C. (1984) *Manipulating the Machine: Changing the Pattern of Government Departments* London: Allen and Unwin.

Pollitt, C. (1986) 'Beyond the Managerial Model: The Case for Broadening Performance Assessment in Government and the Public Service' *Financial Accountability and Management* 12: 115–70.

Pollitt, C. (1992) 'Running Hospitals: The Rise and Fall of Planning' Unit 16 *Running the Country* Milton Keynes: Open University.

Pollitt, C. (1993) *Managerialism and the Public Services* 2nd edn Oxford: Blackwell.

Ponting, C. (1986) *Whitehall: Tragedy and Farce* London: Hamish Hamilton.

Plowden, W. (1994) *Ministers and Mandarins* London: Institute for Public Policy Research.

Putnam, H. (1978) *Meaning and the Moral Sciences* London: Routledge and Kegan Paul.

Pyper, R. (1983) 'The F.O. Resignations: Individual Ministerial Responsibility Revived?' *Teaching Politics* 12: 200–10.

Ranelagh, J. (1992) *Thatcher's People* London: Fontana.

Raub, W. and Weesie, J. (1990) 'Reputation and Efficiency in Social Interactions: An Example of Network Effects' *American Journal of Sociology* 96: 626–54.

Raub, W. and Weesie, J. (1994) 'The Management of Trust Relations' paper presented at World Congress of Sociology, Bielefeld, July.

Rawls, J. (1971) *A Theory of Justice* Oxford: Oxford University Press.

Rayner, Sir Derek (1982) *The Scrutiny Programme – A Note of Guidance*, revised London: Management and Personnel Office.

Reeve, A. and Ware, A. (1992) *Electoral Systems: A Comparative and Theoretical Introduction* London: Routledge.

Richardson, J. J., Maloney, W. A. and Rudig, W. (1992) 'The Dynamics of Policy Change: Lobbying and Water Privatization' *Public Administration*, 70, 157–75.

Ridley, F. F. (1988) 'There is no British Constitution: A Dangerous Case of the Emperor's Clothes' *Parliamentary Affairs* 41: 340–61.

Riker, W. H. and Brams, S. J. (1973) 'The Paradox of Vote Trading' *American Political Science Review* 67: 1235–47.

Rodgers, P. (1991) 'Pay and the Old Boy Network' *Independent on Sunday* 24 November.

Rose, R. (1987) *Ministers and Ministries* Oxford: Clarendon Press.

Rush, M. (ed.) (1990) *Parliament and Pressure Politics* Oxford: Oxford University Press.

Schattschneider, E. E. (1935) *Politics, Pressures and the Tariff* Englewood Cliffs, NJ: Prentice-Hall.

Schwartz, T. (1975) 'Vote Trading and Pareto Efficiency' *Public Choice* 24: 101–9.

Sedgewick, P. (1992) *The Enterprise Culture* London: SPCK.

Siedentopf, H. and Ziller, J. (1988) *Making European Policies Work*, vol 1 London: Sage.

Smith, M. J. (1990) *The Politics of Agricultural Support in Britain* Aldershot: Dartmouth.

Smith, M. J. (1993) *Pressure, Power and Policy* Hemel Hempstead: Harvester Wheatsheaf.

Smith, M., Marsh, D. and Richards, D. (1993) 'Central Government Departments and the Policy Process' *Public Administration* 71: 567–94.

Sober, E. (1993) *The Philosophy of Biology* Oxford: Oxford University Press.

Stanworth, J. and Grey C. (eds) (1991) *Bolton: Twenty Years On* Liverpool: Paul Chapman.

Stevens, J. B. (1993) *The Economics of Collective Choice* Boulder, Col.: Westview Press.

Stinchcombe, A. (1968) *Constructing Social Theories* New York: Harcourt, Brace and World.

Swinbank, A. (1989) 'The Common Agricultural Policy and the Politics of European Decision Making' *Journal of Common Market Studies* 27: 303–22.

Taylor, M. (1987) *Anarchy and Cooperation* Cambridge: Cambridge University Press.

Thain, C. (1984) 'The Treasury and Britain's Economic Decline' *Political Studies* 32: 581–95.

Thain, C. and Wright, M. (1992a) 'Planning and Controlling Public Expenditure in the UK, Part 1: The Treasury's Public Expenditure Survey' *Public Administration* 70: 3–24.

Thain, C. and Wright, M. (1992b) 'Planning and Controlling Public Expenditure in the UK, Part 2: The Effects and the Effectiveness of the Survey' *Public Administration* 70: 193–224.

Trevelyan, C. (1856) *Memorandum on the Examination and Probation of Candidates for Public Employment. Papers on Emoluments in the Public Service* London.

Tullock, G. (1970) 'A Simple Algebraic Logrolling Model' *American Economic Review* 60: 419–26.

Tullock, G. (1965) *The Politics of Bureaucracy* Washington, DC: Public Affairs Press.

Tullock, G. (1990) 'The Costs of Special Privilege' in J. E. Alt and K. A. Shepsle (eds) *Perspectives on Positive Political Economy* Cambridge: Cambridge University Press.

Turpin, C. (1990) *British Government and the Constitution*, 2nd edn, London: Weidenfeld and Nicolson.

Vickers, J. and Yarrow, G. (1988) *Privatization: An Economic Analysis* Cambridge, Mass.: MIT Press.

Waldron, J. (1990) *The Law* London: Routledge.

Warner, N. (1984) 'Raynerism in Practice: Anatomy of a Rayner Scrutiny' *Public Administration* 62: 7–22.

Weber, M. (1978) *Economy and Society* vol 2 ed. G. Roth and C. Wittich, Berkeley: University of California Press.

Weir, S. and Hall, W. (1994) *Ego Trip: Extragovernmental Organisations in the United Kingdon and Their Accountability* London: The Charter 88 Trust.

Wheare, K. C. (1975) 'Crichel Down Revisited' *Political Studies* 26: 390–408.

Wheare, K. C. (1966) *Modern Constitutions* Oxford: Oxford University Press.

Wildavsky, A. (1964) *The Politics of the Budgetry Process* Boston: Little Brown and Co.

Wistow, G. (1992a) 'The Health Service Policy Community: Professionals Pre-eminent or Under Challenge? in D. Marsh and R. A. W. Rhodes (eds).

Wistow, G. (1992b) 'The National Health Service' in D. Marsh and R. A. W. Rhodes (eds) (1992b).

Woodhouse, D. (1993) 'Ministerial Responsibility in the 1990s: When Do Ministers Resign?' *Parliamentary Affairs* 46: 277–92.

Woodhouse, D. (1994) *Ministers and Parliament: Accountability in Theory and Practice* Oxford: Oxford University Press.

Young, H. (1989) *One of Us* London: Macmillan.

Young, H. and Sloman, A. (1982) *No Minister: An Inquiry into the Civil Service* London: BBC.

Young, H. and Sloman, A. (1984) *But Chancellor: An Inquiry into the Treasury* London: BBC.

Index

Note: references which refer to tables are in *italic*; those which refer to figures are in **bold**.